Making Japan's National Game

Making Japan's National Game

A CULTURAL HISTORY OF BASEBALL IN JAPAN

Blair Williams

Carolina Academic Press
Durham, North Carolina

Library of Congress Cataloging-in-Publication Data

Names: Williams, Blair, author.
Title: Making Japan's national game : a cultural history of baseball in
    Japan / Blair Williams.
Description: Durham, North Carolina : Carolina Academic Press, 2020. |
    Includes bibliographical references.
Identifiers: LCCN 2020035907 (print) | LCCN 2020035908 (ebook) |
    ISBN 9781531015312 (paperback) | ISBN 9781531015329 (ebook)
Subjects: LCSH: Baseball--Japan--History. | Baseball--Social aspects--Japan. |
    Japan--Social life and customs.
Classification: LCC GV863.77.A1 B53 2020 (print) | LCC GV863.77.A1
    (ebook) | DDC 796.3570952--dc23
LC record available at https://lccn.loc.gov/2020035907
LC ebook record available at https://lccn.loc.gov/2020035908

Carolina Academic Press
700 Kent Street
Durham, North Carolina 27701
Telephone (919) 489-7486
Fax (919) 493-5668
www.cap-press.com

Printed in the United States of America

In memory of Ken Port

Contents

Acknowledgments

This book evolved from my doctoral dissertation, which was supported by the University of Minnesota History Department. I would like to thank Hiromi Mizuno, JB Shank, Chris Isett, Christine Marran, and Travis Workman for overseeing my doctoral research and training. I also extend my gratitude to the Association of Asian Studies for funding portions of my research that contributed to this book.

Thank you to the numerous archives that permitted me access to their materials: the National Archives and Records Administration in College Park, Maryland; the National Diet Archives in Tokyo, Japan; the Japanese Baseball Hall of Fame Library in Tokyo, Japan; and the microform Prange Collection at the University of California, Los Angeles.

I heartily appreciate the work of Elizabeth Venditto, Nate Holdren, Alex Wisnoski, Julien Sainte, and Huihan Jin in providing comments on the manuscript. Their insights added greatly to the final project. I also want to thank Thomas Chan and Devon Cahill for editing early drafts of this project.

My sincere thanks go to Kenneth Port for his support and guidance on this project. I appreciate the time he spent with me despite ongoing illness, and I will forever appreciate his advice in writing the manuscript.

I want to share my utmost gratitude to my family for supporting me along this journey. Meghan, Elizabeth, Johanna, Aurora, and Devin, thank you for your time and patience in seeing this research come to fruition. Thank you to my dad, Brian, for supporting me along the way and taking me to so many baseball games as a kid. Lastly, thank you to Daniel Patterson and Masashi Fujii for allowing me to use your house as a base for research in Japan and supporting me during my time abroad.

A Note on Transliterations and Translations

This book uses English and Japanese-language sources. Unless otherwise indicated, Japanese names are ordered with the family name first. For example, in the name Abe Isoo, "Abe" is the family name and "Isoo" is the given name. If a place name has a common English transliteration, such as Tokyo or Kobe, then I follow that usage and drop the macrons that accurately represent the Japanese kanji. Where necessary, I have consulted Korean-speaking scholars for translations and transliteration of Korean materials. Many English-language archival resources do not use macrons for Japanese words; in this book, I maintain the original format of the wording seen in the archival material. Unless noted, the author performed all translations appearing in this book. The author assumes all responsibility for any errors, inconsistencies, or oversights.

A Note about Sources

This book uses archival sources acquired from the National Archives and Records Administration (NARA) in College Park, Maryland, and the National Diet Library (NDL, 国立国会図書館) in Tokyo, Japan. In regard to the sources that originate from the period of the Allied Occupation of Japan (formally, 1945–1952): the records housed at the NDL are microfiche facsimiles of materials housed at NARA. This book indicates the origin of these archival materials based upon their box and folder number as indicated by NARA, which is the system used by the NDL as well. This book uses images that have been declassified and are in the public domain. This book also uses materials acquired from the microfiche edition of the Prange Collection housed at the University of California-Los Angeles. The originals of these materials are held at the University of Maryland in College Park, Maryland. Other graphs and images appearing in this book are used under fair use laws.

Foreword
The Transformative Power of Baseball

In the 1970s, Murakami Haruki and his wife ran a popular jazz café in Tokyo, where he spun records and made fresh sandwiches for workers passing through on their lunch hours. As the sun set, Murakami set up a small stage for musicians and poured drinks for patrons who lingered until late in the night. The Murakamis loved the community they had created, but the costs to operate their business had them drowning in debt. The thought of escaping their situation crossed their minds frequently. One night after work, they found a ten-thousand yen note (about three hundred US dollars) on the street. Instead of reporting it to the police as was the Japanese custom, they pocketed the money and hoped that it would provide some financial relief that month.

One summer day, Murakami Haruki went to a Yakult Swallows baseball game in Meiji Jingū Stadium. Completed in 1926 and located in the gardens dedicated to Japan's first modern emperor, the stadium was the oldest sporting venue in Tokyo and the second oldest stadium in Japan. After the extensive damage done to Tokyo in the firebombing of World War II, Meiji Jingū Stadium was one of the oldest structures in Japan's capital. As Murakami stretched out with a beer to watch the game, the sound of a bat hitting a baseball inspired him to escape his stressful work situation and start a new life. Murakami recollected in a 2015 essay:

> Young people like us who were determined to avoid 'company life' at all costs were launching small shops left and right...Although we were doing what we liked, paying back our debts was a constant struggle...My twenties were thus spent paying off loans and doing hard physical labor. Looking back, all I can remember is how hard we worked. I imagine most people are relatively laid back in their twenties, but we had virtually no time to enjoy the 'carefree days of youth.' We barely got by...One bright April afternoon in 1978, I attended a baseball game at Jingu Stadium, not far from where I lived

and worked...The sky was a sparkling blue, the draft beer as cold as could be, and the ball strikingly white against the green field, the first green I had seen in a long while...In the bottom of the first inning, [there was] a clean double. The satisfying crack when the bat met the ball resounded throughout Jingu Stadium. Scattered applause rose around me. In that instant, for no reason and on no grounds whatsoever, the thought suddenly struck me: *I think I can write a novel.*[1]

Regardless of whether one is an elite player or an underdog, when a baseball player succeeds, that moment in the spotlight etches the belief that anything is possible upon the hearts of fans. At that game, Murakami experienced the transformative power of baseball. Baseball, and the community around it — the players, the managers, the stadiums, the crowds, the newspapers and journalists, the politicians and businessmen, the television stations and photographers, the security personnel, the vendors everywhere selling peanuts and beer and soda and gum and programs and jerseys and hot dogs and soba noodles — is a microcosm of society. Inspired by the crack of the bat, for the next six months Murakami spent every night at his kitchen table typing out his first novella, *Hear the Wind Sing*, which went on to win a prize from one of the country's premier literary journals, *Gunzo*. Following the award, Murakami closed his jazz café and set out to be a professional writer. Sparked by the transformative power of baseball, Murakami Haruki became the most celebrated novelist in contemporary Japan.

We can see how baseball transformed the life of one Japanese person. Now, let's begin the journey to understand how baseball shaped the trajectory of the entirety of Japanese society.

---

1. Murakami Haruki, "The Birth of my Kitchen-Table Fiction: An Introduction to Two Short Novels," in *Wind/Pinball: Two Novels* (New York: Alfred A. Knopf, 2015), 2–4.

Introduction

This book tells the story of how the Japanese people imagined and built their country, and it does so through the lens of the baseball communities in Japan. I begin with the first appearance of baseball in 1872, and then illustrate how the Japanese baseball community became the most powerful, influential, and enduring sporting culture within modern Japan. I contend that the nature of baseball and its community evolved within the changing circumstances of Japanese and global society. At times, the Japanese baseball community embraced an ethic of cosmopolitanism, while at other times, it was the vanguard of producing isolationist Japanese nationalism. In other words, at times the Japanese baseball community created new pathways for intercultural communication and cooperation, and at other times, the baseball community created homogeneous communities that delineated who was Japanese and who was not. As an import from the United States, baseball created unique channels of communication, cooperation, and tension between Japanese and American peoples that lasted throughout the twentieth century. However, the Japanese baseball community continuously reinvented itself, and produced a dynamic identity that often contrasted with American baseball communities.

This book illuminates how baseball became the Japanese national game. Because the "national game" is affected by the "nation" — which is a people's concept of ethnicity, culture, history, language, and territory — it is important to know the massive shifts that occurred in Japanese nationality throughout the nineteenth and twentieth centuries. I tie the story of baseball into discussions of Japanese nationalism and discuss *bushidō* philosophy ("The Way of the Samurai") before 1945, *nihonjinron* ("Theories of Japaneseness") during the Cold War, and *kokusaika* ("Internationalization") from the 1980s onward. I also explain how broader athletic cultures, such a physical education systems and mega-events like the Olympics, prepared the Japanese people to strengthen their bodies in the defense of the Japanese nation and state. Therefore, my history of baseball in Japan speaks to how corporate and governmental entities leverage sports, athletics, and recreation to transform the behavior of individuals and communities to meet goals of political and ideological agendas. In this case, I demonstrate how the Japanese baseball community shaped and reacted to nationalist philosophies that emerged throughout the late nineteenth and twentieth centuries. Thus, baseball became the Japanese "national game" not just by means of popularity, but through its imbrication with the very notion of what constituted being "Japanese."

There are two important recurring themes throughout this book that unite my narrative. The first theme is nationalism, or the discourse about the qualities of those people included in the nation. In this book I demonstrate how *bushidō, nihonjinron,* and *kokusaika* philosophies of Japanese nationalism are linked through the community of baseball. Thus, we are able to see ways in which the baseball community shapes nationalism over multiple periods of Japanese history through the actions, thoughts, and writings of politicians, journalists, and pundits. The second theme is of unequal treatment of the Japanese by the Americans, both in terms of general society and in terms of baseball. Like many books about Japanese history, this book divides the history of Japan into "pre-war" and "post-war," with Japanese defeat in World War II in August 1945 being the demarcation point. From 1868–August 1945, Japan's state and empire was predicated upon undoing the humiliating and unequal treaties and colonialism enacted upon Japan — and Asia — by America and the Western powers. After August 1945, Japan spent nearly fifty years under a "subordinate independence" to the United States. Americans treated the Japanese baseball community as inferior and unequal, so the Japanese baseball community sought equality both on the playing field and in global society.

Setting the Stage for Global Baseball Communities: The Age of Imperialism

There is a prevailing belief among Anglophone scholars that the baseball community in Japan is — and has always been — characterized by masochistic and self-sacrificial behavior. Scholars claim these abusive behaviors — both towards oneself and inflicted upon others — are a modern continuation of traditions begun by Japan's ancient warrior class, the *samurai* (侍). I contend that these claims of a transcendent masochistic national character trait of Japanese people are inaccurate and not supported by historical evidence. To address this issue, I will first summarize how baseball developed in the United States and become linked to the American imperial agenda throughout the nineteenth century. As a result of American imperialism, Japan formed into a modern state to protect itself from Western encroachment. The nascent Japanese state studied the West passionately, which led to the formation of a Westernize physical education system and eventually the importation of baseball. The Japanese baseball community then became enmeshed with Japanese nationalism, which laid the foundation for the creation of Japan's national game.

Origin Stories: Baseball Becomes the American Pastime

The sport of baseball is not strictly of American creation; baseball evolved from the British game of rounders. John Thorn, Major League Baseball's current official historian, located evidence that the first reference to "baseball" appeared in the United States in 1791.[2] Throughout the early nineteenth century, baseball spread on the United States' east coast, and in 1845 Alexander Cartwright of Knickerbocker Base Ball Club in New York City codified a set of rules that led to the creation of the first amateur baseball leagues.[3] In 1869, the Cincinnati Red Stockings became the first professional team in the United States, and they were joined shortly thereafter by other professional teams to create Major League Baseball (MLB).[4] By the turn of the twentieth century, baseball had colloquially become the American "national pastime." In 1907, Henry Chadwick — a British essayist who had earned President Theodore Roosevelt's approval for his historical work linking baseball to rounders — joined a group of American writers to write the official history of baseball. However, Chadwick was shouted down by a cadre of American men who insisted that baseball originated in the United States. These American authors created a mythical father of baseball, Abner Doubleday, who was a Civil War general who had no documented interest in baseball. This "lie agreed upon" shifted baseball's origins from Europe to the United States and provided the sport and its players with a military pedigree.[5]

---

2. John Thorn, "The Pittsfield 'Baseball' Bylaw of 1791: What It Means," *Our Game*, August 3. 2011, https://ourgame.mlblogs.com/the-pittsfield-baseball-bylaw-of-1791-what-it-means-940a3ccf08db#.uphpocsu3. Thorn argues that textual evidence shows "baseball" was played as early as the 1750s in the United States, but corroborating evidence has yet to be found.

3. Steven P. Gietschier, "The Rules of Baseball," In *The Cambridge Companion to Baseball*, ed. Leonard Cassuto (Cambridge, UK: Cambridge University Press, 2011), 10.

4. Although not an immediate predecessor, the Red Stockings were a precursor to the current Cincinnati Reds professional baseball team, which formed in 1882.

5. John Thorn, "Abner Cartwright," *Our Game*, https://ourgame.mlblogs.com/abner-cartwright-defba02abf5f.

As participants in the "national pastime," the American baseball community was complicit in American imperialist, colonialist, and militarist endeavors. Broadly speaking, the nineteenth century saw white European settlers displacing Native peoples in the West, and the American Navy was also present in the Caribbean and East Asian countries in efforts to locate colonies, establish trade relationships, and bring American "civilization" to the indigenous peoples. Baseball team owners utilized these expansionist policies to pursue cheap baseball labor and employ players who did not enjoy the same civic rights of the audiences who watched baseball (and thus could be taken advantage of). Beginning in the 1880s, MLB implemented the "Reserve Clause," which permitted team owners to control player contracts indefinitely and effectively treated humans as property. The United States Supreme Court upheld this Reconstruction-era clause — which mimicked aspects of slavery while giving it the appearance of "choice" in labor and wages — twice in the twentieth century, first in 1922 and again in 1970.

The preservation of the Reserve Clause until 1975 encouraged baseball managers and owners to find players willing to work for ever-lower wages.[6] Throughout the late nineteenth and early twentieth century, MLB did not have a coherent policy regarding employment based on race. On the one hand, MLB prohibited the employment of black Americans on their team rosters, which resulted in the creation of the independent Negro Leagues. On the other hand, MLB owners employed Native American, Hispanic-heritage Latinos, and Afro-Caribbean players by the early twentieth century.[7] In 1886, Major League Baseball expanded beyond the borders of the United States and held regular exhibition games between white American teams and Cuban teams, and in 1890 the New York Giants baseball team spent the winter in Havana training with professional Cuban players.[8]

Americans used baseball to justify the spread of American influence and military might. When the USS Maine was sunk in Havana Bay in 1898, newspaper mogul William Randolph Hearst advocated that the United States intervene on behalf of the baseball-loving Cubans to fight the *fútbol*-loving Spanish

---

6. Thomas F. Carter, *The Quality of Homeruns: The Passion, Politics, and Language of Cuban Baseball* (Durham, NC: Duke University Press, 2008), 51.

7. Peter Bjarkman, *Baseball with a Latin Beat* (Jefferson, NC: McFarland and Co., 1994), 204; Jeffrey Powers-Beck, "'Chief': The American Indian Integration of Baseball, 1897–1945," *American Indian Quarterly* 25, no. 4 (Autumn 2001): 508.

8. Carter, *The Quality of Homeruns*, 51.

colonial masters.[9] By 1912, famed author Carl H. Claudy readily equated base-ball to "civilized warfare." Claudy wrote in his book, *The Battle of Base-ball,*

> [W]hen you come to think of it, base-ball is a battle. It has its generals, its captains, its lieutenants, its rank and file. It has its grand strategy, its tactics, its drill. It has its battlefield, its arms, and its equipment. It is a battle with rules, to be sure, but then, a real battle, between real armies, is also fought according to certain rules, called by nations the laws of civilized warfare. These rules prohibit, for instance, the use of expanding or mushroom bul-lets, or poisoned swords or bayonets. The rules of the battle of base-ball pro-hibit certain kinds of balls, shoes, gloves. Civilized warfare recognizes the flag of truce, and will not permit a man carrying one to be shot. He is safe so long as he has the white flag. Base-ball...permits a soldier of the enemy to be safe from danger of being 'put out' so long as he keeps his foot upon any of the white bags used as bases.[10]

Claudy wrote in the context of generalizing warfare from individual actors to broader communities. Sports in the European context had long been an activity to subsume violent tendencies among elite males into socially appro-priate action, with famous examples being fencing, equestrian skills, rowing, shooting, and dancing. Claudy's work remarks on how now the masses are engaged in "civilized warfare," meaning baseball had delivered to the common man the ability to subsume violence in society and instead express aggression on the baseball field.

Therefore, baseball in the American context was well-known for militarist and imperialist affiliations, and the American communities delineated them-selves based upon ethnicity. By treating players—that is, the laborers of the game of baseball—as ownable proxies within ephemeral contests of simulat-ed warfare, the American baseball community created a hierarchy of athletic shows of bravado. As men played baseball, they showcased not only their body's strength and power, but the strength and power of their homeland in relation to other territories. Because most other sporting communities in America did not form a professional league or have the social importance of baseball, this was a trend unseen in other athletic communities.

---

9. Robert Elias, *The Empire Strikes Out: How Baseball Sold U.S. Foreign Policy and Promoted the American Way Abroad* (New York: The New Press, 2010), 38–39.

10. Carl H. Claudy, *The Battle of Base-Ball* (New York: The Century Co., 1912), 4–5. Claudy, a noted speculative fiction writer, noted in the preface of *The Battle of Base-ball* that his parallels between baseball and warfare were authentic and not dramatized.

Revolutionary Beginnings: Japan Becomes a State

This book focuses on the baseball community in Japan during the twentieth century, but in order understand many of those narrative arcs, it is necessary to discuss some aspects of pre-modern Japanese history. The most important aspect of pre-modern Japanese history as it applies to the story of baseball is the social function of the samurai warrior class. In the 1870s, the elimination of the samurai as a privileged class contributed greatly to the emergence of Japan as a modern state. However, it was also the hallmark of this moderni-ty — the arrival of capitalism, the emergence of markets, the appearance of Japan's internal national consciousness and its empire — that Japanese elites *reimagined* the role of the samurai in their country's history. This reimagining happened in the literary and intellectual realms in the form of *bushidō*, which was a late-nineteenth century discursive invention that linked modern Japan to its ancient territorial and cultural roots via the character of the noble and self-sacrificing samurai. Although the majority of nineteenth-century *bushidō* proved to be conjured myth, *bushidō* became foundational to the educational systems of Japan throughout the first half of the twentieth century. Because baseball communities in Japan emerged in these elite schools where *bushidō* was constructed and taught, it is crucial to understand the influence of *bushidō* philosophy upon the creation of the Japanese state and how those powers shaped the Japanese baseball community.

A Brief Overview of the Samurai in Tokugawa Japan

The samurai class emerged gradually over several hundred years, from about 700AD until 1100AD, when a conglomeration of economic, political, and military forces necessitated a landed military elite that was distinct from the aristocrats of the Emperor's court.[11] In the sixteenth century, violence among the samurai class became normalized when the local lords, called *daimyō*, competed for regional hegemony by military or political conquest.[12] However, the samurai became so over-militarized in their defense of individual honor that they began seeking vengeance outside of the jurisdiction of their *daimyo*. The *daimyō* quelled the samurai's cycle of retribution by instituting a policy

---

11. Eiko Ikegami, *The Taming of the Samurai: Honorific Individualism and the Making of Modern Japan* (Cambridge, MA: Harvard University Press, 1995), Chapter 2: The Coming of the Samurai: Violence and Culture in the Ancient World.

12. Ikegami, *The Taming of the Samurai*, 138.

of *kenka ryōseibai,* which delivered "equally severe punishment of all parties to a quarrel regardless of the reason behind a conflict," and it became a law by 1616.[13] At this time, the Tokugawa family had claimed the position of *shogun,* a title reserved for the military leader of Japan who was the *de facto* warlord. The Tokugawa family combined centralized rule in Edo (now Tokyo) under the "great public authority," with local or regional oversight by *daimyo* lords.[14] This *bakufu* system, wherein the Tokugawa shogun led the regional *daimyo,* controlled Japan from 1603–1868 and possessed a near monopoly on formalized violence, forbid a number of non-Japanese customs, and closed the Japanese borders to most Western interaction.

The limited interaction with Western traders was conducted on the island of Dejima near Nagasaki, where Dutch traders were allowed to land. Western scholarship trickled into Japan by means of this trade. Thus, at a time when imperial European powers were racing to control much of the world's landmass and forcing indigenous cultures to adopt "enlightened" Western knowledge, most people in Japan were insulated from this process. Although knowledge of the Western processes of statecraft, capitalism, the industrial revolution, and the scientific revolution seeped into Japan by means of trading with the Dutch, much of that knowledge remained unacted upon until the nineteenth century. Despite rampant European imperialism in Asia throughout the eighteenth and nineteenth centuries, the people living under the Tokugawa *bakufu* remained protected from the military and cultural traumas experienced by their geographical neighbors. By the mid-nineteenth century, the British controlled India and were fighting wars with China; the United States had expanded to the American west coast and were interfering in Hawai'i and the Caribbean, and the Russians had long controlled Siberia.

While the Western imperial powers dissected Central and South East Asia, the Tokugawa shogunate restricted samurai violence, which dramatically shifted samurai from a warrior class into a bureaucratic class. As sociologist Eiko Ikegami summarizes, life for most of the samurai population throughout the Tokugawa era became mundane, "uncolored by power and glory...Increasingly, a strictly defensive attitude crept into the samurai mentality that combined an orientation toward personal safety with procedural perfectionism."[15] Many samurai were monetarily indebted to the socially lower-ranked (yet wealthy)

---

13. Ikegami, *The Taming of the Samurai,* 142.

14. Ikegami, *The Taming of the Samurai,* 152.

15. Ikegami, *The Taming of the Samurai,* 260.

merchants; these merchants became the *de facto* patrons of many samurai families.[16] In summary, by the nineteenth century, the samurai class had not been characterized by their prowess in battle for nearly two hundred years, but were instead known for their prowess in managing the *bakufu's* bureaucracy.

The Meiji Restoration and the End of Tokugawa Japan

Russian and British traders frequently approached the Japanese *bakufu* in the early nineteenth century asking for trading privileges. The *bakufu* responded with increasingly vociferous rejections of foreign encroachment. However, many samurai and *daimyō* wondered if the *bakufu* could effectively reject European encroachment. In 1839, the British commenced a war with China over the right to trade opium. In 1842, the Chinese conceded defeat and signed humiliating treaties that permitted the continued sale of opium and the extraterritorial right of British subjects to be tried by British law on Chinese soil. Many Japanese elites understood that China's failure to resist the West was a foreshadowing of what could happen to Japan if the *bakufu* clung to its traditional isolationism.

In 1854, American Commodore Matthew Perry sailed his steam ships into the harbors outside of Yokohama, and demanded that Japan open their borders and accept trade with the United States. By 1860, the United States had won the right to keep consulates and opened up a total of eight Japanese ports to trade; thus Japan had been subjected to numerous unequal treaties that permitted American influence on Japanese soil.[17] Over the next few years, dissatisfied samurai and peasants revolted against the Tokugawa *bakufu*. In 1868, a group of samurai from the Satsuma and Chōshu domains in Kyūshū defeated the shogunate armies, and installed the hereditary emperor, Mutsuhito, to lead the newly consolidated state of Japan.[18] The new bureaucrats' motto would be to learn from the West through the mass importation of Western industrial, scientific, intellectual, military, and cultural practices in order to undo the humiliating treaties and protect Japan from becoming a colonized territory of a Western power. Although the hereditary samurai elite played a significant role in enacting these changes, it was the reimagining of the samurai as warriors that transformed these Western imports into something truly "Japanese." It is

---

16. Ikegami, *The Taming of the Samurai*, 175.

17. Andrew Gordon, *A Modern History of Japan: From Tokugawa Times to the Present* (Oxford University Press: New York, 2009), 54.

18. Gordon, *A Modern History of Japan*, 59.

within this context that baseball — the American national game — entered into Japanese society, and its adherents began the journey that made baseball the Japanese national game.

Book Trajectory

Chapter one discusses the creation of a Westernized athletic system in Japan from 1868–1890. Although baseball was introduced to Japan four years after the Meiji Restoration, when the country was still in a massive race to "catch up" to the West by using European and American models of science, politics, and industry, Japan lacked any sort of athletic culture where sports could be played. Chapter two discusses the evolution of *bushidō* philosophy, and how it became entangled within the emerging baseball community in Japan. Chapter three briefly discusses baseball within the early twentieth century Japanese empire in Taiwan, Korea, and the Liaodong Peninsula. Chapter four discusses the creation of the National High School Baseball Tournament (*"Kōshien"*), which became the world's largest sporting event in the early twentieth century and brought ethnic minorities from throughout Japan's empire into the Japanese baseball community. Chapter five discusses how the period from 1920–1944 featured numerous Japanese "athletic mega-events," wherein athletics as a whole served to strengthen the bodies of Japanese people and demonstrate loyalty to the emperor, thus creating a connection between individual health and national health. Chapter six discusses how the Japanese baseball community operated in the "Fifteen Year War" from 1931–1945. A brief Interlude follows, which discusses the level of destruction in Japan during World War II and the dire need for recovery, rebuilding, and rehabilitation.

Chapter seven discusses the resumption of baseball after World War II, and the steps the Americans took to control the new athletic environment in post-War Japan. Chapter eight discusses how the Japanese athletic world operated at the onset of the Cold War in 1947 and the subsequent "Reverse Course," wherein the American Occupation authorities remilitarized Japan to serve as a bulwark of democratic capitalism in the defense of Asia from communism. Chapter nine discusses how the Japanese baseball "cold warriors" made intense efforts to connect with the American baseball communities and created Nippon Professional Baseball (NPB) in the image of the United States' Major League Baseball. However, during this period of courting, the Japanese baseball community realized that the Americans were conducting a broader plan to control global baseball organizations, leading to the discussion in chapter ten of how the American and Japanese professional baseball leagues severed official relations throughout the remainder of the Cold War. Chapter eleven discusses how in the context of *nihonjinron* — a form of culturally homogeneous Japanese nationalism — that the NPB yet the league's superstars in the 1960s and 1970s were almost all ethnic minorities. The most iconic figures of Japanese baseball, Oh Sadaharu, played at this time and was neither an ethnic Japanese nor a Japanese citizen. Lastly, in chapter twelve, I discuss the resumption of official relations between the Japanese and American professional leagues in the context of post-Cold War *kokusaika*, or "internationalization" policies that sought to export Japanese culture in the world to protect domestic interests and maintain Japanese global power.

Making Japan's National Game

CHAPTER ONE

Developing an Athletic Culture in the New Japanese State

To protect our country from foreign nations, we must establish a spirit of freedom and independence throughout the entire country. With no distinction between noble and base, high and low, learned and ignorant, blind and sighted, each person must take it upon himself to fulfill his duty as a citizen. Englishmen love England as their native land; Japanese love Japan as theirs. Since the land is ours and not another's, we love it as we do our homes. For the sake of our country, we must willingly sacrifice not only property but our very lives. This is the great principle of repaying the country.[1]

— Fukuzawa Yukichi, "Outline of a Theory of Civilization," 1875

Introduction

Baseball's introduction to Japan occurred during a tumultuous period, when the newly-created Japanese state underwent a massive transition from a completely non-Western system to a model that mixed both Western and Japanese ideas of statecraft. This chapter will highlight how the new Japanese government imported Western athletic cultures and physical education systems from 1868–1890 to create a nation of strong subjects — both male and female — to defend their country physically, mentally, and spiritually against the West. Japan sought to rebalance its unequal treaties with the West and engaged in rapid

---

1. Albert Craig, *Civilization and Enlightenment: The Early Thought of Fukuzawa Yukichi* (Cambridge, MA: Harvard University Press, 2009), 112.

industrialization, the passionate study of Western political and philosophical systems, and the development of a Japanese national identity under the authority of an emperor. I illuminate how a Westernized physical education system and the establishment of a competitive athletic culture set the stage for the emergence of baseball in the late 1890s.

The Meiji Era and the Introduction of Baseball in Japan

The reign of Emperor Mutsuhito lasted from 1868 until his death in 1912, and is referred to as the Meiji era. In this span of forty-five years, Japan shifted from a closed agricultural society to an imperial industrial power. The Meiji government and bureaucracy learned from the imperial powers in order to protect their country from becoming a colonial possession. Japan underwent a triumphant industrial revolution in the late nineteenth century, with the Gross National Product increasing, on average, 3% annually from 1880–1930 alongside a strong agriculture sector.[2] The Meiji government established close ties with Western governments to learn their ways of market capitalism, statecraft, and industrial and metallurgical processes that contributed to manufacturing ships, ammunition, railroads.[3] Japan's rapid industrialization propelled an expansion of both its domestic urban areas and its overseas empire. From 1893–1908, the city of Tokyo doubled in size to over two million people, and Osaka tripled in size to 1.2 million people.[4] Japan fought victorious wars with China (1894–1895) and Russia (1904–1905); by 1910, Japan included Taiwan, the Liaodong Peninsula, and Korea in its imperial holdings.

The Meiji policy of "rich country, strong army" (*fukoku kyōhei,* 富国強兵) resulted not only in a powerful industrial and military sector, but in a Westernized physical education system. The Meiji government hired dozens of British, French, German, and Americans to teach "Western learning" (*yōgaku,* 洋楽) within the newly created Japanese public education system. The introduction

---

2. Koji Taira, "Factory labor and the Industrial Revolution in Japan," in *The Economic Emergen. ce of Modern Japan*, ed. Kozo Yamamura (Cambridge, UK: Cambridge University Press, 1997), 240.

3. E. Sydney Crawcour, "Economic Change in the Nineteenth Century," in *The Economic Emergence of Modern Japan*, 44.

4. *Nihon Teikokuminseki kokōhyō* 日本帝国民籍戸口表 [Report of Households in Imperial Japan], 1891, http://dl.ndl.go.jp/info:ndljp/pid/806017/29; and *Nihon Teikoku jinkō seitai tōkei* 日本帝国人口静態統計 [Statistics of Imperial Japan Population], http://dl.ndl.go.jp/info:ndl-jp/pid/805975.

of baseball to Japan was an accidental byproduct of this Westernized education system.

American Civil War veteran Horace Wilson worked as a teacher of Western learning — called *oyatoi* — at *Kaisei Gakkō*, a school that had been the vanguard of Western learning since the 1850s.[5] As an English teacher, Wilson was largely unnoticed by the school: he earned the minimum wage of 200 yen for one year of service and then returned to the United States.[6] Wilson never wrote about baseball in his personal letters, but it is known that he introduced baseball to his Japanese students as an after school activity.[7] A decade after Wilson's departure from Japan, the Meiji government incorporated *Kaisei Gakkō* into Tokyo Imperial University, which brought the nascent baseball community in Japan into contact with the vibrant hub of Japanese intellectual life during the Meiji era. At Tokyo Imperial University, the baseball community inflected their sport with an emerging philosophy known as *bushidō*, which relied heavily on newly concocted interpretations of history about the elite samurai class.

Thus, the Japanese baseball community's early years should be characterized by its unique brand of Japanese nationalism, rather than as a mimic of America's national pastime. However, the Japanese baseball community remained contained and relatively isolated to the Tokyo Imperial University School system until the 1890s. The pre-requisite for the baseball community to flourish in Japan was the existence of a competitive, non-violent athletic culture. The rest of this chapter will outline how Japanese schools installed a Westernized physical education system, which made the later spread of baseball throughout Japan possible.

Installing a Westernized Physical Education System in Japan

To create a uniform sense of education and shared mindset throughout Japan, an 1872 Educational Order made elementary school attendance compulsory in all parts of the country. The Educational Order did not include any discussion of physical education, and at the time many Japanese did not subscribe

---

5. A summary of *Kaisei Gakkō*'s history is provided in *Tōkyō Kaisei Gakkō ichiran* 東京開成学校一覧 [Summary of Tokyo Kaisei School] (Tokyo, 1875), 1.

6. *Oyatoi gaikokujin ichiran* 御雇外国人一覧 [Catalog of Oyatoi Foreigners] (Tokyo: Chūgaidō, 1872), 8.

7. Theo Balcomb, "Japanese Baseball Began on my Family's Farm in Maine," *National Public Radio: Parallels* (March 28, 2014), http://www.npr.org/sections/parallels/2014/03/28/291421915/japanese-baseball-began-on-my-familys-farm-in-maine. Balcomb is Wilson's great-great-great nephew and current owner of Wilson's documents.

to Western conceptions of the body, physiology, and hygiene.[8] Japan introduced universal male conscription in 1873, but many of the soldiers lacked basic schooling; despite the compulsory Educational Order, throughout the 1870s and 1880s less than half of eligible Japanese students attended school.[9] In 1875, Fukuzawa Yukichi, a prominent intellectual and educator, argued in "An Outline of Theories of Civilization" that the soldiers he saw were not physically fit, trained, or sufficiently loyal to the cause of the Meiji government.[10] With most of the hereditary samurai unfamiliar with battle after two centuries of peace, and with the Americans already forcing the Japanese to sign unequal treaties, Fukuzawa felt compelled to improve the Japanese populace, in mind, body, and national spirit.

The answer to Fukuzawa's desire came in the form of an American physical education system. As part of the early Meiji bureaucracy's efforts to learn from the West, from 1871 to 1873, the Iwakura Mission sent a delegation of Japanese statesmen and scholars to communicate with the Western imperial powers, to understand how they functioned, and to begin re-negotiating the unequal treaties imposed upon Japan. While in the United States, the delegation visited Amherst College in Massachusetts and decided that the "Amherst Program" should become the Japanese physical education model. At the program's founding in 1854, William Stearns, President of Amherst College, said "Physical education is not the number one work in college life, but it's the most important tool in advancing education."[11] The Amherst Program provided students with instruction in exercise, allowed students to get health advice from doctors and hygienists, instructed students on biology and dissection, and directed students to develop exceptional personal character.[12]

However, the Iwakura Mission was cut short when former samurai Saigō Takamori, who had been charged with overseeing a "caretaker" government in Tokyo while so many statesmen were overseas, vociferously argued for a Japa-

---

8. Donald Roden, "Baseball and the Quest for National Dignity in Meiji Japan," *The American Historical Review*, 85, no. 3 (June, 1980): 514.

9. Gordon, *A Modern History of Japan*, 67.

10. Albert Craig, *Civilization and Enlightenment: The Early Thought of Fukuzawa Yukichi* (Cambridge, MA: Harvard University Press, 2009), 112.

11. Ōbitsu Takashi 大櫃敬史, "Rīrando shōhei ni kansuru keii: Ama-suto daigaku shozō bunsho no bunseki wo chūshin toshite," リーランド招聘に関する経緯 : アマースト大学所蔵文書の分析を中心として [The Invitation of Dr. Leland: An Analysis of the Amherst Program], *Hokkaidō Daigaku kyōiku gakubu kiyō*, 73 (1997), 10.

12. Ōbitsu, "Rīrando shōhei ni kansuru keii: Ama-suto daigaku shozō bunsho no bunseki wo chūshin toshite," 12.

nese invasion of Korea. Saigō's invasion proposal was rebuffed by the remaining statesmen in Tokyo, and he returned to his home in Kagoshima prefecture. In Kagoshima, Saigō and his supporters effectively separated themselves from the rest of Japan; they sent no taxes to Tokyo, they followed none of the Meiji government reforms, and they pursued the return of samurai privilege.[13] Hearing of the insurrection and impending uprising at home, the delegates on the Iwakura Mission hastened their return to Japan. As they returned, Horace Wilson introduced baseball to *Kaisei Gakkō* in Tokyo in 1872.

The Amherst Program and the Creation of a Japanese Athletic Culture

Once home in 1873, the Amherst Program began rolling out through Japanese high schools and colleges to strengthen male and female students, to which Fukuzawa Yukichi had expressed as his top desire his 1875 treatise, "Outline of a Theory of Civilization." In 1876, Tanaka Fujimaro (田中不二麿), a former Iwakura Mission delegate working in the newly-created Japanese Ministry of Education, recruited William Clark, a professor of chemistry and biology at Amherst, to teach at Sapporo Agricultural College (札幌農学校).[14] There, Clark instituted "Sports Day," which expanded beyond Sapporo and became a tradition at schools throughout Japan.[15] Although Clark remained in Japan for less than one year, he evangelized Christianity to his students so effectively that many of his students and began evangelizing to their classmates, thus amplifying Clark's teachings and practices — including Sports Day — throughout Meiji Japan.

The winter of 1877 evidenced that the new physical education system and Westernized ways were an improvement on the pre-Meiji Japanese system. The rebellious Saigō Takamori led an army comprised mainly of former samurai on a march from Kagoshima to Tokyo that was halted by conscripts of the new government army who were trained in European tactics and physical education systems. The Meiji government forces soundly defeated Saigō's technolog-

---

13. Gordon, *A Modern History of Japan*, 84.

14. "A History of Physical Education and Sports in Japan: Appendix 1: A Chronological Table of Physical Education and Sports in Japan," 1, Supreme Commander for the Allied Powers: Civil Information and Education Division, Special Projects Branch, Educational Research File, Box 5442, Folder "Research Memo C."

15. Over the next half century, "sports day" evolved within fascist Japan into "*taiiku* day (体育デー)," and after World War II, "sports day" was reborn as a standard component of the Japanese educational system.

ically inferior samurai, which convinced many Japanese people that Western knowledge would defend the state.

In 1878, the Ministry of Education hired Amherst graduate George Leland, who instituted *taisō denshūjo* (体操伝習所, literally, "sites of physical education") as a way to expand physical education instruction throughout Japan. These sites trained Japanese physical education instructors in Western gymnastics and calisthenics, and then placed them into the Japanese school system to replicate the Amherst Program across Japan.[16] Accompanying the physical education program was the American fascination with classifying students both by minute physiological measurements (e.g. chest girth, lung capacity) and instances of disease.[17] Put simply, Japanese officials strengthened the bodies of boys and girls through a program of running, jumping, and body weight exercises, while incessantly measuring their results. Because Leland's program focused on training in calisthenics and hygiene, it left unaddressed how "games" (*yūgi*, 遊技), like cricket or baseball, should be handled by the school system.[18] Japanese educators eventually agreed to use the umbrella terminology "physical education" (*taiiku*, 体育/體育) in the 1890s, and the term included sports, athletic activity, and games.[19] This slippage in terminology would allow local school administrators to adopt baseball in school curriculum at their discretion.

Athletic competitions entered the physical education system in the form of the *undōkai* (運動会, "athletic meet"). In 1886 while working at Tokyo's *Daigaku Yobimon* (大学予備門), a preparatory school for Tokyo Imperial University, Christian missionary Frederick W. Strange introduced to Japan the first *undōkai*. This event differentiated itself from Sports Day by including exercises like running and jumping, and in the spirit of elite British university rivalries, pitting schools against each other in a public spectacle of competition.[20] At

---

16. Ōbitsu, "Rīrando shōhei ni kansuru keii: Ama-suto daigaku shozō bunsho no bunseki wo chūshin toshite," 1–3.

17. Ōbitsu, "Rīrando shōhei ni kansuru keii: Ama-suto daigaku shozō bunsho no bunseki wo chūshin toshite," 15

18. Shinbō Atsushi 新保淳, "Meijiki ni okeru 'taiiku' gainen no kenkyū: ruiji gainen to no konran no genin ni tsuite" 明治期における「体育」概念の研究：類似概念との混乱の原因について [A Study on the Concept of "Physical Education" in the Meiji Era: On the Cause of Confusion with Similar Concepts], *Shizuoka Daigaku kyōiku gakubu kenkyū hōkoku* 37 (1987): 19.

19. Shinbō, "Meijiki ni okeru 'taiiku' gainen no kenkyū," 20.

20. Ikuo Abe and J.A. Mangan, "'Sportsmanship' — English Inspiration and Japanese Response: F.W. Strange and Chiyosaburo Takeda," The International Journal of the History of Sport 19, no. 2-3 (2002): 99.

the first *undōkai*, Strange distributed a fifty-five-page pamphlet titled *Outdoor Games* that summarized his philosophy for the event:

> There are two kinds of exercise, Mental Exercise and Physical Exercise. Scholastic education is mental exercise, thought directed to any object is mental exercise; gymnastics and all kinds of outdoor games constitute physical exercise. In ancient times the Greek doctors and philosophers believed that mental and physical exercises went together.[21]

Strange's student Takeda Chiyosaburō (武田千代三郎) institutionalized Strange's ideas of sportsmanship within the Japanese educational system. Takeda described the philosophy behind the new physical education system, and in doing so, he echoed the origins of the Amherst Program:

> Exercise is not an aim but an instrument. The aim of the training of the body does not solely rest upon the preservation of health or longevity, but it does reside in more than that; the moral training of the playing field evokes human qualities far more than the disciplines of the class room.[22]

From the 1890s onward, Takeda translated Strange's written works into Japanese and promoted them in his capacity as a bureaucrat for the Home Ministry (内務省). In 1913, Takeda became the Vice President of the Japanese Amateur Athletic Association (JAAA) — an organization created to send Japanese athletes to the Olympics — and served on its board for the next decade. From the 1880s until the 1920s, Takeda became a staunch supporter of Western-inspired athletic ideas. Thus, the early incarnation of the physical education system in Japan contained both *physical* and *mental* components, which laid the foundation for baseball to later become integrated with Japanese nationalism.

In summary, the Japanese physical education system began with the Amherst Program and expanded through several Western-inspired athletic competitions from 1870–1890. Within the context of the new school system in Japan and its imported physical education system, events like the *undōkai* and Sports Day created senses of shared national community and later imperial community. These events introduced Western athletics competitions and concepts of physical education to the Japanese masses, and they installed a nascent sense of non-violent athletic competition within the Japanese popula-

---

21. Abe and Mangan, "'Sportsmanship' — English Inspiration and Japanese Response," 101.

22. Abe and Mangan, "'Sportsmanship' — English Inspiration and Japanese Response," 100. Translation of Takeda done by the authors in the original work. Takeda made this statement in 1923.

tion. The first competitive "sport" to emerge within this new environment was the recently created martial art of *jūdō*, which seemed to be a natural choice to become Japan's "national sport." Although *jūdō* became the first competitive sport within Japan — and despite its status as the favored domestic sport with later proponents of Japanese nationalism — *jūdō* lacked one major feature that prevented it from becoming a fascination among the Japanese population: an American audience that Japanese practitioners could defeat.

Budō Martial Arts within the Context of Western Physical Education

Public competitions of martial arts became regular occurrences in Meiji Japan. Historian Inoue Shun explains that the Tokugawa-era term *budō* (武道) was redefined in the context of post-Meiji Restoration Japan: "*Bujutsu* (武術, military arts) and *bugei* (武芸, martial arts) have a long history, but *budō* (武道, warrior arts) is a recent invention."[23] After the Meiji Restoration, *budō* became an umbrella term to describe the combat skills associated with the former samurai class: *kendō* (剣道, sword arts), *jūdō* (柔道, martial arts), *kyūdō* (弓道, archery) and *naginata* (薙刀, halberd arts). In the 1880s, the newly formed martial art of *jūdō* (柔道) quickly surpassed these classical martial arts of Tokugawa-era Japan and represented a Japanese-sourced alternative to the Western physical education system and sporting community.

Jūdō began in the late 1870s, when Kanō Jigorō (嘉納治五郎) created the martial art to elevate Japan as the "new world standard" of martial arts.[24] Kanō modeled *jūdō* after the Tokugawa era martial art *jūjutsu* (柔術), and borrowed many underlying precepts of physiology and mentality from the latter.[25] He evangelized *jūdō* as a universally accessible martial art, available to women and non-Japanese, and by 1905 *jūdō* schools existed in both Europe and the United States.[26] In 1882, Kanō founded the *kōdōkan* (講道館) in Tokyo, a Western-style building where he taught "*kōdōkan jūdō*" and maintained a library of writings on the science of *jūdō* (*jūrigaku*, 柔理学) and the philosophy of *jūdō* (*jūriron*,

---

23. Inoue Shun 井上俊, *Budō no tanjyō* 武道の誕生 [The Birth of Budō] (Tokyo: Yoshikawa kōbunkan, 2004), 2.

24. Maruya Takeshi 丸屋武士, *Kanō Jigorō to Abe Isoo: Kindai supōtsu to kyōiku no senkusha* 嘉納治五郎と安部磯雄：近代スポーツと教育の先駆者 [Kanō Jigorō and Abe Isoo: Pioneers of Modern Sports and Education], (Tokyo: Akashi, 2014), 31.

25. Inoue Shun, *Budō no tanjyō*, 18.

26. Inoue Shun, *Budō no tanjyō*, 9 and 70.

柔理論).[27] The *kōdōkan* began with nine members in 1882, with membership growing to nearly 2,000 people in 1890, over 4,000 people in 1900, and over 10,000 people by 1920.[28]

Martial arts transitioned into a competitive sport in the 1880s, when the Tokyo Metropolitan Police force first practiced *kendō* as a form of military sword arts.[29] Shortly thereafter, the Tokyo Metropolitan Police incorporated Kanō's *jūdō* into their training regimes. Responding to public demand for police-sponsored martial art competitions of *jūdō* and *kendō*, the *dōjō*s holding these competitions became the only place where swords — the former tools of Japan's elite classes — could be used in public. Historian Denis Gainty indicated that these public performances of martial arts competitions were novel to the Meiji era; many Japanese prefectures in pre-Restoration Japan prohibited public contests of martial arts because it was "vaguely inappropriate," with no clear explanation as to why public competition should be avoided.[30] The Metropolitan Police's public competitions brought the newly revamped *jūdō* and *kendō* martial arts under the approving gaze of Emperor Meiji.[31] By training its constables in *budō* martial arts, the Tokyo Metropolitan Police became the first organization in Japan to have physical education crossover into discussions of national identity. Although Japanese people enjoyed the public performances of martial arts, Leland's *taisō denshūjo* ("sites of physical education") system — rooted in instructing students in Western physiology and kinesiology — blocked the entrance of martial arts into public schools and sparked a lively debate among intellectuals about the place of martial arts within Japan's modernization program.[32] This will be discussed more in the next chapter.

Conclusion

This chapter illustrated how a Westernized physical education system developed within Meiji Japan. The Meiji government installed Western physical education systems as part of their process to strengthen the Japanese nation and resist future aggression from the West. By 1890, athletic contests had become infused with notions of emerging Japanese nationalism, and the first public

---

27. Inoue Shun, *Budō no tanjyō*, 18.
28. Inoue Shun, *Budō no tanjyō*, 44.
29. Gainty, *Martial Arts and the Body Politic in Meiji Japan*, 30.
30. Gainty, *Martial Arts and the Body Politic in Meiji Japan*, 27.
31. Gainty, *Martial Arts and the Body Politic in Meiji Japan*, 28–30.
32. Gainty, *Martial Arts and the Body Politic in Meiji Japan*, 32.

sports contests appeared within the *jūdō* community. However, simultaneous to the emergence of *jūdō*, the baseball community within Japan emerged from its insulation in the Tokyo Imperial University system. Whereas *jūdō* practitioners used their own internally developed philosophies, the baseball community in Japan latched onto a virulent strain of Japanese nationalism that propelled the game to a prominent status at the turn of the twentieth century. The next chapter will discuss the growth of the Japanese baseball community in late Meiji Japan.

CHAPTER TWO

Bushidō Baseball

*Martial skills that train the physique and form the spirit are not nec-
essarily limited to those that use the sword and spear, but also include
football, rowing, and baseball. These are originally products of the West,
and although I do not know what the Westerners used these skills to
prepare for, when these skills are brought to Japan and we apply our true
Japanese bushi-like spirit to them, with regard to training the physique
and forming the spirit, they bear comparison with our ancient martial
skills. Baseball, especially, is truly a civilizational martial skill, and at
the same time a bushi-like sport.*[1]

—Oshikawa Shunrō, journal entry written while traveling in the
    United States, 1905

Introduction

In this chapter, I argue that it was baseball's unique relationship with *bushidō*
discourse, particularly the emperor-centric variant promoted by philosopher
Inoue Testujirō, that enabled the sport to transform Japanese modernity, develop national identities within the broader empire, and become symbolic of
the Japanese people's physical and mental strength. Through *bushidō* philosophy's imbrication into Japanese athletic culture, baseball became the *de facto*
Japanese national game and possessed an internal cultural coherency that was
no longer rooted in American culture. Therefore, this chapter treats the Japanese baseball community not as a banal symptom of Westernization, but as an
integral part of Japan's efforts to create a modern empire. As Japanese baseball
players engaged with American baseball players, they did so with the intention

---

1. Quoted in Oleg Benesch, *Inventing the Way of the Samurai*, 134.

not only of winning the immediate game, but of restructuring the treaties and policies that the United States used to control Japan.

The Reimagining of the Samurai

Shortly after the Meiji Restoration in 1868, the samurai class was abolished and its hereditary privileges revoked, although many former samurai preserved their social power by working in positions for the new government. By the 1880s, several writers, who were descended from samurai families and disenchanted with Japan's rapid implementation of Western technology and educational systems, reimagined the samurai's role in the formation of modern Japan. Many of these writers de-emphasized the samurai's bureaucratic utility in the Tokugawa era and instead highlighted their more ancient roles as warriors (*bushi*, 武士). Accordingly, *bushidō* ("the way of the warrior," 武士道) emerged in the Meiji era as a genre for authors to discuss both the samurai's military utility, and as a forum for debate about how Japanese ideologies and morals operated inside and outside of Westernization. Any claims that the samurai were elite warriors obsessed with pride in battle harkened back to social practices that were not regularly seen in Tokugawa Japan. Therefore, the contention that *bushidō* philosophy is a metaphor for a transcendent Japanese national character — which is a core component of the contemporary historical narrative about baseball in Japan — fails to recognize that *bushidō* was a rhetorical form originating in the modern era.

Inoue Testsujirō and the Emergence of Imperial *Bushidō*

Historian Oleg Benesch demonstrates that the early Meiji era writers on *bushidō* philosophy did not adhere to a uniform definition. Benesch argues that many of these authors of *bushidō* philosophy had "a pronounced nostalgia for a vanished martial ideal that the writers had not personally experienced, but were convinced had existed in the past."[2] This resulted in many Meiji-era Japanese authors poring over literary sources, both Western and Japanese, to interpret samurai morality and virtues, thus creating stories that often better reflected the author's political agenda than actual historical evidence. Benesch contends:

---

2. Oleg Benesch, *Inventing the Way of the Samurai: Nationalism, Internationalism, and Bushidō in Modern Japan* (Oxford: Oxford University Press, 2014), 15.

Bushidō is treated primarily as an invented tradition and ideology, with the understanding that these concepts can overlap significantly. Not all invented traditions are ideologies, and certainly not all ideologies are invented traditions... [A]s a traditional samurai ethic and/or defining trait of the Japanese 'national character,' *bushidō* is best treated as an invented tradition... From the late 1880s onward, *bushidō* has been continually reinvented in different ways, often by the same individuals. Sometimes these have been cases of almost pure invention with no connection to earlier history aside from the term '*bushidō*,' while in other cases specific historical sources and terminology have been used in attempts to reanimate what were believed to be historical traditions.[3]

In this book, I contend that the Japanese baseball community's relationship with Inoue's brand of Imperial *Bushidō* was constructed at the turn of the twentieth century, and this relationship enabled the baseball community to transform Japanese nationalism throughout the first half of the twentieth century.

Benesch demonstrates that from about 1890 until 1945, the dominant understanding of *bushidō* philosophy, both by the common Japanese person and political elites, evolved from the writings of Inoue Tetsujirō, who was a professor of philosophy at Tokyo Imperial University. Inoue attended *Kaisei Gakkō* in 1875 (three years after baseball was introduced there), and from 1884–1890 he traveled throughout Europe to study Western languages and political philosophy.[4] From this European trip, Inoue discovered German nationalism, and he believed that Japan should similarly protect its unique "Japanese spirit."[5] In 1890, he returned to Japan and assumed a position as professor of philosophy at Tokyo Imperial University, where he used Herbert Spencer's concept of Social Darwinism to argue against permitting Westerners to live alongside Japanese. Inoue feared that if Japan permitted "mixed residence," then the Japanese people "might be completely overwhelmed by the foreigners and become extinct."[6] Inoue's 1891 book, *Chokugo Engi* (*Commentaries on the Imperial Rescript*) sold over four million copies and nearly one in ten Japanese owned a copy.[7] Mod-

---

3. Benesch, *Inventing the Way of the Samurai*, 8.

4. Davis, "The Civil Theology of Inoue Testujirō," 7.

5. Benesch, *Inventing the Way of the Samurai*, 98.

6. Davis, "The Civil Theology of Inoue Tetsujirō," 8.

7. Inoue's books sales from Davis, "The Civil Theology of Inoue Tetsujirō," 9. Population data derived from the Statistics Bureau of the Japanese Ministry of Internal Affairs and Communications, http://www.stat.go.jp/data/chouki/zuhyou/02-01.xls.

ern philosopher Winston Davis summarized Inoue's stance in *Chokugo Engi* as "the promotion of a national morality that would enable Japan to resist the political, economic, and intellectual pressure from the West."[8] In short, Inoue constructed a defense of Japanese national characteristics by using snippets of historical accounts to justify Meiji Japan's very modern agenda. By appealing to the extinct elite samurai class yet universalizing the samurai ethos to all Japanese people, Inoue compelled citizens to imagine a continuity between Japan's insulated heritage and the imperialist, capitalist, and modernizing agenda as seen in the late nineteenth century.

Inoue espoused an ahistorical model of "defensive nationalism" that promoted the uniqueness of the Japanese spirit, patriotism and ultra-nationalism, intolerance of dissenting ideas, the people's close relationship to military education, and loyalty to the emperor.[9] Inoue's brand of "Imperial *Bushidō*" gained traction through state-sponsorship under the moniker of "National Morality" (*kokumin dōtoku*, 国民道徳), which Benesch describes as "constructed around a desire to redefine Japanese society in terms of a 'national family' with the emperor at its head as the benevolent father figure."[10] In the early twentieth century, Inoue amended his views to permit foreign ideas with the understanding that such ideologies did not distract from one's patriotism.[11] The looseness of Inoue's later models of *bushidō* — called "tendentious" and "artificial" by philosopher Winston Davis — allowed it to deal with foreign ideas like Christianity, capitalism, and eventually baseball.[12] By the turn of the century, Inoue's "Imperial *Bushidō*" defined Japanese values as "patriotism and loyalty to the emperor...a close relationship with the military as an educator and ideologist; ultranationalism and the emphasis on a unique Japanese spirit; [and] pronounced anti-foreignism framed in the rhetoric of Japanese superiority..."[13] Thus, Inoue's philosophy can be seen as putting into practice the Meiji Era goal of driving out the West, although with a philosophy that was contrived to be "Japanese" instead of "Western."

---

8. Davis, "The Civil Theology of Inoue Tetsujirō," 9.

9. Benesch, *Inventing the Way of the Samurai*, 97–100.

10. Benesch, *Inventing the Way of the Samurai*, 115.

11. Benesch, *Inventing the Way of the Samurai*, 117. In this dissertation, I use the English-language translation of "National Morality" as used by Carol Gluck and Oleg Benesch. *Dōtoku* could also be translated as "virtues."

12. Winston Davis, "The Civil Theology of Inoue Testujirō," *Japanese Journal of Religious Studies* 3, no. 1 (March 1976): 5, and Benesch, *Inventing the Way of the Samurai*, 117.

13. Inoue Tetsujirō 井上哲次郎, *Bushidō* 武士道 (Tokyo: Heiji Zasshi Corporation, 1901), 2 and Benesch, *Inventing the Way of the Samurai*, 99.

Questioning *Bushidō* and Masochism: The *Hagakure*

A peculiar strain of *bushidō,* which appeared in the throes of fascist wartime Japan in the 1930s and 1940s, promoted the belief that *bushidō* ideology created masochistic baseball communities that represented enduring Japanese national character. Inoue's Imperial *Bushidō* provided the groundwork for these fantasies of an unbroken Japanese nation-state with an Emperor of divine descent. However, it was author Matsunami Jirō in 1938 who mobilized an obscure pre-modern work on samurai aesthetics, the *Hagakure,* and intertwined it with Imperial *Bushidō* to justify wartime Japanese national character as a "philosophy of death" and "the true *bushidō,*" which "provided a possibility to understand Japan's unique *bushidō* and the importance of loyalty and willingness to give one's life for the emperor."[14] Written in the early eighteenth century in Saga Prefecture, Yamamoto Tsunetomo penned the *Hagakure* (葉隠) with a famous opening line that proclaimed the way of the warrior was discovered in death (武士道と云うは死ぬ事見つけたり) and that a loyal warrior should — at all times — be prepared to lay down their life for their master.[15] In the case of fascist Japan, Matsunami universalized this relationship to conceptualize all individuals as self-sacrificing samurai who bowed down to the Emperor.

The *Hagakure* was a late-blooming phenomenon among *bushidō* literature, and it was not even published in its entirety for a mass audience until 1906.[16] Even in the early twentieth century, Inoue Tetsujirō found the *Hagakure* inconsequential for his National Morality project. Therefore, for *Bushidō* Baseball practitioners in the early twentieth century, it was their duty to remain loyal to country and emperor, but for the most part, it was not any characteristic of Japanese national character by which baseball players were to be self-sacrificial. Although there are several notable examples of baseball players dying for the war effort in the 1940s, the government generally held baseball players back from the war front to continue competitive play and symbolize the importance of physical strength and national power to their domestic audiences. Therefore, in the first part of the twentieth century, the relationship between *bushidō* philosophy and baseball was characterized by discussions of respect, fair play, procedure, and nationalism instead of brutal training regimens or self-sacrificial ideologies.

---

14. Benesch, *Inventing the Way of the Samurai,* 202–203.

15. Yamamoto Tsunetomo, *Hagakure: The Secret Wisdom of the Samurai,* trans. Alexander Bennett (Tokyo: Tuttle Publishing, 2014), 28.

16. Benesch, *Inventing the Way of the Samurai,* 202–203.

Baseball's Emergence in the Home of Imperial *Bushidō* Philosophy

I contend that proximity to the imperial court was important to baseball's emergence as a Japanese sport that differentiated it from its American heritage. Baseball, school athletic competitions, *jūdō*, and Imperial *Bushidō* discourse all emerged within four kilometers of the Japanese imperial palace. This fact is often overlooked because the names of the involved schools often changed. Baseball was introduced to *Kaisei Gakkō* in 1872, and after several transformations the school became Tokyo Imperial University in 1886. The *kōdōkan*, built in 1882,

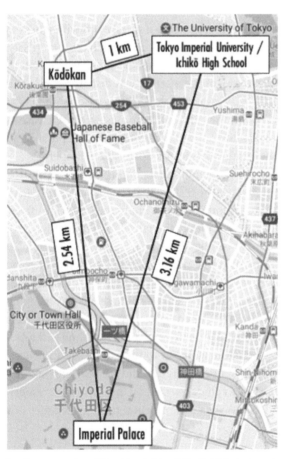

was one kilometer away from Tokyo Imperial University. In 1887, *Daigaku Yobimon*, the home of the *undōkai* and the instigator of sports competitions in Japan, became the official preparatory school for Tokyo Imperial University and was renamed *Daiichi Kōtō Gakkō*, which was nicknamed "Ichikō" (第一高等学校, hereafter "Ichikō"). By 1896, Ichikō was a hotbed of Imperial *Bushidō* discourse and became the first school in Japan to engage United States nationals in a game of baseball.

Locations accurate from 1890 positions in Tokyo. Ichikō High School relocated to Tokyo's Meguro Ward in 1935.[17]

17. Map and distance calculations from http://maps.google.com.

The First Baseball Game Between Japanese and American Players

The unequal treaties provided the background for the first baseball game between Japanese high school boys and American sailors. Beginning in the 1890s, the professional organization in the United States, Major League Baseball, had focused its recruiting efforts entirely into the Caribbean. Therefore, the first Americans to play baseball with the Japanese were sailors who did not represent any serious American sporting interests. However, for the Japanese, the American sailors represented a pseudo-colonial presence: the American sailors were proxies for the men who had opened Japan fifty years earlier and forced the Japanese to sign humiliating treaties. The sailors lived under American laws in the treaty port of Yokohama, and treated the neighboring Japanese with disdain.

Historian Donald Roden described the first baseball game between Ichikō and a group of United States sailors in 1896 in the context of what he called the Japanese quest for "national dignity" that symbolized the "'new *bushidō*' spirit of the age."[18] Under the protection of American extraterritoriality in the treaty port of Yokohama, the Yokohama Athletic Club, a social club for white American sailors, hurled insults at their "primitive" Japanese neighbors for wearing dirty clothes. Roden argued that these Americans were "undoubtedly the first to play baseball on Japanese soil," and they did so as:

> [T]he means of preserving a frontier spirit of daring and adventure that had brought them to this curious and distant land in the first place. By smashing home runs, a young bachelor from the Midwest compensated for the demoralizing effects of settlement brothels and grog shops while safeguarding the integrity of his national identity. Such activity was important in order to maintain social and cultural distance from the Japanese...[19]

On May 23, 1896, the Ichikō baseball team traveled to Yokohama wearing spotless new uniforms to thwart any accusation by the Americans that they were "primitive," and Ichikō crushed the Athletic Club team by a score of 29–4.[20] At the end of the game, the American sailors escorted the Japanese high school boys off the field, a gesture interpreted by Ichikō students as an assertion of

---

18. Donald Roden, "Baseball and the Quest for National Dignity in Meiji Japan," *The American Historical Review* 85, no. 3 (June, 1980): 520. Roden's article is the second-most cited work on Japanese baseball, trailing only Robert Whiting's book *You Gotta Have Wa*.

19. Roden, "Baseball and the Quest for National Dignity in Meiji Japan," 518.

20. Roden, "Baseball and the Quest for National Dignity in Meiji Japan," 523–524.

United States extraterritorial rights.[21] Throughout the summer of 1896, the Ichikō students played three more teams comprised of sailors from the United States Navy, winning the "series" three games to one.[22]

Ichikō's victories evidenced that physical education and intellectual strength associated with Imperial *Bushidō* ideology could defeat the Americans at the sport that was synonymous with American strength, militarism, and imperial prowess. Because Japan remained under American extraterritorial jurisdiction, the Ichikō team became the first group of Japanese to defeat the United States on symbolically "American soil." Historian Ariyama Teruo indicated that Ichikō's baseball team treated victory in these baseball matches as a matter of cultural superiority, which echoed Inoue's appeal to soldiers to be metaphorical representatives of the "survival of the fittest."[23] On the field, Ichikō students reflected the cultivation of their moral education through knowledge of the true spirit of *bushidō* philosophy.[24] This sentiment is echoed in Ichikō's fight song, which portrays the team emerging victorious from battle with a decimated foe. The first verse of the song goes,

> Every day we must show the strength of the blood and tears in our youth, facing the Emperor filled with the spirit of truth...the troops [軍, *gun*] waving our flag in victory...Baked under the scorching sun and stained with sweat and soil our boys are strongly disciplined...We slaughter all of our enemies (全部の敵を屠り)...[25]

At this early stage, Ichikō's emerging brand of "*bushidō* baseball" defeated the Americans at their own game, on a field where American laws dominated, and did so without shedding a drop of American blood or invoking the American military's wrath. Thus, the Meiji-era program of learning from the West in order to expel the West found footing in Japan's nascent baseball community.

---

21. Roden, "Baseball and the Quest for National Dignity in Meiji Japan," 525.

22. Guthrie-Shimizu, *Transpacific Field of Dreams*, 36–37.

23. Ariyama Teruo 有山輝雄, *Kōshien Yakyū to Nihonjin: Media no tsukutta ibento* 甲子園野球と日本人:メディアのつくったイベント [Japanese People and Kōshien Baseball: A Media Created Event] (Tokyo: Yoshikawa Kobunkan, 1997), 26.

24. Ariyama, *Kōshien Yakyū to Nihonjin*, 27.

25. Excerpt from *Yakyūbu ōenka* 野球部應援歌 [Baseball Club Cheering Songs], http://www5f.biglobe.ne.jp/~takechan/S10P1-8seiki.html. Composed in 1923, the song has four verses and extends for 120 measures.

Conclusion

This chapter illustrated the development of Imperial *Bushidō* philosophy as outlined by Inoue Tetsujirō. Inoue's brand of *bushidō* became the dominant strain of Japanese nationalism throughout the twentieth century and was incorporated as mandatory education into the Japanese public education system. Because Japan's nascent baseball community emerged in the same school system as Inoue's Imperial *Bushidō* philosophy, the young players were steeped in its teachings and incorporated its lessons into their baseball games. Baseball players were demonstrating their understanding of the Japanese nation — subjectivity to the emperor, the defense of the country, the expulsion of the foreign and the promotion of the domestic — as they trained and competed. When the Ichikō players defeated a group of American sailors, they symbolized the success of the long Meiji-era project of learning from the West in order to defeat the West.

CHAPTER THREE

Imperial Baseball

*On April 4 [1905], we were scheduled to depart by steam train from Shin-
bashi at 9:30 PM, so we assembled at the station at 9 PM. There were 12
players, wearing brand new baseball caps and uniforms that spoke to their
bravery; each of their families and closest friends saw them off... Including the Waseda athletic department, there were several hundred people
standing on the platform shouting "Banzai" to us as we left.*[1]

— Abe Isoo, journal entry, 1905

Introduction

Where the Japanese empire expanded, baseball followed. No comprehen-
sive account exists of the baseball communities within the Japanese colonies
from 1895–1945, and this chapter provides only a very brief overview of how
baseball operated in the Japanese colonies in the early twentieth century.
Japan began its empire by taking the islands of Ezo and Ryūkyū shortly after
the Meiji Restoration and incorporating them into the Japanese state as the
prefectures of Hokkaidō and Okinawa. Then in 1895, the Japanese empire
expanded again through conquest to include Taiwan. By the time the Meiji
Emperor died in 1912, the Japanese empire had expanded to include Korea
and the Liaodong Peninsula.

Baseball was not limited to a group of like-minded elites in Tokyo, but because those influential elites in Tokyo were key creators of nationalist thought

---

1. Abe Isoo 安部磯雄, *Wadai yakyūbu yōbei ki* 早大野球部渡米記 [Waseda Baseball Club
Trip to America Journal], quoted in Itami Yasuhiro 伊丹安広, *Yakyū no chichi: Abe Isoo Sensei*
野球の父: 安部磯雄先生 [The Father of Baseball: Teacher Abe Isoo] (Tokyo: Waseda daigaku
shuppanbu, 1965): 43.

and members of baseball communities, baseball became a critical element to building Japan's empire. Baseball was not considered a leisure activity in the colonies; it was used at first to maintain physical prowess among the Japanese colonists and later to instruct Japanese civilization to the colonized subjects. As Japanese colonists and colonial enterprises introduced baseball to their subjected peoples, they at first re-implemented the unequal treatment that they had learned from the Japanese. However, by the mid-1920s, most Japanese colonists were playing alongside their colonial subjects in the effort to create a multiethnic Japanese empire.

Baseball in Taiwan

Emboldened by two decades of army training and the Imperial *Bushidō*-driven belief that Japanese culture was superior, many within Japan wanted to use Japan's newfound industrial might and intellectual prowess to acquire its own empire. In order to defend against the European and American powers and rewrite the unequal treaties, many Japanese believed that the Japanese army should be used offensively to extract land and concessions from its geographical neighbors. The first target was Japan's long-time rival, China. Japan defeated China militarily in 1895, gaining as its concession the island that became known as Taiwan.

After European arrival in the 1600s, Taiwan became a trading hub and home to indigenous Taiwanese, Han Chinese migrants, and Portuguese traders. After Japanese annexation in 1895, Gotō Shinpei (後藤新平), a Japanese doctor who became the head of Taiwan's civilian affairs, turned the island into a productive and profitable sugar colony. Within two decades, Taiwanese sugar met the increasing demand in Japan proper.[2] Gotō promoted athletics and sports among the Japanese settlers to protect them from what he considered the troublesome Han Chinese living in Taiwan and the "savage" aborigines. Ethnic Japanese teachers in the Taipei region played the first regular baseball games in Taiwan in 1906.[3] Taiwanese sugar plantations became company towns and gave rise to a flourishing baseball culture among Taipei's ethnic Japanese residents.[4] Historian Andrew Morris posits that many ethnic Japanese feared that if they lost a baseball game to the capable Taiwanese players, it would humiliate them

---

2. Chih-Ming Ka, *Japanese Colonialism in Taiwan: Land Tenure, Development, and Dependency, 1895–1945* (Taipei, Taiwan: SMC Publishing, Inc., 1995), 53–66.

3. Andrew D. Morris, *Colonial Project, National Game: A History of Baseball in Taiwan* (Berkeley, CA: University of California Press, 2011), 10.

4. Morris, *Colonial Project, National Game*, 11.

and undermine their status as colonial masters. Their fears echoed and underscored the cultural significance of Ichikō's triumph over the United States in Yokohama, which was a port under American jurisdiction. So strong were the Japanese settlers' fears that the first documented baseball game between ethnic Japanese and ethnic Han Chinese did not occur until 1919.[5]

Baseball in Korea

Historian Ono Yasuteru demonstrates that Koreans first encountered baseball in 1896 when American naval soldiers visited the city that later became Seoul (*Keijyō*, 京城).[6] At the time, Korea was still a semi-autonomous entity under China's protection. From 1896–1910, baseball spread through Korea by two means: the Young Men's Christian Association (YMCA) and Korea's pre-colonial physical education curriculum.[7] A missionary working for the YMCA, P.L. Gillett, introduced baseball to Korea. Once introduced, the Seoul YMCA became home to many baseball teams formed of ethnic Koreans. Baseball then entered Korea's physical education curriculum through secondary schools, first at Hanseong High School (漢城高等學).[8] In 1909, a team of ethnic Japanese foreign exchange students living in Korea formed a baseball team and acquired uniforms and other equipment from Tokyo in order to look more "Japanese."[9] Japan forcibly annexed Korea in 1910, and Japanese colonial officials segregated Korean and Japanese students' participation in athletic events based on their ethnicity.[10] Only after 1920 did regular baseball matches between ethnic Japanese and ethnic Koreans occur on Korean soil.[11] Whereas Korea had been a target of muscular Christian evangelism prior to annexation, baseball re-oriented Korean athletes toward the Japanese emperor.

5. Morris, *Colonial Project, National Game*, 12–13.

6. Ono Yasuteru 小野安輝, "Chōsen ni okeru yakyū juyō: Chōsen de 'bēsubōru' ha ikanish-ite 'yakyū' ni natta no ka" 朝鮮における野球の受容：朝鮮で「ベースボール」は如何にして「野球」になったのか [On the Reception of Baseball in Korea: How "Baseball" Became "Yakyū"] in *Kanryū, Nichiryū: Higashi Ajia bunka kōryū no jidai* 韓流・日流：東アジア文化交流の時代 [Korean Flow, Japanese Flow: The Period of Exchange in East Asia], ed. Yamamoto Joho (Tokyo: Bensei Publishing Corporation, 2014), 106.

7. Ono, *Chōsen ni okeru yakyū juyō*, 106.

8. Ōjima Katsutarō 大島勝太郎, *Chōsen yakyū shi* 朝鮮野球史 [Korean Baseball History], (Tokyo: Chosen Publishing Co., 1932), 2.

9. Ōjima, *Chōsen yakyū shi*, 4.

10. Ono, *Shokuminchi Chōsen no yakyū*, 51.

11. Ōjima, *Chōsen yakyū shi*, 4.

Baseball in Dalian

Whereas Yokohama was the first city in Asia to host a baseball game between Japanese nationals and Americans, the second city was Dalian, a port city located at the edge of the Liaodong Peninsula about halfway between the Korean peninsula and the Chinese port city of Tianjin.[12] The 1905 Portsmouth Treaty that concluded the Russo-Japanese War leased Dalian to Japan. Within a decade, Dalian became the main hub of the South Manchuria Railway—owned and operated by the Japanese company known as *Mantetsu* (満鉄)—which supported the formation of Dalian's first baseball team. In 1910 Gotō Shinpei, who had relocated from Taiwan to Dalian and now presided over the *Mantetsu* company, encouraged a team comprised of Japanese company employees to play a group of American sailors who were passing through the port.[13] Although the *Mantetsu* team lost the game, the players immediately began discussions to form a team that included players outside of the South Manchurian Railway employees. In 1913, the "Dalian Manchuria Club" (大連満州倶楽部) was established, and in 1916, baseball teams from the nearby region—now called *Kantōshū* (関東州)—began playing in an annual tournament, the *Kantōshū* Tournament (関東州大会).[14] Like in Taiwan and Korea, baseball communities in the Kantōshū region remained largely segregated by ethnicity until the early 1920s and reinforced the superiority of Japanese settlers and business operations. However, as ethnic Japanese baseball teams began traveling throughout the colonies to compete, teams formed of colonized players would eventually play against—and in some cases, compete alongside—ethnic Japanese players.

Japanese Baseball on Tour

No individual spread baseball throughout the Japanese empire more than Abe Isoo (安部磯雄), the "father" of baseball in Japan. Abe held university degrees from the United States, Germany, and Japan, and in 1899 he took a professor-

---

12. Dalian can also be transliterated as "Dairen" in accordance with its Japanese kanji, 大連. In this book, I use the common English transliteration of "Dalian."

13. Hata Genji 秦源治, *Wagakuni yakyū wo rīdo shita: Dairen yakyū kai* わが国球界をリードした：大連野球界 [Our Country Was the Leader of Baseball: The Dalian Baseball World] (Kobe: Twentieth Century Dairen Conference, 2009), 43.

14. Hata, *Wagakuni yakyū wo rīdo shita*, 44. Tokyo, the center of baseball in Japan, is in the *Kantō* (関東) region of Japan, which coincidentally shares nomenclature with the home region of Dalian (*Kantōshū*).

ship at Tokyo's Waseda University and became the coach of its baseball team. A Unitarian Christian, Abe helped establish the Social Democratic Party of Japan in 1903, and he was long-interested in the social welfare aspects of Karl Marx's teachings.[15] In the middle of the Russo-Japanese War in 1905, Abe took his Waseda baseball team on a privately financed tour of the United States. From 1905 to 1910, the Waseda University baseball team hosted American teams from Wisconsin, Hawai'i, and St. Louis. From 1910 through 1915, Abe took his baseball team to the United States, the Philippines, and Taiwan. In 1917, he took his team on a long tour of the Japanese imperial territories in the Liaodong Peninsula and Korea to play against established high school teams.[16]

Conclusion

Baseball in Japan emerged as an imperial endeavor almost immediately after its inception, part and parcel of Meiji Japan's quest for international legitimacy and colonial conquest. Abe wanted his students to recognize that fair play was socially constructed and demand fairness on an unfair playing field, echoing Japan's decades-long concern with correcting its "unequal treaties" with the United States. Similarly to how the United States had expanded its baseball interests throughout its imperial interests in the Caribbean, the Japanese baseball communities created baseball communities in its imperial possessions. However, an important distinction emerged by the end of World War I: whereas the United States was enlisting colonized and imperiled players for cheap labor, the Japanese baseball community was transforming their community into an imperial baseball community that connected all people within a diverse empire. The mechanism by which the Japanese created this unified community was the national high school baseball tournament, which the next chapter discusses in depth.

---

15. See Katayama Tetsu 片山哲, *Abe Isoo den* 安部磯雄伝 [Biography of Abe Isoo], (Tokyo: Ōzorasha, 1991).

16. Waseda University, "Baseball Team History," http://www.waseda.jp/9a-baseball-team/history.htm.

CHAPTER FOUR

The Kōshien Tournament

Baseball is done with such zeal as to completely neglect one's academic work, the result of which is nothing but the stagnation of knowledge for baseball players. The harm from the popularity of baseball and the trend towards brashness in baseball players has resulted in a problem of public morals.[1]

— Nitobe Inazō, "Baseball Poisons," *Tokyo Asahi Shinbun*, 1911

Introduction

Enhanced by Inoue Tetsujirō's Imperial *Bushidō* philosophy, baseball in early twentieth-century Japan dismantled social barriers and created a uniform baseball community across an empire that spanned thousands of miles and nearly a dozen ethnicities. The mechanism that enabled this uniform community was the National High School Baseball Tournament, which began as a small tournament in 1915. By 1926, the National High School Baseball Tournament included teams from all corners of the Japanese empire, all social classes, and had spurred discussion about women playing baseball. This yearly tournament became synonymous with the stadium built to accommodate the vast audiences attending the games: *Kōshien*.

Additionally, the *Kōshien* Tournament began within the context of another shift in Japanese society: the Meiji Emperor passed away in 1912, leaving his frail son, Yoshihito, as Emperor. During this period, which became known as the Taisho era, political parties began taking power away from the emperor's

---

1. Quoted in Ariyama Teruo 有山輝雄, *Kōshien Yakyū to Nihonjin: Media no Tsukuta Ibento* 甲子園野球と日本人：メディアのつくったイベント [Japanese People and Kōshien Baseball: A Media Created Event], (Tokyo: Yoshikawa Kobunkan, 1997), 53.

office, thus weakening Imperial *Bushidō*. However, I argue that the baseball community in Japan created a public "examination" of Imperial *Bushidō* discourse. Teenage boys at the center of public scrutiny became a metaphor to judge the development and spread of Imperial *Bushidō* and, concomitantly, the evolution of Japan's national character. In this way, the Japanese baseball community created a "national game," one which helped transform and define domestic and imperial identities, and kept Imperial *Bushidō* thriving in the vacuum created by the weak leadership of the Taisho Emperor.

The "Baseball Evils" Debate (野球害毒論)

The creation of the National High School Baseball Tournament began with a newspaper editorial feud. In 1911, Oshikawa Shunrō, a famous adventure novelist and alumni of Waseda University and its baseball team, began a newspaper editorial quarrel with the famed "Christian Bushidō" author, Nitobe Inazō. The debate about "baseball evils" could also be translated as "baseball poison," indicating the broader concern among many Japanese intellectuals about American culture poisoning Japanese culture. Additionally, the debate pitted two drastically different versions of *bushidō* ideology against each other: Oshikawa deployed the predominant narrative of Imperial *Bushidō*, which sought to defend Japan against external pressure; Nitobe countered with his own methodology — popular among Anglophone audiences — that adherents of *bushidō* should value above all else a sense of righteous decorum and respect for one's station in society.

Nitobe Inazō (新渡戸稲造) attended Sapporo Agricultural College, where William Clark had instituted "Sports Day," and while there Nitobe converted to Christianity. For most of the last two decades of the nineteenth century, Nitobe traveled throughout the United States working, researching, and writing in English to the extent that he felt more comfortable in his adopted tongue than his native language.[2] In 1900, he published the English-language book, *Bushido: The Soul of Japan*. Nitobe insisted that the ethical standards of the samurai persisted within the post-Meiji social orders. In this way, Nitobe distinguished Japanese modernity from European modernity by arguing that the moral compass of his version of *bushidō* endured within industrialized Japan's people. Europe, comparatively, was engrossed in individualism and losing its

---

2. Benesch, *Inventing the Way of the Samurai*, 91.

religiosity.[3] Nitobe's version of *bushidō* had a positive reception among English-language audiences and a negative reception among Japanese audiences, so he did not publish a Japanese-language edition of *Bushido: The Soul of Japan* until 1908. Ultimately, Western audiences believed Nitobe symbolized the totality of Japanese *bushidō* philosophy, but in reality Nitobe was inconsequential to the domestic Japanese *bushidō* discourse.

Although at odds with Inoue Tetsujirō's Imperial *Bushidō* ideology, Nitobe served as headmaster of Ichikō High School from 1906 until 1913. This position put him into regular contact with Japan's pre-eminent youth baseball team while also putting him into conflict with Inoue, Japan's pre-eminent ideologue. Recognizing that he was out of his element at Ichikō, Nitobe promoted social cohesion among proponents of the multiple versions of *bushidō* discourse.[4] When Nitobe learned of an incident on a baseball field that he believed to be counter to his doctrine of social cohesion, he wrote a newspaper editorial and sent it to the Asahi Shinbun newspaper, one of the premier news organizations with multiple hubs in Japan.

In August 1911 and continuing through autumn of that year, Nitobe lambasted Abe Isoo's Waseda baseball team — renowned for its international travels — in the Asahi Shinbun. Abe's Waseda University team had played an exhibition game against a team of Americans located in the resort town of Karuizawa in Nagano Prefecture. During the game, an American umpire hurled racial epithets in English at Waseda player Takasugi Takizō. Unbeknownst to the umpire, Takasugi had studied in the United States and spoke fluent English. As Coach Abe had taught, Takasugi verbally defended himself to the umpire, an act that eventually symbolized to many in the baseball community Japan's rejection of the United States' unequal treatment.[5]

Nitobe argued that Takasugi's resistance against an umpire's authority as symbolic of how the Japanese baseball world operated contrary to his idealized, chivalrous *bushidō*.[6] In Nitobe's words:

Japanese baseball players do not know manners, or how to behave… Whereas in any school kendo and judo players perform their matches with cour-

---

3. Nitobe, *Bushido*, 175. Nitobe highlights Friedrich Nietsche's trope of the death of God and Hegel's assertion of history unfolding to reveal freedom (*Bushido*, 125).

4. Kobayashi Ryūichi 小林竜一, "Dai Ichikō tōgakkō kōchō toshite no Nitobe Inazō" 第一高等学校校長としての新渡戸稲造 [Nitobe Inazō as Headmaster of Ichikō High School], *Shigakken ronshū* (March 25, 2011): 84.

5. Abe, "Muscular Christianity in Japan," 724.

6. Abe, "Muscular Christianity in Japan," 724.

tesy, baseball players do not. In America, it is by no means the case that baseball players do not know proper manners of play. They know the 'sportsmanlike' and behave courteously most of the time. [This concept] can be translated into Japanese as *undōka rashii* [運動家らしい, "sports-manlike"], but because the Japanese sportsman behaves as a man of mean character, it is only perceived as something like *reigi wo shiranu gorotsuki* [礼儀を知らぬ破落戸, "an ill-bred character"].[7]

Nitobe remarked that baseball "harmed" or "poisoned" (*gaidoku*, 害毒) the Japanese national character because the game distracted students from their education and instead encouraged players to violate decorum. Additionally, Nitobe was concerned that charging money for admission tickets would turn these high school students into professional baseball laborers rather than students.[8] Responding to Nitobe's critiques in a book published later that year, Abe Isoo, who had recently become Chairman of the Japanese Amateur Athletic Association in preparation for Japan's entrance into the International Olympic Committee, emphasized that charging admissions for tickets had nothing to do with paying players or giving money to their families for performance. It was a mere business transaction that paid for the costs of the fields and team upkeep. Abe further explained that American universities had long charged admission for sporting events without losing their amateur athletic standing.[9]

Oshikawa Shunrō defended Takasugi and the Waseda baseball program in several editorial responses in the Asahi Shinbun. Oshikawa, a supporter of Inoue's Imperial *Bushidō*, lectured Nitobe on the irony presented by chivalrous *bushido* discourse:

> While Dr. Nitobe applauds the decorum shown by the American attitude to-wards [sporting] games, he declares on the other hand, that Japanese sports-men as a whole are men of mean character. I hope millions of students in Japan will never forget his remarks. Despite the fact that he does not know anything about this field, he behaves like an expert and avows logically that we are mean in character... On the one hand, he not only argues and writes

---

7. Abe, "Muscular Christianity in Japan," 724. This is Abe's translation and I have included his own parentheticals.

8. Abe, "Muscular Christianity in Japan," 724.

9. Abe Isoo 安部磯雄 and Oshikawa Shunrō 押川春朗, *Yakyū to gakusei* 野球と学生 [Baseball and Students] (Tokyo: Kobundō, 1911), 30.

on moralistic *bushidō* and gives an account of character, while on the other hand he exposes his own mean character.[10]

Abe followed with his own retort to Nitobe, explaining that students were not harmed by baseball, but instead developed a sense of national character:

> [The students] play baseball because they just want to, because it is interesting...Since the players are thinking of school honor in the interscholastic matches and of the honor of Japan in international baseball tours, they can develop the sense of prudence...that will enhance the character of athletes.[11]

Much to Nitobe's displeasure, the debate spiked newspaper sales and, for the first time, brought baseball beyond its usual confines of elite universities and preparatory schools and led to the creation of the National High School Tournament. [12]

In the late nineteenth and early twentieth centuries, the baseball community in the Japanese empire, influenced by Imperial *Bushidō*, began identifying characteristics of how a Japanese person should play baseball. The baseball community in Japan was predominantly interested in leveling an unfair playing field, epitomized by Abe Isoo's teams and world tours. Prior to World War I, much of the baseball community in Japan borrowed heavily from the European and American sporting contexts of creating social distance: baseball was played predominantly in elite schools, discussed by writers from families of privilege, and segregated by ethnicity. Because of the "baseball evils debate," however, Japan's first annual baseball championship tournament began, and this resulted in baseball's spread throughout the empire to all schools and all social classes, which transformed athletics into a vehicle for national identity.

The Making of a Japanese Game: The "Kōshien" High School Baseball Tournament

"The National Secondary School Championship Baseball Tournament" (全国中等学校優勝野球大会 *Zenkoku Chūtōgakkō Yūshō Yakyū Taikai*) began in 1915 in Hyōgo (located between the cities of Osaka and Kobe). The tournament had several important effects: it broke down social barriers within

---

10. Abe, "Muscular Christianity in Japan," 724–725.

11. Quoted in Abe, "Muscular Christianity in Japan," 730.

12. Ono, "Shokuminchi Chōsen no Kōshien Taikai," 45.

Japanese society, it incorporated players from the entirety of the empire, and it shifted the landscape of how baseball was played in Japan with the construction of the massive stadium that would lend its name to the tournament and became its home for the next century, *Kōshien* (甲子園球場). Annually, over 5,000 male students from across the empire participated in qualifying rounds for the tournament, and about 250 students from 22 teams from across the empire competed for the championship on *Kōshien*'s famous dirt infield (*Kōshien no do,* 甲子園の土, "Kōshien soil").[13] The *Kōshien* Tournament was the world's largest single-sport competition for most of the first half of the twentieth century, and at times it was two-to-three times as large as the Summer Olympics.

Hoping to match the increased newspaper sales seen during the "baseball evils debate," in 1915 rival Osaka newspaper branches of the Asahi Shinbun and the Mainichi Shinbun organized and sponsored the first high school baseball tournament in Japan.[14] Ultimately, the Asahi and Mainichi newspapers did see the surge in sales they predicted: in a market about 75% the size of Tokyo, the Osaka edition of the Asahi Shinbun outsold the Tokyo edition by an average of two to one throughout the first decade of the Kōshien tournament.[15] A picture published in the Asahi Shinbun of the tournament's ceremonial first pitch became one of the most enduring images in Japanese baseball history. Seen below, the President of the Osaka Asahi newspaper, Murayama Ryōhei (村山龍平), threw the first pitch of the tournament while dressed in a traditional hakama; Araki Torasaburō (荒木虎三郎), President of Kyoto Imperial University, stood behind him in a top hat and frock coat. The juxtaposition of the men — Murayama a former Meiji politician representing Japanese "tradition" and Araki the academic dressed in contemporary Western fashion representing Japanese modernity — demonstrated the tournament's intent to look to both Japan's past and future.

The ceremonial first pitch of the high school baseball tournament on the Toyonaka Grounds.[16]

---

13. Ariyama, *Kōshien Yakyū to Nihonjin,* 147.

14. Ono, "Shokuminchi chōsen no Kōshien Taikai," 45.

15. Data compiled from Japanese Population statistics and Ariyama, *Kōshien Yakyū to Nihonjin,* 75.

16. Image from Asahi Shinbun, 全国高校野球選手権大会 *Zenkoku kōkō yakyū senshuken taikai* [The National Baseball Championship Tournament], http://www.asahishimbun-saiyou. com/project/baseball.html.

Most significantly, the national high school tournament redefined the relationship between baseball and the space where it was played. From baseball's inception in Japan until the late 1910s, baseball was played on "grounds" (グランド), which were flat spaces located close to natural environments and featured few if any risers or bleachers for spectators. The Toyonaka Grounds (豊中グランド) in Osaka hosted the first two years of the national tournament (1915–1916). Spectators sat on short risers near the playing field, as seen in the picture below.

A play at home plate during the 1915 high school baseball tournament at Toyonaka Grounds.[17]

The high school baseball tournament increased in popularity and quickly outgrew Toyonaka Grounds. In 1917, tournament organizers relocated the competition to the recently constructed multipurpose Naruo Stadium (鳴尾球場) in Osaka. In addition to a baseball grounds, Naruo featured a horse racing track, a running track for humans, tennis courts, and swimming pools. Although Naruo Stadium could seat 10,000 spectators, it was a poor venue for baseball; the stadium's layout situated the tennis courts closer to the baseball ground than the spectators.[18]

The national tournament's popularity continued to grow and prompted the construction of a massive single-use baseball stadium, Kōshien Stadium (*Kōshien kyūjō*, 甲子園球場). Kōshien Stadium was one of the most significant buildings in Japan's first half-century of statehood. Completed in Hyōgo prefecture (about halfway between the prefectural capital of Kobe and its neighboring metropolis, Osaka) in 1924, it had a maximum capacity of 55,000

17. Image from Asahi Shinbun Digital, *Kōkō yakyū 100 nen* 高校野球100年 [100 Years of High School Baseball], http://www.asahi.com/koshien/100years/photo_gallery/1.html.

18. Ariyama, *Kōshien Yakyū to Nihonjin*, 119. Ariyama has a simple diagram of Naruo Stadium.

people. It was the first single-purpose baseball stadium in Asia, and remained the highest capacity baseball stadium in Japan for sixty years until the Tokyo Dome's completion in 1988.[19] On a global scale, Kōshien Stadium was the second biggest baseball stadium in the world when it was finished, only smaller than the original Yankee Stadium in New York, which was completed in 1923 (the Polo Grounds, located across the river from Yankee Stadium, later expanded to be larger than Kōshien Stadium).[20] Whereas Yankee Stadium and the Polo Grounds were home to the most famous professional baseball teams in the United States and in a metropolis of nearly six million people, Kōshien Stadium was the center of a high school baseball tournament where the nearest three prefectures — Kyoto, Osaka, and Hyogo (Kobe) — had six million people combined.[21]

Kōshien, both the stadium and the tournament, created unprecedented audiences throughout the empire and simultaneously expanded the market of *bushidō* baseball philosophy. Although a world-class stadium hosted the championship games, about 95% of the Kōshien tournament occurred in its local qualifying tournaments, held in each Japanese prefecture. By 1924, qualifying tournaments included each of the colonized territories.[22] The qualifying tournament for the *Kōshien* championship had over 5,000 participants annually, and was five times bigger than any Summer Olympics before World War II. The quest to play on *Kōshien* Stadium's dirt infield consumed most of the academic year and put students under incessant pressure to exemplify national strength and discipline in addition to stellar baseball play. Less than ten years after Nitobe Inazō feared that baseball was distracting from student learning, *bushidō* baseball had become a year-round occupation for boys to demonstrate both baseball skill and adherence to Imperial *Bushidō* philosophy.

The Transformative Power of Baseball *Bushidō*

The power in the relationship between Imperial *Bushidō* and the Japanese baseball community was visible early in the *Kōshien* Tournament's existence. Within a few years, Japanese intellectuals began discussing the intersections of art

---

19. Yōsensha 洋泉社, *Shōwa puro yakyū kyūjō taizen* 昭和プロ野球「球場」大全 [Professional Baseball Stadiums of the Shōwa Era] (Tokyo: Yōsensha, 2014).

20. Statistics from www.ballparksofbaseball.com.

21. Population data derived from the Statistics Bureau of the Japanese Ministry of Internal Affairs and Communications, http://www.stat.go.jp/data/chouki/zuhyou/02-05.xls.

22. Ariyama, *Kōshien Yakyū to Nihonjin*, 147.

and business within the context of national character. As early as 1919, essayist Yokoi Kakujō (横井鶴城) recalled the baseball evils debate when he wrote a semi-regular column in the seminal baseball magazine, *Yakyūkai* (野球界, "Baseball World") titled "Discussing Baseball *Bushidō*" (野球武士道を論ず). In September of 1919, Yokoi wrote:

> The spirit of baseball virtues [野球道徳] are "baseball *bushidō*," but the difference between baseball virtues and general virtues are not often discussed. Generally, business people follow business virtues and industrialists follow industrial virtues, but what is the origin of this thing called "baseball virtues?"... The spirit of baseball virtues are that the thing called "baseball *bushidō*" can be witnessed and discussed, and right now in the many games that we watch, we recognize actions that violate current "baseball *bushidō*"... and most students in secondary school can be corrected ...[23]

Writing at the end of World War I, Yokoi emphasized that whereas the world often acted with cruelty and maliciousness, "baseball *bushidō*" offered a sense of "fairness" or "openness" or "acceptance" (正々堂々, *seisei dōdō*) compounded with "righteousness" (正義, *seigi*).[24] Using this as his basis, at the end of 1919 Yokoi lambasted a group of *Kōshien* umpires for permitting a game to continue while two teams hurled insults at each other, which recalled the original baseball evils debate. Yokoi wrote:

> The Asahi Newspaper should apologize to its readers... the Hiroshima Commercial High School acted without a *bushi* attitude, and the boys should be ashamed. In permitting this attitude of the Hiroshima Commercial High School, the tournament organizers have a similar lack of gentlemanly *bushi* attitude.[25]

In other words, Yokoi extrapolated the values of baseball not only to the boys on the field, but to the tournament and to its corporate sponsors. Although Yokoi defended "baseball *bushidō*" on the ground of strengthening the Japanese empire and its population, he also vindicated Nitobe's concern that baseball would consume student lives and become a mechanism for generating profit.

---

23. Yokoi Kakujō 横井鶴城, "Yakyū bushidō wo ronzu" 野球武士道を論ず [Speaking of Baseball Bushido], *Yakyūkai* 1, no. 9 (1919): 1. Yokoi later changed his name to Yokoi Haruno.

24. Yokoi, "Yakyū bushidō wo ronzu," 1.

25. Yokoi, "Yakyū bushidō wo ronzu," 1.

The Kōshien Tournament's success in transforming public dialogue about national character also centered on whether women were allowed to play baseball. Although the early Meiji-era physical education programs sought to strengthen young women's bodies, this trend had waned throughout the early twentieth century as many Japanese men preferred a more domesticated image for women. After the formation of a women's baseball team at a Nagoya high school 1919, several articles in *Yakyūkai* discussed whether women should participate in baseball. Writing on behalf of the members of the Nagoya women's team, team captain Koshihara So (越原租) indicated that a lack of research into women's physical education caused discrimination about women playing baseball.[26] Because men had long been the focus of physical education curriculum, they naturally became physically stronger, and Koshihara believed that a focus on women's physical education could similarly promote healthy and strong female bodies that would complement the formation of a strong Japanese nation. Although Koshihara advocated for the improvement of women's health through the playing of baseball, she framed it within the context of expectations for Japanese women to remain distinctly non-masculine. Women would have more modest and subdued uniforms than men, and instead of focusing on competition, women's baseball would focus on the building of close relationships that were useful in "domestic life."[27] Although women's baseball continued on a small scale throughout the 1920s, by the 1930s the physical education curriculum had shifted so strongly toward militarization that women's baseball had disappeared almost entirely from Japan.

The Nagoya Women's Baseball Team in 1919.[28]

---

26. Koshihara So 越原租, "Jyoshi ni yakyū wo shōreisu," 女子に野球を奨励す [Encouraging Women to Play Baseball], *Yakyūkai* 1, no. 6 (1919): 12.

27. Koshihara, "Jyoshi ni yakyū wo shōreisu," 14.

28. *Yakyūkai* 1, no. 6 (1919): 1.

Playing a game at Kōshien Stadium acted as the ultimate examination for aspiring baseball acolytes. Newspapers across the empire recorded baseball performance statistics — runs scored, innings pitched, errors made — and made a public record of how teenage boys played before some of the largest audiences yet seen in human history. Additionally, the teams represented at the tournament were from all corners and social classes of the Japanese empire. Whereas baseball's progenitors in Japan were elite preparatory schools and universities located in Tokyo (Ichikō and Waseda, among others), the championship game of the Kōshien Tournament in 1924, for example, was played between two prefectures on the relative periphery of the Japanese baseball community, Nagano and Hiroshima. In 1926, the championship game of the Kōshien Tournament was played between Shizuoka Prefecture and the Dalian baseball team, demonstrating that even the imperial territories could compete with the elite teams from the Japanese metropolises.[29]

Kōshien Stadium in 1924. Unlike the previous layouts of baseball "grounds," the stadium permitted an elevated audience to surround the baseball players.[30]

---

29. All Kōshien Tournament data is provided by the Asahi Shinbun at http://www.asahi.com/koshien/stats/.

30. Image available: http://www.asahicom.jp/koshien/100years/history/images/bg/bg1915.jpg.

The "*bushidō* baseball" that expanded throughout the Japanese empire in the early twentieth century was not a replication of the "American pastime" but the appearance of Japan's national game. Fueled by conversations about how a baseball player should act within the context of Imperial *Bushidō* — including whether women should play — the Japanese baseball community and viewing public debated and constructed their own "national game" that had had a history that entangled with Meiji-era discussions of Japan's cultural uniqueness. Despite the early success of the Kōshien Tournament, baseball was not yet an official component of state policy. The baseball community embraced Imperial *Bushidō* more than policy makers embraced baseball. Inoue's Imperial *Bushidō* popularized several "national" concepts like the "national body" (*kokutai*, 国体) and "national morality" (*kokumin dōtoku*, 国民道徳), but baseball was not yet formally the Japanese "national game" (*kokugi*, 国技). From the start, Inoue aspired for *budō* martial arts, not baseball, to become Japan's "national game." The next stage for baseball to become Japan's national game involved a period of athletic mega-events, wherein athletic communities integrated mental, physical, and national characteristics within practitioners.

Conclusion

The National High School Baseball Tournament, or *Kōshien* Tournament, began from a newspaper editorial feud and expanded into the world's largest athletic competition by 1926. The tournament was at all times an evaluation of Imperial *Bushidō* spirit, and it drove discussions of "Japanese-ness" among audiences from all corners of the empire and among all social classes. By 1924, the Japanese baseball community had included teams from every colonial possession into the *Kōshien* Tournament, and the community had built a world-class stadium where baseball could be enjoyed by one of the world's largest audiences. The *Kōshien* Tournament's success inspired several other athletic "mega-events," which would characterize the next twenty years of Japanese culture.

CHAPTER FIVE

The Era of Athletic Mega-Events

Sports are a kind of peaceful conflict. When there's social competition everywhere among all people, the emergence of beast-like characteristics among men is unavoidable. In these chaotic competitive situations, we obey the rules of sports as the rules that protect human dignity.[1]

— Abe Isoo, "The Educational Value of Sports," 1926

Introduction

On December 25, 1926, the frail Taishō Emperor passed away and his first son, Hirohito, officially ascended to the imperial throne after five years as regent. Among the many things in the empire that Hirohito and his government inherited, they controlled within Tokyo the most impressive, concentrated collection of sporting venues that existed in the world. In total, the outer gardens devoted to the memory of Emperor Meiji held over forty percent of Tokyo's athletic space and placed almost the entirety of the Japanese athletic world under the imperial family's immediate gaze.[2] Emperor Hirohito's younger brother, Prince Chichibu, patronized Japanese athletics and was called "the sporting prince" by an affectionate public.[3] Under Hirohito and his parliaments, athletics be-

---

1. Abe Isoo 安部磯雄, *Supōtsu no Kyōikuteki Kachi* スポーツの教育的価値 [The Educational Value of Sports], quoted in Itami Yasuhiro 伊丹安広, *Yakyū no Chichi: Abe Isoo Sensei* 野球の父: 安部磯雄先生 [The Father of Baseball: Teacher Abe Isoo, (Tokyo: Waseda Daigaku Shuppanbu, 1965), 116. Translation mine.

2. Japanese Ministry of Education, "Result of Survey on Current Condition of Sport Equipment Throughout Japan," Supreme Commander for the Allied Powers, Civil Information and Education Section, Education Division, Special Projects Branch 1945–1952, Box 5727, Folder 29, 1–2.

3. The Imperial Household Agency, "Their Imperial Highness Prince and Princess Chichibu," http://www.kunaicho.go.jp/e-about/history/history12.html.

came the fertile soil from which a militarized, athletic, and *bushidō*-inflected Japanese national identity sprouted. Ultimately, the Ministry of Education, the Ministry of Home Affairs, and the Ministry of Health and Welfare became important proponents of creating and maintaining these athletic mega-events. This chapter discusses how these early twentieth century processes massively expanded Japanese sporting culture and laid the groundwork for the formal incorporation of the Japanese baseball community under the umbrella of the imperial family, thus becoming Japan's "national game."

The Era of Mega-Events in Japan's Empire

Sociologist Maurice Roche defines "mega-events" as:

Large-scale cultural (including commercial and sporting) events which have a dramatic character, mass popular appeal and international significance. They are typically organised by variable combinations of national governmental and international non-governmental organisations and thus can be said to be important elements in 'official' versions of public culture.[4]

Athletic mega-events became increasingly common for Japan during the first part of the twentieth century, and they transformed the way Japanese understood their concept of an integrated culture and empire. There was a nearly twenty-year span from 1923–1942 in which Japan participated in two athletic mega-events per year. Throughout the 1930s and 1940s, an average of 20–30,000 total athletes participated in these events, with 1941 topping all other years at 60,000 participants.[5] The following subsections will discuss how Japan's poor performances in the Olympics led to the creation of nationalized athletics in the *Meiji Jingū Taikai* and a series of loosely-related tournaments in the puppet state of Manchūkuo. The chart below tracks the occurrences of Japanese athletic mega-events from 1912–1942, whether hosted or participated. It is beyond the scope of this book to focus on the Far East Championship Games, which the Japanese promoted as an Asian-alternative to the Western-driven Olympics.

---

4. Maurice Roche, *Mega-Events and Modernity: Olympics and Expos in the Growth of Global Culture* (London: Routledge, 2000), 1.

5. Data compiled from Ariyama, *Kōshien yakyū to Nihonjin*, 147; Irie, *Shōwa supotsu shi ron*, 3; and Takashima, Teikoku Nihon to supōtsu, 77.

	Far East Championship Games	Summer/ Winter Olympics	Kōshien Baseball Tournament	Meiji Jingū Taikai	East Asian Tournament in Manchūkuo
1912		X			
1913	X				
1914					
1915	X		X		
1916			X		
1917	X (Hosted)		X		
1918			X		
1919	X		X		
1920		X	X		
1921	X		X		
1922			X		
1923	X (Hosted)		X		
1924		X	X	X	
1925	X		X	X	
1926			X	X	
1927	X		X	X	
1928		X	X		
1929			X	X	
1930	X (Hosted)		X		
1931			X	X	
1932		X	X		X
1933			X	X	
1934	X		X		
1935			X	X	
1936		X	X		
1937			X	X	
1938	(planned host)		X		
1939			X	X	X
1940		(planned host)	X	X	X
1941			X	X	
1942			X	X	X

Japanese athletic mega-events from 1920–1942, either hosted or participated, indicated with an X.

Athletic Mega-Events and Imperial *Bushidō*

As historian Irie Katsumi noted, "Essentially as imperialist thinking was nor-malized, it was domestic policy to emphasize the strength of the military as the physical strength of the people."[6] Imperial lawmakers and statesmen increas-ingly used the physical education system as a training grounds for militarist ideology, and the athletic mega-events became the pinnacle moments where these ideologies were showcased for the wider empire. In 1917, the Japanese Ministry of Education established the Special Council for Education, which mandated: "students above middle school should be trained to be a soldier with patriotic conformity, martial spirit, obedience, and toughness of mind and body."[7] Following World War I, Japanese state politics was controlled by multi-party cabinets that "ruled as partners of other elites," and these parties promoted the image of the emperor as the center of imperial ideology and made it illegal to critique the imperial family or its agenda.[8] Within the frequent-ly-shifting cabinets, multiple special councils formed to control school physical education, but all shared the common goal of continuing the militarization of physical education. In April 1925, the Ministry of Education enacted military drill in high schools and installed military officers to oversee its instruction. In 1931, in accordance with Imperial *Bushidō*, the Ministry of Education ordered that all middle and high school students train in *jūdō* and *kendō* to help edu-cate about the "origin of the nation."[9] These skills would then be displayed at mega-events, which became a recurring mechanism to keep students involved in the strengthening of their body for the purposes of defending the empire.

Athletic mega-events were possible, in part, because of earlier efforts at con-structing venues to improve Japanese performances in international sporting competition. The outer gardens of Emperor Meiji's shrine, which Kanō Jigorō wanted to use to improve Japanese physical education and Olympic perfor-mance, were finished in 1920. The foundation for a multi-use athletic stadium was laid in late 1922. Then, over the first two days of September 1923, three earthquakes—magnitude 8.1, 6.4, and 7.8—levelled three-quarters of the city of Tokyo, killed upwards of 200,000 people, and destroyed nearly 600,000

---

6. Irie Katsumi 入江克己, *Shōwa supōtsu shi ron* 昭和スポーツ史論 [Discussions of Shōwa Sports History] (Tokyo: Fumidō Shuppan, 1991), 59.

7. Ikuo Abe, Yasuharu Kiyohara, and Ken Nakajima, "Sport and Physical Education Under Fascistization in Japan," *In Yo: Journal of Alternative Perspectives* (June 2000), 3.

8. Gordon, *A Modern History of Japan*, 170.

9. Abe, Kiyohara, and Nakajima, "Sport and Physical Education Under Fascistization in Japan," 3.

buildings.[10] The earthquake damaged the foundation and framework of the "National Athletic Stadium" (*Meiji Jingū Gaien Kyōgijō*, 明治神宮外苑競場), and construction halted for foundation repair. The stadium opened a year later, on October 25, 1924, in the outer gardens of the shrine to Emperor Meiji. Five days later, the first *Meiji Jingū Kyōgi Taikai* (明治神宮競技大会, "Meiji Shrine Athletic Meet," hereafter "Meiji Jingū Taikai") began, putting on display over 3,000 athletes in various Olympic-style athletic competitions.[11]

Baseball fans in the heart of Tokyo envied Kōshien Stadium in Hyōgo and wondered if they too could have a stadium to host games for the recently incorporated "Tokyo Big 6" College League that formed in 1925. Their wishes were fulfilled on October 22, 1926, when *Meiji Jingū* Stadium (*Meiji Jingū Kyūjō*, 明治神宮球場, literally "Meiji Shrine Stadium") opened to the public. Located within the Meiji Jingū Outer Gardens, *Meiji Jingū* Stadium featured meeting rooms, an art gallery, inviting gardens, and an adjoining *sumō* ring.[12] Tokyo-based athletes now had modern, world-class stadiums and venues all located within the confines of the Meiji Jingū Outer Gardens.

The Meiji Jingū Taikai

Officially, the Meiji Jingū Taikai directed people to "aspire to the imperial virtues of the Meiji Emperor" (明治大帝の御聖徳を憬仰する), a sentiment which more closely matched the 1920s legislation promoting the Emperor as the nation's moral compass.[13] The *Taikai* was an athletic meet that featured Olympic-style events like track-and-field and swimming; non-Olympic Western sports like baseball, basketball, and hockey; and *budō* martial arts like *kendō*, *jūdō*, *kyūdō*, and *naginata*.[14] Although lacking the empire-wide qualification rounds seen in the Kōshien Tournament, the Meiji Jingū Taikai had more baseball players participating in its championship games at Jingū Sta-

---

10. Gordon, *A Modern History of Japan*, 140, and United States Geological Survey, "Significant Earthquakes — 1923," https://earthquake.usgs.gov/earthquakes/browse/significant.php?-year=1923.

11. Irie, *Shōwa supōtsu shi ron*, 3.

12. Size information from Yōsensha, *Shōwa puro yakyū kyūjō taizen*; Construction information from 神宮球場の歴史 *Meiji Jingū Kyūjyō no rekishi*, http://www.jingu-stadium.com/about_kyujo/history/.

13. Takashima, Teikoku Nihon to supōtsu, 121.

14. Irie, *Shōwa supōtsu shi ron*, 78–81.

dium than did the Kōshien Tournament.[15] Because the Meiji Jingū Taikai included people of all ages, it was not controlled by the Ministry of Education; instead, it was first sponsored by the Ministry of Home Affairs (内務省). Over the next decade, the Meiji Jingū Taikai integrated the school physical education system, amateur sports, the emperor system, and *bushidō* philosophy.[16] The tournament boomed in participation from 3,000 participants in 1924 to 50,000 participants by 1940, and moved into the purview of the larger Ministry of Health and Welfare (厚生省).[17] Annually, almost half of the participants in the Meiji Jingū Taikai were in the "mass games," which was a public display of calisthenics and gymnastics.[18] Because the Ministry of Education had formally designed school gymnastics after World War I to develop soldier's mentality in accordance with Imperial *Bushidō*, the "mass games" were a demonstration of bodies fortified for both health and military service.

Alongside the first Meiji Jingū Taikai, the first "National Physical Education Day" (全国体育デー) was held on November 3, 1924, to commemorate Emperor Meiji's birthday.[19] The holiday's purpose was to disseminate physical education ideas among Japanese society by expanding beyond the school system to include businesses, banks, and civic centers in athletic discussion and performances.[20] The National Physical Education Day's official guidebook made it abundantly clear that all Japanese citizens should have access to contemporary knowledge about physical education. The text explains: "As for the outcry for the revival of people's physical education, it resounds in every nook and cranny of the country, and the voices spreading physical education fill the rural areas and urban areas alike."[21] According to historian Noguchi Hodaka, National Physical Education Day allowed the Ministry of Education to create over 15,000 student and civic organizations that sponsored over 30,000 separate events in relation

---

15. To date, there are no significant research projects into the baseball community at the Meiji Jingū Taikai. This would be an area for future research.

16. Takashima, *Teikoku Nihon to supōtsu*, 119–121.

17. Irie, *Shōwa supōtsu shi ron*, number of participants from p.1, sponsorship from p. 14.

18. Irie, *Shōwa supōtsu shi ron*, 1.

19. Secretary of the Ministry of Education School Hygiene Section 文部大臣官學校衛生課, "Taiiku de- jisshi gaikyō" 體育デー實施概況 [*Physical Education Day Implementation Guideline*] (1924), http://kindai.ndl.go.jp/info:ndljp/pid/939870, 1 (location 5/51).

20. Secretary of the Ministry of Education School Hygiene Section, "Taiiku de- jisshi gaikyō," 6–7 (location 8/51).

21. Secretary of the Ministry of Education School Hygiene Section, "Taiiku de- jisshi gaikyō," 1 (location 5/51).

to the holiday.[22] Athletic day activities varied from organization to organization and included lectures on athletics and hygiene, field trips, and full-scale athletic tournaments.[23] The Ministry of Education's official stance was lenient as to what events were considered, and stated that events should "not be limited to the body, but should include discussion of how the body (肉体) and spirit (精神) are inseparable."[24] Through the instrument of National Physical Education Day, the Ministry of Education spread their militarized physical education agenda beyond schools and into the general public and private businesses.

The Manchurian *Undōkai* and Olympic Committee

The use of athletic mega-events in the foundation of the Manchūkuo puppet-state further exemplified the Imperial Japanese state's early efforts to use athletics to create a uniform national identity. In late 1931, the Japanese Kwangtung Army purposefully sabotaged a section of the Japanese-operated Manchurian Railway located within Chinese territory. Chinese soldiers engaged in skirmishes designed to reassert Chinese sovereignty in the area, and as a result the Kwangtung Army destroyed a section of railroad, blamed Chinese rebels, and then mobilized to "protect" Japanese interests along the railroad by occupying the area. In February 1932, Japan created the puppet state of Manchūkuo (満州国) and installed as the head of state Pu-Yi, the last emperor of China's Qing Dynasty that had abdicated in 1911. Simultaneous to the creation of Manchūkuo, Japanese soldiers battled Chinese soldiers in a brutal battle in Shanhai. While these conflicts did not become a sustained war in 1932, they set the stage for years of tense relations and skirmishing followed by a formal declaration of war in 1937. The invasion of Manchuria effectively began Japan's involvement in what is popularly called the "Fifteen Years War" that spanned its invasion of Manchuria, its war with China beginning in 1937, and its war with the United States beginning in 1941.

Less commonly known, however, is the role that athletics played in setting up the puppet state of Manchukuo and beginning the "Fifteen Years War." In

22. Noguchi Hodaka 野口穂高, "1924 nen no daiichi zenkoku taiiku no de- no katsudō jōkyō ni kan suru—kōsatsu," 1924 年の第一回全国体育デーの活動状況に関する一考察 [An Inquiry into the Conditions and Activities of the First All Japan Physical Education Day in 1924], *Tamagawa Daigaku kyōiku gakubu kiyō* (2013): 51–52.

23. Noguchi, "1924 nen no daiichi zenkoku taiiku no de- no katsudō jōkyō ni kan suru—kōsatsu," 61.

24. Quoted in Noguchi, "1924 nen no daiichi zenkoku taiiku no de- no katsudō jōkyō ni kan suru—kōsatsu," 50.

the spring of 1932, the League of Nations intervened in China to establish peace in Shanghai and formed a multinational committee to investigate the bombing in Manchūkuo. The commission's results, the Litton Report, were released in October 1932. The Japanese government tried to sway the findings of the European and American investigators — many of whom were military or colonial officers — through demonstrations of national unity by the people of Manchūkuo.[25] About two months after Manchūkuo's creation in April 1932, the Japanese government forced the people of Manchūkuo to publicly celebrate their nation's creation with a huge athletic meet (*undōkai*, 運動会). About one in five Manchurians participated in the event.[26] The athletic meet lasted several weeks, featured 100,000 participants, and had an audience of nearly 160,000.[27] The Yomiuri Shinbun newspaper reported the athletic meet was a routine among the people of Manchūkuo, noting that "every student from every school" would go to their local sports grounds at 8:30 in the morning.[28] Another report from the Yomiuri wistfully described a day in which the sun shone on a crowd of 30,000 people, filled with Koreans, Japanese, and Manchu who were in a state of "harmonious union" (*yūwa ketsugō*, 融和結合) as they watched the athletic events.[29] Although the athletic meet did not sway Litton Report's findings, it demonstrated that the Japanese government saw mega-events as critical to the formation of national unity and a colonial consciousness, and also as a vehicle to deflect international criticism of their imperialist endeavors.

Continuing the effort to bolster support for the international recognition of Manchūkuo as a sovereign state, in May 1932 the Manchūkuo Physical Education Association (*Manshūkuo Taiiku Kyōkai*, 満州国体育協会) submitted a last-minute application for admission into the 1932 Los Angeles Summer Olympic Games.[30] The Manchūkuo Physical Education Association believed

25. Takashima, *Teikoku Nihon to supōtsu*, 24.

26. Numbers calculated using population grid provided by Irie, *Shōwa supōtsu shi ron*, 4.

27. Takashima, *Teikoku Nihon to supōtsu*, 23.

28. "Manshū kenkoku dai undōkai" 満州建國大運動会 [The Great Athletic Meet of Manchuria's Founding] *Yomiuri Shinbun*, May 22, 1932, Morning Edition, 5.

29. "Supotsu ni musubu: Nichiman no mangeki, kenkoku dai undōkai hiraku" スポーツに結ぶ：日満の感激、建國大運動會開く [Connected Through Sports: The Passion of Japan and Manchuria, The Opening of the Great Nation-Founding Athletic Meet] *Yomiuri Shinbun*, May 1, Evening Edition, 2.

30. Takashima Kō 高嶋航, "Manchūkuo" no tanjyō to kyokutō supōtsu kai no saihen 「満州国」の誕生と極東スポーツ界の再編 [Reevaluating the Birth of Manchūkuo and the Far East Sports World], *Kyoto University Bulletin of Linguistic Research* 47 (2008): 142.

that representation at an international sporting event — especially one held in the United States — would help legitimize the Manchūkuo government. However, there were insurmountable challenges, foremost the fact that Manchūkuo had existed for less than two months and did not have the prerequisite International Olympic Committee approval.

As part of their proposal to enter the Olympics, Japanese officials in Manchūkuo chose Liu Chang-Chun to represent the country in the 100-and 200-meter track and field sprint races. Liu was a 23-year-old college student at Northeastern University in Manchūkuo who majored in physical education. Born and raised in Mukden, the site of the 1931 Manchurian Railroad sabotage by the Kwangtung Army, Liu was disdainful of the Japanese after watching his home become a Japanese puppet state. He wrote a note to the Chinese Olympics Committee stating that he wanted to participate in the Olympics not as a representative of Manchūkuo, but as a representative of China.[31] By June 24, 1932 faculty at Northeastern University funded $1,600 dollars to cover Liu's travel expenses. After Liu's graduation on July 1, he fled Manchūkuo and arrived in the port of Shanghai. By July 8, Liu was in Los Angeles as China's only Olympic athlete.[32] One of Liu's supporters commented, "His hope was that all Chinese people would fight for the [Chinese] state the way that he had fought for it."[33] Thus while athletics served as a state tool to inculcate national consciousness and a colonial subjectivity, they also provided a contested space where athletes could assert their own political beliefs and undermine the Japanese state's efforts to create a uniform national consciousness.

Conclusion

This chapter discussed how the Japanese athletic world created athletic mega-events with Japanese-sourced traditions that tied into imperial ideology and buffeted existing discussions of Imperial *Bushidō*. Japan's school physical education system promoted preparation for national defense, and subsequent government policies extended this beyond the school system and into the public sphere. Japan did not draw nearer to the West via athletic mega-events, but instead Japanese athletic communities created their own Olympic-inspired events to amplify existing narratives of national consciousness and inculcate

---

31. Takashima, "Manshūkuo" no tanjō," 142.
32. Takashima, "Manshūkuo" no tanjō," 143.
33. Takashima, "Manshūkuo" no tanjō," 143.

imperial ideology. In the next chapter, I build on this discussion of athletic mega-events to discuss how the Japanese baseball community transformed Japanese nationalism during the fascist era of the 1930s and 1940s.

CHAPTER SIX

Baseball during the Fifteen Years War

*From the beginning of time in Japan, sportsmanship has been entirely
unified with a bushidō spirit, and the Kōshien tournament is not a
direct translation of the corporatized American baseball, but a game
that spread and encourages the foundation of Japanese baseball in a
bushidō spirit.*[1]

— Editorial in the Asahi Shinbun, 1929

Introduction

This chapter analyzes baseball's militarization during the Fifteen Years War
from 1931–1945. I argue that the baseball community became entangled in the
creation of the fascist fantasy of Japan, which gave the sport cachet to promote
the emperor system and the belief in a transcendental and unified Japanese
identity. The political situation in Japan was tumultuous in the 1930s. Formally, Japan remained a democratic capitalist system throughout most of the
1930s, yet increasingly the government ignored the results of popular votes,
espoused ideology that contradicted Western capitalism and science, demanded unwavering loyalty to the stated or inferred wishes of Emperor Hirohito,
and controlled what social practices were considered acceptable conduct. In
this chapter I argue that the "*bushidō* baseball" that became increasingly well-
known in the 1930s was an instrument of capitalist critique that substituted
fascist narratives of unity and strength in place of capitalist unevenness. In
other words, the Japanese baseball community purposefully integrated across
ethnic and social classes to oppose the racism and elitism seen in American
baseball. The Japanese critique of American baseball was also greatly affected

---

1. Quoted in Ono Yasuteru, "Shokuminchi Chosen no Kōshien Taikai," 46.

by the influence of the increasingly fascistic tendencies of the Japanese government, which assumed control of the Japanese baseball community in 1932.

I contend that baseball in Japan under fascistization in Japan erased the notion of unevenness seen in American baseball. For example, MLB included Caribbean players only to extract higher profits for team owners and prohibited black men from playing alongside white men. In contrast, during the 1930s the Japanese baseball community — both in the professional and amateur leagues — included players not only from Japan, but also Taiwan, Korea, the Soviet Union, and American white and black players. Although there were several Major League Baseball goodwill tours to Japan in the late-1920s continuing through much of the 1930s, I argue that scholars should not see these through the familiar narrative of American benevolence, but instead as reminders of Japan's inequality to the United States and the unevenness of capitalism. For the United States, the unevenness of capitalism justified why their baseball programs were superior and the programs of the Japanese inferior. Babe Ruth, the luminary American baseball player whose 1934 visit to Japan is discussed in this chapter, did not need the Japanese to validate that he was the homerun king of American baseball. Thus, the increasingly fascist Japanese state promoted images of multicultural unity among its imperial subjects and offered a solution to the ongoing unequal treatment. As anthropologist Marilyn Ivy wrote of the fascist fantasy:

> [T]he fascist fantasy…comes in to regulate the dangerous excesses of capitalism…Capitalism utterly depends on unevenness, and its state of normalcy is one of hysterical, excessive production…If we think of the fascist fantasy as an integral part of the structure of capitalism…then we won't find it illegitimate to think of Japan as permeated with something we would call fascism in the interwar years…That fantasy is always cultural…the notion of culture — emerges as that which *also* works precisely to erase the political (that is, class division and unevenness) and the traumas of capitalism…[2]

In other words, the Japanese baseball community was the culture that erased the traumas of the capitalist West; instead of a hierarchical Japanese baseball community, baseball gave the impression that the Japanese state — and the empire it defended — were unified in harmony.

---

2. Marilyn Ivy, "Fascism, Yet?" in *The Culture of Japanese Fascism*, ed. Alan Tansman (Durham, NC: Duke University Press, 2009), vii–xi.

Yet at the height of the war, the fantasies of fascism no longer promoted the joyous unification of imperial identities, but instead a hyper-national, homogeneous, masochistic Japanese identity. Even as Japanese casualties grew at horrifying rates in the later third of the Pacific War, baseball players continued games before domestic audiences to symbolize the strength of the Japanese army and the enduring unity of the Japanese nation. As such, this era of Japanese baseball represents a period where Japanese government bureaucrats demanded overtures of fanatical Japanese nationalism and self-sacrificial, masochistic athletic practices in defense of a concocted national spirit.

Government Intervention in School Baseball

A watershed moment occurred in 1931, when a baseball team from Taiwan demonstrated *bushidō* baseball's power to Japanese fans, and ultimately led to the Japanese government's complete takeover of school baseball and the later creation of Japan's first professional baseball league. Of Japan's colonies, Taiwan was the last to join the *Kōshien* Tournament, when a mostly ethnic Japanese team from Taiwan first participated in 1923. However, less than ten years later, Taiwan had one of the most successful showings of any colonial team when the Jiayi Agriculture and Forestry Institute (nicknamed "Jianong" in Chinese[3] and "Kanō" in Japanese[4]) made it to the championship game of the 1931 *Kōshien* Tournament, eventually losing by a score of 4–0. Despite that loss, the Kanō team received special attention from the Japanese government because of its unprecedented multiethnic starting lineup: four aboriginal Taiwanese, two Han Taiwanese, and three ethnic Japanese players.[5] The team's ethnic Japanese coach, Kondō Hyōtarō, innovated the use of multi-ethnic teams; of the previous teams representing Taiwan at *Kōshien* from 1923–1930, 94% of the players were ethnic Japanese.[6] Therefore, the Kanō team represented the image of a unified, strong, and loyal baseball program that represented imperial might.

Kondō's preference for multi-ethnic teams stemmed from his espousal of a brutal *bushidō*-inspired training regimen he learned as a youth. From 1904 to 1907, Kondō attended Ichikō High School while Nitobe Inazō was headmaster, and he spent the next decade coaching a successful team in rural Matsuyama

---

3. Junwei Yu, *Playing in Isolation: A History of Baseball in Taiwan* (Lincoln, NE: University of Nebraska Press, 2007), 19.

4. Morris, *Colonial Project, National Game*, 31.

5. Morris, *Colonial Project, National Game*, 31.

6. Morris, *Colonial Project, National Game*, 36.

prefecture.[7] After being recruited to work in Taiwan in the late 1920s, Kondō built a reputation for his "Spartan" style (スパルタ式) practices in the summer heat. One student, Hong Tai-Shan, recollected in an interview about the practices, "They weren't Spartan. They were just short of murder. Of fifty people who entered one year, eighty percent quit."[8] In other words, Kondō recruited a diverse team regardless of ethnicity because most of the players could not endure his training regimen.[9]

The success of Kondō's *bushidō*-inspired team at the Kōshien Tournament drove a faction in the Ministry of Education to pull baseball within the government's jurisdiction. At the same time as the massive Manchūkuo *undōkai* in spring 1932, the Ministry of Education swiftly implemented a set of regulations (統制令) upon school baseball throughout Japan proper and declared complete control over elementary-through-college level baseball's tournaments, participation, and rules.[10] As part of these regulations the Ministry of Education corporatized student baseball and set admission prices for spectators, diverting those fees from schools and into the government coffers.[11] The Ministry of Education justified these regulations based upon Nitobe Inazō's 1911 critique about the unregulated nature of school baseball. Nitobe had argued that unifying baseball under one set of regulations would align the sport with national thought, but the sport remained largely unregulated until 1932. Nitobe did not live to see much of the baseball regulation's effects: at the time of their enactment, he was traveling in the United States as an ambassador making the case for the legitimacy of the state of Manchūkuo, and he passed away in October of 1933.[12]

---

7. Lin Sheng-Lung 林勝龍, *Nihon tōchika Taiwan ni okeru bushidō yakyū no jyuyō to kaiten* 日本統治下台湾における武士道野球の受容と展開 [The Infusion and Popularization of the Japanese Samurai Baseball Culture in Taiwan During the Period of Japan's Colonization], Dissertation, Waseda University, 2012, 239. English title is provided by Lin.

8. Lin Sheng-Lung, *Nihon tōchika Taiwan*, 243.

9. There is a significant contemporary resonance with Kondō's manner of managing, with a 2014 Japanese language movie having been made of his storied 1931 team, called "KANO 1931 海の向こうの甲子園" [Kanō's 1931 Overseas Trip to Kōshien]. The website's flash introduction states in Japanese, "Did you know / That one time at Kōshien / Taiwanese representatives made an appearance?" Such wording implies that the selling point of the movie was less about the Kanō team's multi-ethnic heritage and more the fact that Kanō was a team from Taiwan. However, Taiwan was eligible for upwards of 17 appearances at the national high school baseball tournament from 1923–1940. The movie website is at http://kano1931.com/.

10. Kaga Hideo 加賀秀雄, "Wagakuni ni okeru 1932 nen no gakusei yakyū no yōsei ni tsuite" わが国における1932年の学生野球の統制について [Regarding Our Country's 1932 Student Baseball Regulations], *Hokkaidō Daigaku kyōiku gakubu kiyō* 51, no. 3 (1988), 6.

11. Kaga, "Wagakuni ni okeru 1932 nen no gakusei yakyū no yōsei ni tsuite," 9.

12. Benesch, *Inventing the Way of the Samurai*, 211.

Many in the Japanese baseball community realized their game's popularity and the admissions fees — including the Kōshien Tournament — had transformed baseball from having any sense of "play" into a game that funded the Japanese state.[13] Although historian Andrew Gordon notes that the Japanese bureaucracy's attempts to control private enterprise began in earnest in the mid-1930s, I contend that the state's takeover of school baseball is a precursor to these events. Historian Kaga Hideo described these regulations as the moment of rupture in the history of baseball in Japan; he argues that the Japanese baseball community had previously critiqued capitalism, but that the 1932 regulations made concrete the relation between sports and fascist trends within the Japanese government.[14] Writing in 1988 during a wave of anti-American nationalism in Japan, Kaga wanted to discourage his contemporary baseball fans who longed for a strict, disciplined, and masochistic form of student baseball. This kind of disciplined baseball, Kaga noted, was the result of a militarist state that was trending toward fascism.

After the 1932 baseball regulations, the Japanese government ministries controlled most of the Japanese athletic world: they operated the National Athletic Stadium and Meiji Jingū Baseball Stadium in the Meiji Jingū Shrine Outer Gardens, they redirected Kōshien Tournament's profits away from Osaka newspapers into government coffers, and they operated the Meiji Jingū Taikai, which had become the world's largest athletic mega-event. With the Manchūkuo *undōkai*, the government expanded the role of sports beyond expressing loyalty to the emperor and creating strong physical bodies by creating fantasies of "harmonious unity" of Manchuria's subjects. Baseball also fell into the purview of the fascist fantasy, aided by a 1934 tour of Japan by American all-star players headed by Babe Ruth.

Babe Ruth's Tour of Japan in the Context of Fascism

Historian Robert Fitts quotes the American ambassador to Japan, Joseph Grew, as saying in November 1934: "Babe Ruth... is a great deal more effective Ambassador than I could ever be."[15] Babe Ruth was unarguably the face of American baseball, and his arrival in 1934 was celebrated by throngs of fans jamming train station platforms to greet his arriving team. However, baseball players from the

---

13. Kaga, "Wagakuni ni okeru 1932 nen no gakusei yakyū no yōsei ni tsuite," 10–12.
14. Kaga, "Wagakuni ni okeru 1932 nen no gakusei yakyū no yōsei ni tsuite," 10.
15. Fitts, *Banzai Babe Ruth*, 83.

United States — both professional and amateur, both black and white, both celebrity and unknowns — had visited Japan since 1905 when Abe Isoo first helped establish these connections. Lou Gehrig, probably the second most famous baseball player behind Babe Ruth, had visited Japan with several other all-star players in 1931 in a well-documented trip that produced far less frenzy.[16] What, then, made the 1934 appearance of a 39-year-old and out-of-shape Babe Ruth a case for hysteria in Japan? In the immediate scope, Shōriki Matsutarō (正力松太郎), owner of the Yomiuri Shinbun newspaper, cast the tour as a precursor to the emergence of the first Japanese professional baseball league that operated outside the government's control. In the long run, the "immortal pitcher," Sawamura Eiji (沢村栄治), emerged as a popular figure who narrated and eventually symbolized a brand of sacrificial Imperial *Bushidō* during World War II.

Shōriki Matsutarō was a graduate of Tokyo Imperial University who spent most of the Taishō era as a police enforcer before purchasing the Yomiuri Shinbun in 1924. Competing newspapers sponsored baseball tournaments, most famously the Asahi's sponsorship of the Kōshien Tournament, and to a lesser degree, the Mainichi-sponsored local city tournaments. One day in 1928, an employee offering ideas to improve newspaper sales suggested that Shōriki invite Babe Ruth for a tour of Japan.[17] Ruth, nicknamed by his American fans the "Sultan of Swat" or "King of Swat" for his homerun prowess, had just finished his legendary 60 homerun season in 1927.[18] Additionally, Ruth was familiar with traveling abroad, having toured Cuba in 1920. With nothing to lose, Shōriki petitioned Major League Baseball to send Ruth to Japan.[19] At the time, the thirty-three-year-old Ruth was one of the United States' biggest celebrities and had an affinity for visiting speakeasies; he had no interest in traveling to Japan and resisted Shōriki's continuing efforts in the following years. Six years later in 1934, a group of friends and family finally convinced Ruth, who was 39 years old, to tour Japan. His body muddled by drink, Ruth agreed to go to Japan as a kind of farewell tour.[20] As incentive, Shōriki ensured that the Japanese-lan-

---

16. Vintageball.com has several helpful pictures indicating the team and where they visited at http://www.vintageball.com/1931Tour.html.

17. Izumino Seiichi 五十公野清一, *Shōriki Matsutarō puro yakyū ikusei sanjyūnen* 正力松太郎プロ野球育成三十年 [Thirty Years of Shōriki Matsutarō's Professional Baseball] (Tokyo: Tsuru Shōbō, 1966), 10–12.

18. Data from www.baseball-reference.com.

19. Roberto González Echevarría, *The Pride of Havana: A History of Cuban Baseball* (Oxford University Press, New York, 1999), 161.

20. Fitts, *Banzai Babe Ruth*, 29.

guage promotional posters called Ruth "The King of Baseball" (野球王), giving him an even grander nickname than he had in English.[21] The "King" spent much of the boat voyage by boat to Japan using the ship's exercise rowing machine trying to regain a respectable physique.

Having secured Ruth as the head of an American all-star team, Shōriki then assembled an "all-star" Japanese baseball team, which was a difficult challenge in a country where formal organized baseball did not exist beyond the college level. Complicating matters, the recently-implemented 1932 baseball regulations prohibited high school-age baseball players from engaging in matches with professional touring teams.[22] With Abe Isoo's help, Shōriki recruited popular college and high school players—some of whom dropped out of school to circumvent the newly implemented regulations—to join Japan's first professional baseball team, the "Greater Japan Tokyo Baseball Club" (大日本東京野球倶楽部).[23] It is critical to understand that this was not a Japanese national team, but a team of "greater Japan," which included the Soviet-born pitcher Victor Starfin and Horio "Jimmy" Fumito, a United States citizen of Japanese descent.[24] Having non-Japanese players on the team, it underscored Shōriki's vision of Japanese baseball, which included foreign-born players, as compared to United States baseball, which excluded almost all minorities except Latinos.

The legacy of the Greater Japan Tokyo Baseball Club was created by a 17-year-old pitching phenom, Sawamura Eiji. Sawamura dropped out of Kyoto Commercial High School before his senior year to ensure his eligibility to play against the American all-stars.[25] Had Nitobe Inazō not died the previous year, he certainly would have said something about Sawamura's disregard of school in favor of baseball. Furthermore, the professionalization of the Greater Japan Tokyo Baseball Club enabled Shōriki to take ticket proceeds and split them between his newspaper and the touring American players instead of handing them over to the government.[26] Although the fact that the Greater Japan team lost all eighteen of its exhibition games to the American team is often forgot-

21. Besuboru Magajin Sha ベースボールマガジン社, *Puro yakyū 70 nen shi* プロ野球70年史 [70th Anniversay History of Professional Baseball] (Tokyo: Besuboru Magajinsha, 2004), 19.

22. Robert Fitts, "Babe Ruth and Eiji Sawamura," *Baseball Research Journal* 41, no. 2 (Spring 2012), http://sabr.org/research/babe-ruth-and-eiji-sawamura.

23. Besuboru Magajin Sha, *Puro yakyū 70 nen*, 18.

24. Besuboru Magajin Sha, *Puro yakyū 70 nen*, 20.

25. Suzuki Sōtarō 鈴木惣太郎, *Fumetsu no daitōshu: Sawamura Eiji* 不滅の大投手：沢村栄治 [The Immortal Pitcher: Sawamura Eiji] (Tokyo: Kobunsha, 1975), 61.

26. Fitts, *Banzai Babe Ruth*, 27.

ten by Japanese fans, Sawamura symbolized Japanese strength in the face of adversity when he struck out four consecutive Major Leaguers, including Babe Ruth and Lou Gehrig.[27]

An assassination attempt on Shōriki on February 22, 1935, halted baseball's continued professionalization in Japan. The attempt was likely sponsored by a competing newspaper, the Mainichi Shinbun, which enlisted the ultranationalist Nagasawa Katsusuke to attack Shōriki with a samurai sword as he entered the offices of the Yomiuri Shinbun. After the attack, Shōriki, who was a master *jūdō* practitioner and quite fit, stumbled his way to the office infirmary before collapsing and being rushed to the hospital. When Nagasawa turned himself into the police later (refusing to identify his patron), he explained that "Shōriki had defiled the memory of Emperor Meiji by allowing Babe Ruth and his team to play in the stadium named in the ruler's honor."[28] Although the United States team had traveled throughout Japan and played in numerous stadiums and fields — including Kōshien Stadium, which had a Shintō shrine on site — Nagasawa's emphasis on Babe Ruth's appearance at *Meiji Jingū* Stadium revealed the degree to which Imperial *Bushidō* discourse had rendered Tokyo-centered athletics sacred and distinctively Japanese.

The Creation of the Japanese Baseball Federation

After a period of convalescence, in late 1935, Shōriki used the Greater Japan Tokyo Baseball Club as the basis to create Japan's first professional baseball organization, the Japanese Baseball Federation (日本野球連盟) and renamed the Greater Japan Tokyo Baseball Club the "Yomiuri Giants." Shōriki reveled in his league's ethnic integration, which included the Soviet Victor Starfin, white American Bucky Harris and black American Jimmy Bonner, and Taiwanese players that filled up a quarter of the Tokyo Senators' roster.[29] In 1936, Shōriki's Giants' team traveled to the United States to play against teams of all levels. Featuring both the Soviet Victor Starfin and the *nikkei* player Horio "Jimmy" Fumito, the Yomiuri Giants were effectively one of the first "integrated" professional baseball teams to appear on United States soil.[30] Major League Baseball

---

27. Fitts, "Babe Ruth and Eiji Sawamura."

28. Fitts, *Banzai Babe Ruth*, 235–238.

29. Place of birth data from www.baseball-reference.com.

30. Nagata Yōichi 永田陽一. *Tokyo Giants hokubei tairiku enseiki* 東京ジャイアンツ北米大陸遠征記 [*Record of the Tokyo Giants North American Tour*] (Tokyo: Tohō shuppan, 2007), 141.

would not admit its first player outside of the United States' sphere of colonialism, Alex Carrasquel of Venezuela, until 1939.[31]

Sawamura Eiji became the young star of the league, reaching his peak in 1937 when he struck out 21% of the batters he faced.[32] That year, the Yomiuri Giants opened their new stadium, *Kōrakuen* (後楽園), located precisely in between the *kōdōkan* and the Imperial Palace. Despite Shōriki's flaunting of the school baseball regulations and clear intention to take profits for his own newspaper instead of handing them over to the government, Japanese bureaucracy overlooked these actions because of a tumultuous political environment that shifted the country into Total War.

Japanese Athletics in the "Time of Crisis"

Already at odds with the West, Japanese bureaucrats in the early 1930s began instituting agricultural, economic, labor, and political reforms that aimed to inculcate a coherent sense of national identity. Although popular elections continued, after 1934 the political cabinets contained fewer and fewer popularly elected members and more and more political elites, military members, and imperial family members. Those who advocated for rule by non-elected officials became part of the Imperial Way Faction, while those who sought to continue reforms through the electoral process joined the Control Faction.[33] These groups came into conflict in February 1936 when the Imperial Way Faction led the "Shōwa Restoration" uprising that attempted to undo party politics and leave the emperor as the sole holder of political power in Japan. One of the Imperial Way faction's leaders, Kita Ikki, had long argued that proper interpretation of *bushidō* philosophy would eliminate the government ministries and bureaucrats and permit the Emperor direct rule over the Japanese people.[34] The coup d'état failed, and its leaders were executed.

The military leaders in the Control Faction were empowered and political reforms accelerated. In February 1937, the Ministry of Education published and distributed throughout schools "The Cardinal Principles of the National Polity" (*Kokutai no Hongi*, 国体の本義), which promoted an unbroken line of imperial authority dating from antiquity and declared that all Japanese

---

31. Place of birth data from www.baseball-reference.com.

32. Data from www.baseball-reference.com.

33. Gordon, *A History of Modern Japan*, 196.

34. Benesch, *Inventing the Way of the Samurai*, 196.

subjects should accept the emperor's will as their own.[35] Then on July 7, 1937, the Second Sino-Japanese War officially began. In the subsequent "time of crisis" caused by the failed *coup d'état* and the onset of war with China, Prime Minister Konoe Fumimaro—a hereditary prince from pre-modern Japan's aristocratic class—enacted the National General Mobilization Law of 1938, which:

> gave the government sweeping powers to control almost all aspects of economic and social life in support of the war effort...The totalitarian concentration of power at the centre was accompanied by massive education campaigns and propaganda activities to promote the 'New Order' against dangerous ideas including individualism, socialism, communism, and other 'un-Japanese' philosophies.[36]

The government enforced the militarization and unification of the "Japanese spirit" through cultural activities, from *kabuki* theater to jazz.[37] Simultaneously, the government distributed pamphlets on *bushidō* that incorporated the *Hagakure* (葉隠), a formerly minor eighteenth-century tract that "actively promoted self-destructive behavior as the highest *bushidō* virtue."[38]

In the "time of crisis," athletic mega-events demonstrated how men and women prepared their bodies for war. In 1937 the Osaka Mainichi newspaper sponsored the First Osaka Youth School National Defense Sports Contest (第一回大阪府青年学校国防スポーツ競技大会), and it received support from the newspaper's Tokyo branch for the second annual tournament in 1938.[39] In 1939, the National Defense Sports Contest was integrated into the Meiji Jingū Taikai, and the Ministry of Health and Welfare encouraged secondary school students to practice military marching, the obstacle course, grenade throwing, sandbag-carrying relay races, and competitive towing of loads using teams of men with ropes.[40] These "national defense contests" (国防競技) had a total of 1,331 combined male and female participants; comparatively, there were 310 baseball players that year in the *Meiji Jingū Taikai*.[41] By 1943, the national defense contests expanded to include "battle-

35. Gordon, *A Modern History of Japan*, 198.
36. Benesch, *Inventing the Way of the Samurai*, 198.
37. Benesch, *Inventing the Way of the Samurai*, 200.
38. Benesch, *Inventing the Way of the Samurai*, 199.
39. Takashima, *Teikoku Nihon to supōtsu*, 136.
40. Takashima, *Teikoku Nihon to supōtsu*, 137.
41. Irie, *Shōwa supōtsu shi ron*, 185.

field exercises" (戦場運動), military marching (行軍訓練), and bayonet arts (銃剣道).[42] "Military marching" is better known as "drill" in English, and was a large group exercise that required the participants to accurately respond to commands shouted at them by an official.

Baseball During Total War

Japan continued athletic mega-events until the fall of 1942 and continued professional baseball until 1944, when raw materials became scarce and hunger the norm among Japanese people. The persistence of athletic events and baseball contests was the consequence of the Japanese state spending sixty years treating athletics as the key to maintaining a strong army and national cohesion. Professional baseball fell under spell of the Japanese fascism in 1940, coinciding with Shōriki Matsutarō's entrance into the Imperial Rule Assistance Association, which was an organization that replaced Japan's political parties.[43] Under the Imperial Rule Association, Emperor Hirohito directed his will onto the Japanese people directly through a small, select cabinet. No longer could Japan under Total War purport to be a democracy. Shōriki would, in 1943, become Japan's Information Minister, a position that earned him a place in jail charged as a war criminal after the end of World War II, a topic that will be covered in more detail in the next chapter.

After 1940, war permeated baseball, even among the seemingly independent professional baseball leagues. As part of the Japanese bureaucracy's efforts to create a distinctly Japanese history and society, baseball was reimagined as a uniquely Japanese game. This process went far beyond the Meiji-era idea of "*bushidō* baseball," which still used American terminology and was regularly played alongside Americans. After 1940, English loan words were eliminated entirely from the Japanese baseball community and replaced with Japanese terminology. Formally, "*bēsubōru*" (ベースボール, written in *katakana*, the Japanese alphabet for foreign loan words) became "*yakyū*" (野球). Teams exchanged their English names for monikers of Japanese uniqueness or strength: the Yomiuri Giants became the Yomiuri *Kyojin* (巨人, "giants" or "great men"); the Kōrakuen Eagles became the *Yamato Gun* (大和軍, "Yamato Troop," named after the unique "Japanese spirit"); the Tokyo Senators

---

42. Takashima, *Teikoku Nihon to supōtsu*, 135–139.

43. Kikkawa Takeo 橘川武郎 and Nara Takashi 奈良堂史, *Fan kara mita puro yakyū no rekishi* フアンから観たプロ野球の歴史 [History of Professional Baseball from a Fan's Point of View] (Tokyo: Nihon keizai hyōron sha, 2009), 20.

moved to Nagoya and became the *Kinshachi* (金鯱, "golden *sachi*," a mytho-logical creature with a lion's head and a carp's body that adorned the parapets of Nagoya castle).[44] Other teams adopted names of their parent newspaper company or railroad company. Government ministries imposed new termi-nology that moralized every pitch: strike became a "correct pitch" (正球), a ball became a "bad pitch" (悪球), a fair hit was "good" (よし) and a foul hit was "bad" (だめ), among other changes.[45] Many baseball terms were directly taken from the military: the batting team was the "attacking side" (攻撃側, *kōgekigawa*), the shortstop was the "hit-and-run attacker" (遊撃手, *yūgeki-shu*), the catcher was the "capturer" (捕手, *hoshu*, a term that originated as a *jūdō* hold). English letters were removed from uniforms and replaced with Japanese kanji, but more frequently baseball players appeared in public in military uniforms.

Compare the stylistic changes on the covers of Yakyūkai magazine.[46]

---

44. Kikkawa and Nara, *Fan kara mita puro yakyū no rekishi*, 20.

45. Kikkawa and Nara, *Fan kara mita puro yakyū no rekishi*, 20.

46. Magazines courtesy Japanese National Diet Library. Modifications mine.

The Yomiuri Kyojin "force displays its hard training."[47]

Perhaps more than any other demographic, the Japanese public celebrated the departure of baseball players to the warfront. In October 1943, the elite Japanese colleges Keio and Waseda played their last baseball game before sending their students to the warfront.[48] Fans packed the National Athletic Stadium beyond its 35,000-person capacity to bid farewell to not only the players in one of Japan's longest-held sporting rivalries, but the symbolic future of the Japanese empire.

Departure ceremony for students destined for the war front, October 21, 1943, held at Meiji Jingū Athletic Stadium.[49]

---

47. *Yakyūkai*, March 1, 1941.

48. http://www.waseda.jp/student/weekly/contents/2005a/061e.html. The event also was turned into a movie in 2008 and a play in 2015.

49. Image available from http://www.asahi.com/articles/ASHD95VQCHD9UTIL03Y.html.

Sawamura Eiji — the pitcher who had dropped out of high school to become a professional baseball player and became the face of the Yomiuri Giants — became a battlefront celebrity. He participated in Japan's invasion of the Philippines and was present at the infamous Bataan Death March. In November 1943, Sawamura wrote an article for *Yakyūkai* praising the bravery of Japanese soldiers and claiming that United States troops poured boiling water over the heads of Japanese prisoners of war. Robert Fitts notes that Sawamura's popularity and the mass circulation of *Yakyūkai* likely made this article one of the war's most widely-read pieces of Japanese propaganda.[50] Although there was no empirical evidence for Sawamura's claims, they fit into the narrative of the Pacific War shared by both the Japanese and Americans, which John Dower described as an "obsession with extermination…a war without mercy."[51] Japanese troops fought to eradicate the narrative of American baseball, with multiple reports of Japanese soldiers shouting, in English, "To hell with Babe Ruth" as they fought American troops.[52] Such sentiment twisted the American narrative in which baseball was a savior to colonized peoples, as seen in the liberation of baseball-loving Cubans during the Spanish-American War. In this case, baseball-loving Japanese defended their country and their national sport against imperialist Americans.

The Japanese were losing the war, but Japanese professional baseball continued fielding teams of men in their young twenties as a symbolic source of physical strength until 1944. The players' waning performance demonstrated that any claim of physical strength was an illusion. The chart below demonstrates the precipitous decline of homeruns — which are correlated with physical strength — as people in Japan proper endured the depletion of food resources.[53] The Japanese Baseball Federation played a half season in 1944, after which baseball in Japan went on hiatus until the end of the war.

---

50. Fitts, "Babe Ruth and Eiji Sawamura."

51. John Dower, *War Without Mercy: Race and Power in the Pacific War* (New York: Pantheon Books, 1986), 11.

52. Fitts, *Banzai Babe Ruth*, xiii.

53. Data compiled from www.baseball-reference.com. Chart created by the author.

Japanese Baseball Federation Homeruns per Game

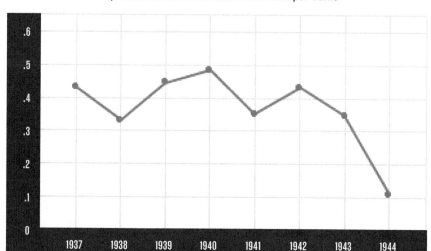

Whatever fantasy of physical strength that baseball provided ended in November 1944, when the "immortal pitcher" Sawamura Eiji's transport ship was sunk *en route* to the Philippines, a final ignominious defeat at the hands of the Americans.[54]

Conclusion

In this chapter I argued that baseball under fascistization contributed to the fantasy of the physical strength of the Japanese military endeavor. Coinciding with the government's sponsorship of Olympic-style athletic mega-events, the Japanese government took control of student baseball and the *Kōshien* Tournament. When the American celebrity Babe Ruth finally came to Japan in 1934, his visit set in motion a series of events that the government had not planned for, but ultimately understood as representative of their agenda. The formation of a professional baseball league in Japan included players from all corners of the empire and did not conform to the system of Major League Baseball. The government took additional steps to control professional baseball by requiring all terminology to be in Japanese, literally rewriting the language of the game and providing a Japanese-sourced heritage. Men continued

54. Fitts, "Babe Ruth and Eiji Sawamura."

to play professional baseball into the depths of World War II, but the decline in homeruns underscored the fantasy of national strength at a time when food and material resources became scarce.

Interlude

An Empire in Ruins

The war's damages to the Japanese empire in the five-month period from March through August 1945 were nearly unprecedented in human history. Beginning March 9–10, 1945, the United States Air Force firebombed Tokyo over a twenty-four hour period, killing one-hundred thousand Japanese civilians and leaving a million survivors homeless.[1] Although Tokyo endured years of bombings, according to scholar Mark Selden this particular night stood out in its calculated precision to "instill terror:" American Commander Curtis LeMay wanted to have Tokyo "wiped right off the map" and sent 334 B-29 airplanes loaded to capacity with incendiary materials that were dropped on an area estimated to be about 85% residential.[2] The United States' Strategic Bombing Survey's official report of the raid stated that:

> probably more persons lost their lives by fire at Tokyo in a 6-hour period than at any time in the history of man. People died from extreme heat, from oxygen deficiency, from carbon monoxide asphyxiation, from being trampled beneath the feet of stampeding crowds, and from drowning. The

---

1. Mark Selden, "A Forgotten Holocaust: US Bombing Strategy, the Destruction of Japanese Cities and the American Way of War from World War II to Iraq," *The Asia-Pacific Journal: Japan Focus*, http://www.japanfocus.org/-Mark-Selden/2414. Selden notes that the mechanism of death — fire — was so prevalent that it is possible that thousands of bodies may never have been discovered and the death toll could easily reach 150,000. Furthermore, the toll could have been much higher had Tokyo not enacted a mass evacuation of children to the countryside at the end of 1944.

2. Selden, "A Forgotten Holocaust: US Bombing Strategy, the Destruction of Japanese Cities and the American Way of War from World War II to Iraq."

largest number of victims were the most vulnerable: women, children and the elderly.[3]

Following the Tokyo bombings, the United States expanded its firebombing across the remainder of Japan throughout July, attacking sixty-seven cities in total, killing an estimated 300,000 people and injuring another 400,000. The Japanese metropolises of Osaka (population of over three million) and Kobe (population of about one million) endured a near forty percent rate of destruction.[4] On the ground, the United States' invasion of Okinawa in April and May 1945 resulted in a quarter-million Japanese deaths, almost sixty percent of whom were Okinawan civilians.[5] Five Japanese metropolises remained untouched by American firebombs in early August, 1945, and these became the potential drop sites for the newly-developed American atomic bomb. Hiroshima was hit by a uranium-powered bomb on August 6 and Nagasaki was hit by a more powerful plutonium bomb on August 9; the two cities combined for over 100,000 immediate deaths caused by heat burns, and over the next five years the radiation left by the bombs contributed to an overall death toll estimated at 350,000 people.[6] Following the atomic bombs, the United States continued conventional bombings and killed another 15,000 Japanese, even as American intelligence translators picked up radio messages on August 10 that the Japanese government was preparing to surrender.[7] In the three-month period from May 1945 until August 1945 alone, about 800,000 Japanese people died and another million were injured, which was about forty percent of the Japanese death toll during the entire Pacific War. Most Japanese metropolises had at least half of their territory destroyed.[8]

---

3. Selden, "A Forgotten Holocaust: US Bombing Strategy, the Destruction of Japanese Cities and the American Way of War from World War II to Iraq."

4. Population statistics from the 1940 Japanese census, http://www.e-stat.go.jp/SG1/estat/GL08020103.do?_toGL08020103_&tclassID=000001026559&cycleCode=0&requestSender=-search

5. Gordon, *A Modern History of Japan*, 221.

6. Gerard DeGroot, *The Bomb: A Life* (Cambridge, MA: Harvard University Press, 2005), 95, 101.

7. DeGroot, 102, and Marc Gallicchio, *The Cold War Begins in Asia: American East Asian Policy and the Fall of the Japanese Empire* (New York: Columbia University Press, 1988), 59.

8. Numbers are compiled by adding the death tolls from fire bombings, atomic bombs, and the Invasion of Okinawa and dividing by the total war dead as provided by Andrew Gordon in *A Modern History of Japan*, p. 223. The percentage of destroyed city territory is derived from Selden, http://www.japanfocus.org/-Mark-Selden/2414.

As the Potsdam Conference closed on August 2, 1945, the Americans suspected that Japanese surrender was near.[9] Due to the large area occupied by Japanese troops — extending from Burma to Papua New Guinea to the Sakhalin Islands to the imperial puppet state of Manchūkuo — the Americans wanted to coordinate a Japanese surrender with the Soviet Red Army, the Chinese Kuomingtang, and the British in order to represent each state's colonial and national interests.[10] A week after the atomic bombings, on August 15, 1945, Emperor Hirohito ordered Japanese soldiers to lay down their weapons even as Joseph Stalin threatened to continue the Red Army's southward advance toward Hokkaido with the intention of occupying the island. Forced to act unilaterally, United States President Harry Truman diplomatically rebuffed Stalin's threat and managed to protect the United States' interest in being the primary occupier of Japan.[11]

The simultaneous geographical dismemberment of the Japanese empire, the psychological disintegration of Imperial-era cultural values and the humanization of the Emperor, and the physical depreciation of bodies due to malnutrition caused an unprecedented shift in Japanese national consciousness. Following this intense period of widespread destruction, most Japanese people were exhausted and uncertain about a future directed by the American government that had just caused such widespread destruction. John Dower notes that the plight of the mainland Japanese was both psychological and physiological in nature, highlighted by two terminologies that came into common use after the Pacific War: *kyodatsu* (虚脱, despondency, demoralization) and *takenoko seikatsu* (筍生活, "bamboo-shoot existence"), the latter a metaphor for people who stripped their possessions and clothes, like stripping a bamboo shoot, to acquire food.[12] There was an additional burden of deciding what to do about the enormous population of orphaned and vagrant children, which the Japanese Ministry of Education estimated in 1948 to be 123,511.[13] These

---

9. Gallicchio, *The Cold War Begins in Asia*, 59.

10. Gallicchio, *The Cold War Begins in Asia*, 64–75.

11. The Soviet Union's entrance into the Pacific War was important to hastening Japanese surrender and setting the context for American occupation. For more information, see Andrew Barshay, *The Gods Left First: The Captivity and Repatriation of Japanese POWs in Northeast Asia, 1945–1956* (Berkeley, CA: University of California Press, 2013), 19.

12. Dower, *Embracing Defeat*, 84–95.

13. Hemmi Masaaki 逸見勝亮, "Dai niji sekai taisengo no Nihon ni okeru furōji・Sensō koji no rekishi," 第二次世界大戦後の日本における浮浪児・戦争孤児の歴史 [Juvenile Vagrants and War Orphans after World War II in Japan], *Nihon no kyōikushi gaku: Kyōikushi gakkai kiyō* [Japan Society for the Historical Studies of Education] 37 (1994): 100. The numbers were cal-

impoverished children often made a living by scalping tickets at train stations, selling tobacco, shining shoes, pickpocketing, or extortion.[14]

Approximately seven million ethnic Japanese located in Manchuria, Taiwan, Korea, and other former imperial territories struggled to return to Japan proper amid hostilities from the Chinese Kuomintang, the Chinese Communist Party, and the Soviet Red Army. Many returnees' psychological and physiological condition was often worse than those people in Japan proper. In general, the returnees from the overseas territories had served the interests of the imperial Japanese state as soldiers, colonial overseers, or settlers. However, those who had remained in Japan proper viewed these former colonials as the embodiment the imperial total war machine's failure.[15] These Japanese nationals abroad included almost the entire 600,000-man Kwangtung Army — the organization central to Japanese imperial interests in northeast Asia throughout the early twentieth century — who were interred in the Soviet gulag system. The Soviets returned Japanese citizens and soldiers alike in staggered exchanges that continued through the mid-1950s.[16]

The Stabilizing Force of Baseball

One day in Shinkyō, the capital of the former puppet state of Manchūkuo, six young men knocked on baseball essayist Nakazawa Fujio's door asking, "There are about seventy baseball players in Shinkyō, and we were thinking about having a baseball tournament with the troops and municipal government. Would you please approach them?"[17] Nakazawa organized the event, but he was not prepared for such a turnout of fans. Three years removed from celebrating a massive *undōkai* as the "fuse of a new world order," Nakazawa found himself on a baseball diamond in front of 30,000 Japanese colonials who would be returning to Japan. Many of the young people had never actually seen

---

culated by the Ministry of Health and Welfare in 1948. Within this count, 10,000 children were orphaned within the former colonial territories, and another 4,000 were unable to independently live without full time care.

14. Hemmi, "Dai niji sekai taisengo no Nihon ni okeru furōji・Sensō koji no rekishi," 99.

15. Dower, *Embracing Defeat*, 60.

16. Barshay, *The Gods Left First*, 1–5.

17. Nakazawa Fujio 中澤不二雄, *Bokura no yakyū* ぼくらの野球 [Our Baseball] (Tokyo: Yamanoki Publishing, 1948), 13–14. Nakazawa was one of the most important baseball writers in Japan and was posthumously inducted into the Japanese Baseball Hall of Fame in 2002. His hall of fame induction information is available online at: http://www.baseball-museum.or.jp/baseball_hallo/detail/detail_141.html.

Japan, but it was to be their new "home" after the Japanese empire's dissolution. Grabbing a megaphone, Nakazawa addressed the crowd:

> These baseball players play with precision and fairness. Everybody, support your home team with a big roar of applause and have some fun. This baseball tournament will communicate the road home to Japan to those Japanese who are waiting to return, but in the meantime, they will feel safe and secure here as long as they can play baseball in Shinkyō.[18]

The residents of Shinkyō were not alone in thinking that baseball could provide safety and security in a time of turmoil. In Japan proper, measures were already underway to revive baseball, even as people struggled to find food and lodging.

---

18. Nakazawa Fujio, *Bokura no yakyū*, 13–14.

CHAPTER SEVEN

Baseball in the Aftermath of Total War

There is no material for the needed equipment [to play sports], and the condition of the play-grounds is not what it should be. Food is also a great problem. The Government subsidy has been cut by half. There are other points which would, needless to say, make the up-hill walk a pretty steep one to climb. [sic]

But the greater the obstacles the stronger our love for Sports grows. From now on, we must spread Sports to furthermost ends of the country and do our utmost to bring it to perfection whereby we may attain a healthy development of Sports to bright and lighten the newly reconstructed Japan.[1]

— Kiyoshi Saburō, Director of the Japanese Amateur Athletic Association, January 1946

Introduction

This chapter covers the end of the war in August 1945 until the initiation of what historians now call the Reverse Course in April 1947. This period of intense change was characterized by the policies of the Supreme Commander of the Allied Powers (SCAP) General Douglas MacArthur and the American General Headquarters (GHQ) to democratize, to demilitarize, and to end the will to war in Japan.[2] In this chapter I argue that the Japanese baseball com-

---

1. Saburo Kiyoshi, "New Constitution of The Great Japan Physical Culture (*Dai Nippon Tai-Iku-Kai*), Jan 12th 1946;" Supreme Commander for the Allied Powers: Civil Information and Education Division, Physical Education and Youth Affairs, Topical File 1945–1951, Box 05724, Folder 1. The quote is from the English copy that the GHQ was provided.

2. Dower, *Embracing Defeat*, 77.

munity created opportunities to rehabilitate Japanese men by renouncing militarism and imperialism and promoting a program where baseball became the means of instructing American-style peace and stability. The Japanese baseball community adopted a pro-American identity, which contrasted to the community's anti-American and militaristic actions prior to 1945. For these overtures, SCAP and GHQ rewarded the Japanese baseball community with space and equipment — both rarities in postwar Japan's devastated landscape — but these rewards came with a catch: an enduring dependent and subservient relationship with the GHQ.

A Nation Passes Time: The Resumption of Baseball in Occupied Japan

On August 16, 1945, the day after Emperor Hirohito announced Japan's surrender in World War II, Saeki Tatsuo (佐伯達夫), a truck driver during the war, walked to the Tokyo headquarters of the Asahi Shinbun newspaper to inquire whether the company was interested in resuming its sponsorship of secondary school baseball tournaments.[3] Saeki, a Kōshien Tournament organizer of the during the 1920s, believed that the resumption of baseball would help the postwar recovery efforts.[4] Asahi managers quickly approved Saeki's appeal, which created an interesting tension between the existing devastation and the promise of renewal in Japan. Immediately, high schools in Fukushima, Miyazaki, and Yamagata prefectures sent young men out to play baseball wherever they could with whatever equipment they could find.[5] These ad-hoc tournaments became a place where people received their food rations and bonuses of rice for good performance. In the first postwar Kōshien Tournament in August 1946, victorious teams received a rice ration as they advanced further in the tournament. The team from Kagoshima Prefecture on the island of Kyūshū promised their families that they would succeed and bring home as many rations of rice as they could win.[6]

---

3. Morioka Hiroshi 森岡浩, *Kōkō yakyū 100 nen shi* 高校野球100年史 [100 Year History of High School Baseball] (Tokyo: Tokyo Shuppudan, 2015), 158.

4. The Japanese Baseball Hall of Fame and Museum, 佐伯達夫 *Saeki Tatsuo*, http://www.baseball-museum.or.jp/baseball_hallo/detail/detail_070.html. After his work to resume baseball after the Pacific War, Saeki became president of the Kōshien Tournament from 1967–1980 and was inducted to the Japanese Baseball Hall of Fame in 1981.

5. Morioka, *Kōkō yakyū 100 nen shi*, 161.

6. Morioka, *Kōkō yakyū 100 nen shi*, 181.

The baseball community in post-war Japan focused on their game's social aspects instead of equipment or statistics. Using improvised balls and bats, people played what they called "town ball" (タウンボール).[7] In rural areas, "farm field leagues" (田んぼリーグ) appeared, using natural landmarks as bases and bamboo sticks as bats.[8] When there were not enough people to field a team, people played "catch ball" (キャチボール), a game in which two or more people tossed a ball back and forth to pass time and distract themselves from the surrounding devastation. Yamamoto Kōji, who grew up in the rebuilding city of Hiroshima and later became a well-known professional baseball player, explained that spending ten minutes a day playing catch ball with a friend added up to nearly three hundred hours of shared time over the course of five years.[9] Beginning with these "baseball-like" games of catch ball and town ball, the Japanese baseball community created opportunities for revitalization and caught the attention of the Occupation Forces of the United States military.

The Resumption of Baseball in Japan

The American's initial plan to use baseball to revitalize the Japanese public formed in mid-August 1945, as General Douglas MacArthur sailed north on the *USS Missouri* from the Filipino Leyte Gulf to finalize the Pacific War's surrender documents. MacArthur served as the Supreme Commander of the Allied Powers (SCAP) and overseer of the Allied Occupation of Japan until his dismissal at the start of the Korean War in April 1951. MacArthur's military career began in Asia when he followed his father, Arthur MacArthur, as an American observer stationed in Manchuria during the Russo-Japanese War in 1905.[10] After serving in World War I, Douglas MacArthur served as the President of the 1928 United States Olympic Committee in Amsterdam, where Japan became the first East Asian state to win a gold medal. MacArthur served as Chief of Army Forces in the Pacific, and as early as July 11, 1945, he drew up a plan for the occupation

---

7. Sayama Kazuo 佐山和夫, *Nichibei rimenshi: Bishōjo tōshū kara dai Bebu Rusu made* 日米野球裏面史：美少女投手から大ベーブルースまで [The Secret History of Japan-America: From Female Pitchers to Babe Ruth] (Tokyo: NHK Publishing, 2005), 17.

8. Yamamoto Kōji 山本浩二, *Yakyū to Hiroshima* 野球と広島 [Baseball and Hiroshima] (Tokyo: Kadokawa, 2015), 89.

9. Yamamoto, *Yakyū to Hiroshima*, 92.

10. Rotem Kowner, *The A to Z of the Russo-Japanese War* (Lanham, Maryland: Scarecrow Press, 2006), 214.

of Japan, known as Operation Blacklist.[11] During his free time, MacArthur encouraged his troops to engage in the "MacArthur Cup," an informal sporting competition among shipmates.[12] Because of MacArthur's affinity for sports, he was receptive to policies that used sports to promote democratization and demilitarization.

The American idea to use baseball as part of the GHQ agenda for revitalizing Japan came from one of the crewmembers on board the *USS Missouri* with General MacArthur, the *nisei* American soldier, Harada "Cappy" Tsuneo (原田恒男). Harada was born and raised in California by his Japanese parents who had immigrated to America. Proficient in the Japanese language, Harada had spent the better part of three years working in military intelligence and was assigned to the Pacific Theater instead of the famed ethnic Japanese 100th Battalion/442nd Infantry Regiment that endured heavy casualties throughout Europe.[13] Harada wrote in his autobiography about the stress he endured from fighting his ethnic kin. Unable to sleep one night *en route* to Japan, he went to the ship's bathroom so as not to wake his crew mates. Examining his unruly beard in the mirror, he realized he had not seen himself out of uniform in weeks. He thought to himself, "This isn't me, is it?"[14]

This self-probing question prompted Harada to consider his life before the war, when he played minor league baseball throughout the American West Coast. There he met Uno "Buddy" Kazumaro, a newspaper journalist who was also a *nisei* raised in California. Although they shared a similar upbringing, Uno's career trajectory was very different from Harada's. Uno was upset with the racism he experienced while growing up in early twentieth century America. In 1937, he moved to Japan at the start of the Second Sino-Japanese War and joined the Imperial Army Press Corps.[15] Like many Japanese during wartime, Uno was immersed in racially-charged propaganda that described

---

11. Gallicchio, *The Cold War Begins in Asia*, 60.

12. Ōkubo Hideaki 大久保英明 and Yamagishi Kōji 山岸孝吏, "Makkasa Gensui mai supōtsu kyōgikai no seiritsu to haishi" マッカーサー元帥枚スポーツ競技会の成立と廃止 [The General MacArthur Cup Competitions: Regarding their Establishment and Dissolution] (Kanazawa: Kanazawa University Education Department Bulletin, 2004), 92.

13. Richard S. Oguro, *Senpai Gumi* [Our Teachers], 4. http://www.100thbattalion.org/wp-content/uploads/Senpai-Gumi.pdf.

14. Harada Cappy 原田キャッピ, *Taiheiyō no kakehashi: Sengo yakyū fukkatsu no rimenshi* 太平洋のかけはし：戦後・野球復活の裏面史 [Bridging the Pacific: The Secret History of Baseball Revival] (Tokyo, Baseball Magajin Sha, 1980), 47.

15. Yuji Ichioka, "The Meaning of Loyalty: The Case of Kazumaro Buddy Uno," *Amerasia Journal* 23, no. 3 (1997): 50–51.

Americans as demons who knew nothing but brutality.[16] Looking at himself in the mirror of the ship's bathroom, Harada wondered how he could possibly re-habilitate men like Uno — who were exhausted, demoralized, and indoctrinat-ed — to follow the American agenda of democratization and demilitarization. Harada believed the best way he could help was to call upon his skills from his pre-military days: baseball.

On August 30, 1945, alongside the Supreme Commander, Harada disem-barked from the *USS Missouri* in Yokohama, a city of almost a million peo-ple, many of whom were homeless after American bombers destroyed nearly half the city.[17] Glass broke under Harada's feet as he walked to the New Grand Hotel, the charred ruins of buildings giving him the image of a "ghost town" because "there wasn't a soul on the streets."[18] At the New Grand, Harada wait-ed in a separate room while the Supreme Commander toasted to victory with the officials of his advance troops with a steak dinner. Assisted by Harada, the professional Japanese Baseball Federation resumed in 1946 under the watchful eye of GHQ officials.

Because the stadiums of the *Meiji Jingū* Outer Gardens in Tokyo housed some of the world's best athletic venues and were sites of wartime Japanese athletic mega-events, GHQ confiscated *Meiji Jingū* baseball stadium for Unit-ed States troops to use as entertainment. This left Kōrakuen Stadium, built in 1936, as the only venue to host the remaining six professional baseball teams in Tokyo, and it became the *de facto* home of amateur baseball clubs as well. The Kōrakuen Company, the stadium's Japanese owners, benefitted greatly from the near-monopoly on baseball in eastern Japan, earning a profit of 19 million yen in 1950 (approximately $52,000 in 1950 dollars, equivalent to $520,000 in current US dollars).[19] With Kōrakuen a two-mile walk from GHQ headquar-ters in the Dai Ichi Insurance Building, United States servicemen were often present in Kōrakuen's stands either for recreation or surveillance.

Baseball's revival in Japan was not a matter of saying, "play ball." For as ephemeral and mundane as baseball seemed to the casual observer, the game's

---

16. Dower, *War Without Mercy*, 244.

17. Mark Selden, "A Forgotten Holocaust: US Bombing Strategy, the Destruction of Japanese Cities and the American Way of War from World War II to Iraq."

18. Harada, *Taiheiyō no kakehashi: Sengo yakyū fukkatsu no rimenshi*, 55.

19. Supreme Commander for the Allied Powers: Economic and Scientific Section, Programs and Statistics Division, Zaibatsu Corporation, Box 7719, Folder 49. During Occupation, the ex-change rate of yen to dollars was set at 360 yen to 1 dollar. Conversion of 1950 dollars to current dollars provided by the Bureau of Labor Statistics' Inflation Calculator: http://data.bls.gov/cgi-bin/cpicalc.pl?cost1=52777&year1=1950&year2=2016.

resumption in Japan was the product of layered SCAP and GHQ policies and a broader plan to redirect Japan's male population away from the imperial era militarism seen in athletics. Throughout Occupation, two distinct bureaus of the General Headquarters — the Civil Information and Education (CIE) section and the Economic and Scientific Section (ESS) — managed athletic affairs in Japan. The CIE was responsible for research, policy, and communication among the numerous Japanese athletic organizations; the ESS was responsible for allocating equipment, payments, and handling financial requests. These bureaus began overhauling of the Japanese athletic world by addressing what they perceived to be the source of imperial-era militarism: school physical education programs.

School Physical Education under Democracy and Demilitarization

Within thirty days of landing on Japanese soil, the GHQ changed the Japanese physical education curriculum to demilitarize athletics and promote an American-inspired curriculum of individualist democracy. To do this, GHQ developed and implemented a complex system of regulations to rewrite the relationship between physical education and militarism. The regulations replaced the former *budō*-and *bushidō*-inspired curriculum with a curriculum steeped in American sporting culture, and reallocated land to non-physical education purposes. However, the events that actually contributed to the relationship between militarism and athleticism in Imperial Japan were the mega-events conducted by the Japanese ministries, like the Olympic-style Meiji Jingū Taikai, the Kōshien Baseball Tournament, and the *undōkai* athletic meets in Manchuria. The GHQ overlooked these mega-events — and would permit their resumption in 1946 — and instead focused their attention on what they believed to be the foundation of militarist ideology in Japan: the school physical education curriculum.

On October 22, 1945 — less than twenty-five days after the beginning of the Allied Occupation of Japan — GHQ required schools to submit physical education curriculum for GHQ review to eliminate militaristic influences.[20] On November 6, 1945, GHQ issued Order No. 80, which explicitly banned *budō*

---

20. General Headquarters Supreme Commander for the Allied Powers, "Administration of the Education System of Japan," excerpted in "Reinstatement of [Budō Sports] Physical Education Activities in the Schools and Universities of Japan," 1; Supreme Commander for the Allied Powers: Civil Information and Education Division, Physical Education and Youth Affairs, Topical File 1945–1951, Box 05725, Folder 25.

martial arts (*kendō, jūdō, kyūdō*, and *naginata*) as well as the children's games popular during Total War like "Warship Play," "Soldier Play," and "Torpedo Boat."[21] On May 15, 1946, Kiyoshi Kitazawa, the Chief of the Physical Education Section of the Japanese Ministry of Education, clarified the government's policy in a radio broadcast directed at all Japanese schools.[22] The first directive, translated by CIE officials, is worth quoting at length:

> You should completely eliminate from your thinking any relationship between physical education and military activity. While it is true that during the war, physical education was used to train for combat; yet it should be realized that physical education can also contribute just as surely to peace, understanding, and democracy provided the activities are carried out in a wholesome, cheerful atmosphere of cooperation, and friendly competition. The attitude of the teachers and pupils is the important difference, and it is the responsibility of every teacher of physical education in Japan to develop the spirit of play in all physical education activities. If this is done, the wholesome development of body, mind, and spirit will be more likely to result.[23]

Additionally, Kitazawa communicated that the CIE prohibited calisthenics, gymnastics, and marching. These practices were replaced with:

> A new schedule of physical training, and it is important to instruct sports in the right way. Such sports as basketball, soccer, volleyball, football...baseball, and others are valuable for physical training and also to cultivate the spirit of cooperation through team work, and to develop fair play and friendly rivalry.[24]

Kitazawa's statement, which was overseen by the CIE, emphasized that the Occupation-era changes to Japan's physical education curriculum promoted Japanese children's "bright spirits and morality," saying "In order to promote democratic education, the respect of individual character is necessary."[25] This

---

21. Vice-Minister of Education, "Hatsutai no. 80: Re: 'Handling of Post-War Course in Physical Education," 2; Supreme Commander for the Allied Powers: Civil Information and Education Division, Physical Education and Youth Affairs, Topical File 1945–1951, Box 05725, Folder 25.

22. Whereas Kitazawa's original copy said "orders," he was requested to change it to "directives." This demonstrates SCAP's utmost concern over terminology that could be considered militarist.

23. Kiyoshi Kitazawa, "Broadcast for Schools (Teacher's Hour): About the Instruction-Method of the Physical Training in Schools," 1; Supreme Commander for the Allied Powers: Civil Information and Education Division, Physical Education and Youth Affairs, Topical File 1945–1951, Box 05725, Folder 30.

24. Kitazawa, "Broadcast for Schools (Teacher's Hour)," 3.

25. Kitazawa, "Broadcast for Schools (Teacher's Hour)," 3.

wording rejected the wartime Japanese 1938 National General Mobilization Law, which discouraged individualism. As Kitazawa explained in his address, Japanese teachers should ask students, "What do you want to play today," and if no consensus was reached, the students should take a vote.[26]

Such a statement clarified school physical education policy in Japan that separated *budō* martial arts from Imperial *Bushidō* philosophy. Japanese physical education teachers — many of whom were hired during the war based on their qualifications for teaching *bushido* philosophy instead of physical activity — were confused why *budō* martial arts were banned while the orders they received did not speak directly to militarist *bushidō* discourse.[27] The GHQ seemed either unaware or insouciant about the difference between *budō* martial arts and the militarist *bushido* philosophies of wartime Japan; the documented evidence indicates that they treated *budō* martial arts as the equivalent of *bushidō* philosophy. After banning *budō* martial arts, CIE officials restricted physical education spaces by reassigning them "practical" uses for rebuilding the devastated state. In December 1945, most existing athletic spaces for schools were transformed into "school farms," becoming sites that ameliorated the food crisis. GHQ authorities ordered that students, from elementary age to high-school age, cultivate sixty square meters of food crops per student and spend time farming during their normal school days and holidays, with no more than fifty days per school year spent for land reclamation.[28]

One Out Baseball

In the midst of enacting physical education reforms, GHQ introduced to Japanese schools a new form of baseball game that accounted for the lack of equipment and space. In January 1946, Major John Norviel of the CIE developed a baseball variation he first called "Burn Out," and then, upon considering the nature of the damage to Japan, renamed "One Out Baseball."[29] Although

---

26. "Supplementary Notes for Kitazawa's Radio Talk," 1; Supreme Commander for the Allied Powers: Civil Information and Education Division, Physical Education and Youth Affairs, Topical File 1945–1951, Box 05725, Folder 30.

27. Kitazawa, "Broadcast for Schools (Teacher's Hour)," 1.

28. "Production of Foodstuffs by the Students," Supreme Commander for the Allied Powers: Ministry of Education — Bureau of Physical Education #1, Box 5492, Folder 12.

29. "Special Report: Recent Physical Education Conferences," 23; Supreme Commander for the Allied Powers: Civil Information and Education Division, Special Projects Branch, Educational Research File 1941–1951, Box 5432, Folder 5, Research Memos A.

well-intentioned, One Out Baseball did not become popular in Japan because it was too complex. Its rules were twenty-six paragraphs long, and many rules referenced the parent sport of American baseball, which itself was not explained. One Out Baseball called for fifteen players per team, and the "batting" team was somehow expected to stand in a space seven meters wide. To compensate for the lack of equipment, Norviel proposed that One Out Baseball be played with rejected baseballs that had failed Japanese manufacturers' quality assurance examination.[30] Any baseball fan would chortle at One Out Baseball's chaos and disorganization. Conversely, people unfamiliar with baseball likely felt overwhelmed by the rules that were more complex than the original game of baseball. At best, the game showed CIE's intentions to support Japanese physical education but more importantly, One Out Baseball demonstrated the CIE's unfamiliarity with the logistics of resuming competitive athletic events in Japan.

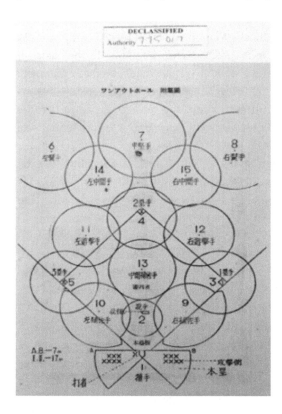

The Japanese-language diagram of how fifteen defensive players should position themselves while playing a game of One Out Baseball. The opposing fifteen offensive players stood in the semi-circular "home plate" space between letters A and B at the bottom of the image, an area which was seven meters wide. The distance between the bases was 17 meters.[31]

---

30. "Special Report: Recent Physical Education Conferences," 22.

31. Major John Norviel, "One Out Baseball," Supreme Commander for the Allied Powers: Civil Information and Education Division, Physical Education and Youth Affairs Branch, Topical File, 1945–1951, One Out Ball to Property Book, Box 5721. Folder 1 (One Out Ball). Image is declassified and in the public domain.

Social Physical Education under Democratization and Demilitarization

The GHQ had installed a new physical education system that the Japanese teachers were ill-prepared and poorly equipped to instruct, and they seemed unaware that Japanese physical education teachers hired in the 1930s and 1940s possessed little training in Western physiology and sports. Additionally, the GHQ turned most athletic spaces into farms, and there was a country-wide shortage of athletic equipment. To remedy this situation, GHQ created a series of state-wide education campaigns that served two purposes: first, to train physical education instructors and the public in the basics of Western sports and athletics, and second, to create a dependent relationship with the Japanese athletic communities. This dependent relationship encouraged Japanese athletic communities to adopt the early Occupation period's democratization and demilitarization agenda to receive disbursements of equipment and space provisions.

In May 1946, a series of meetings about "social physical education" (*shakai taiiku,* 社会体育) attempted to quell Japanese physical education instructors' concerns that they could not manage the new American physical education system. Social physical education sought to end militarism and ultra-nationalism while simultaneously promoting physical strength, hygiene, self-confidence, and women's inclusion into athletics.[32] Social physical education created a self-renewing process by which the entire Japanese populace — not just students — used athletics to adopt and maintain GHQ's early Occupation-era agenda of democratization and demilitarization.

From June 3–5, 1946, representatives from every prefecture in Japan assembled in Tokyo for a physical education conference. Chaired on the American side by Major John Norviel and on the Japanese side by Kitazawa Kiyoshi, the conference aimed to solve the severe equipment shortage, unfamiliarity with the sports curriculum, and the lack of knowledge about Western physiology and kinesiology. On the first day of meetings, the representative from Niigata Prefecture lamented the pressure that Westernized curriculum and space limitations placed upon physical education instructors:

> Teachers of physical education have too heavy responsibilities, too many hours per week, and too many pupils in each class...Give more time for teachers to study. Increase the number of teachers in physical education...It

---

32. "Special Report: Recent Physical Education Conferences" Supreme Commander for the Allied Powers: Civil Information and Education Division, Special Projects Branch, Educational Research File 1941–1951, Box 5432, Folder 5, Research Memos A, 4–8, 11.

is not possible for one teacher to handle 50 students and try to do activities which students prefer...the natural result is dry, uninteresting calisthenics in a large group.[33]

In response, Major John Norviel clarified SCAP's stance on calisthenics by explaining that teachers could lead group exercises in a "pleasant, non-militaristic manner," and outlined how participants should count, line up, and perform without assuming a militaristic attitude.[34] Satisfied with Norviel's clarification, the Niigata representative then lamented that school athletic spaces "are still utilized as cultivated land for the production of food stuffs. We want our play grounds back as soon as possible."[35] Major Norviel, understanding that food cultivation of remained a priority for preventing famine, refused to address this issue. Ultimately, the three-day conference provided opportunities for Japanese physical education instructors to relate their challenges using the new curriculum and achieving the end goals of democratization and demilitarization.

Following the Physical Education Conference in Tokyo, the CIE initiated multiple "Short Course for the Popularization of Social Physical Training" conferences that traveled from prefecture to prefecture — and often to multiple municipalities within each prefecture — from the end of June until the end of July 1946. The "short course" aimed to "[encourage] the formation of physical training bodies, as well as for development in various working places among groups of the same kind of business and in special regions which are to be the bases in carrying out social physical training."[36] Each conference lasted three days, during which a flurry of activity occurred: city representatives reported on their city's plans for rebuilding athletic infrastructure, and teachers received training in physiology and athletic games like volleyball,

---

33. "Report of the Conference of Prefectural Officials of Physical Education," 6; Supreme Commander for the Allied Powers: Civil Information and Education Division, Special Project Branch, Educational Research File, 1941–1951, Box 5439, Folder 22. The reports are only archived in the original English translations for GHQ officials. The names of the representatives were not recorded, and they were identified only by their place of origin.

34. "Untitled Memo to Minister of Education Kotaro Tanaka, May 4, 1946," Supreme Commander for the Allied Powers: Civil Information and Education Division, Special Projects Branch, Educational Research File 1941–1951, Box 5432, Folder 5, Research Memos A, 14–15.

35. "Report of the Conference of Prefectural Officials of Physical Education," 6.

36. "Particulars Concerning the Short Course for the Popularization of Social Physical Training," Supreme Commander for the Allied Powers: Civil Information and Education Division, Special Projects Branch, Educational Research File 1941–1951, Box 5432, Folder 5, Research Memos A.

basketball, and baseball. Due to the massive number of people participating in the conferences, each municipality's representatives were burdened with purchasing athletic clothes, travel tickets, and three days' worth of meals out of their own funds. The ambitious program was onerous to many locales that were preoccupied with growing food, rebuilding, and finding capable physical education teachers.

Educating About the Democracy through Baseball Magazines

Occupation-era baseball magazines, which GHQ officials oversaw and censored, provide researchers a clearer understanding of how messages of democracy, individualism, dependency, and subservience were delivered to the Japanese baseball community's many readers. During the Occupation-era, thirteen new baseball-related magazines began publishing, serving a monthly audience of over 50,000 people. Although *Yakyūkai* — the Imperial-era's famed baseball magazine — resumed publication, it was quickly surpassed by a new upstart, *Besuboru Magajin* (Baseball Magazine). *Besuboru Magajin* skyrocketed in sales and reached monthly publication runs of 20,000 by 1949.[37] In contrast to *Yakyūkai*, which continued using imperial Japanese-language word for baseball, *yakyū* (野球), *Besuboru Magajin* used the previously banned English loan word *bēsubōru* to indicate its desire to leave Imperial-era militarism in the past.

Besuboru Magajin demonstrated how the Japanese baseball community strove to meet GHQ expectations about democratization and demilitarization. The most notable author about democratic ideals in the Japanese baseball community was Suzuki Sōtarō (鈴木惣太郎). Suzuki, born in 1890, studied at Columbia University and long desired to connect American and Japanese culture, which his biographer described with a metaphor as building "bridges" across the Pacific.[38] Suzuki often worked with newspaper mogul Shōriki Matsutarō and was a key figure in securing Babe Ruth's 1934 Japanese tour.[39] Whereas Shōriki, the wartime Information Minister, languished in Sugamo

---

37. "Shūki yakyū yomimono gō" 秋季野球読物号 [Fall Reading Issue], *Besuboru Magajin*, Fall 1949, cover. The SCAP censor's comments about publication numbers are written on the cover. In this chapter, I use the familiar romanization of *Besuboru Magajin*, which does not use diacriticals.

38. Hatano Masaru波多野勝, *Nichibei yakyū no kakehashi: Suzuki Sōtarō no jinsei to Shōriki Matsutarō* 日米野球の架け橋：鈴木惣太郎の人生と正力松太郎 [Bridging Japanese-American Baseball: The Life of Suzuki Sōtaro and Shōriki Matsutarō (Tokyo: Fuyushobo, 2013), 6–8.

39. Hatano Masaru, *Nichibei yakyū no kakehashi*, 101–110.

Prison charged as a Class A War Criminal in early 1946, Suzuki, who did not hold government office during the war, received a rare face-to-face meeting with General Douglas MacArthur.

In April of 1946, the first issue of *Besuboru Magajin* appeared for sale on newsstands, and as readers opened it they were greeted with Suzuki's long-form article, "The Question of Baseball Democracy" (野球デモクラシイの問題). Suzuki recounted meeting General MacArthur on a quiet night at a hotel. The two men discussed the merits of using baseball to teach American-style democracy, and to help familiarize the Japanese population with American culture.[40] Suzuki explained his foremost concern to MacArthur: in general, Japanese people understood that they needed to embrace democracy to create "a new Japanese state." However, Suzuki believed that most Japanese people did not fully comprehend how to be a member of a democratic society, asking, "Just what *is* democracy? (デモクラシイとは何ぞや?)"[41] MacArthur sympathized with this problem. Suzuki and General MacArthur agreed that the long-established relationship between baseball and major newspapers — most notably Shōriki's Yomiuri Shinbun — suggested that baseball could be another way to help disseminate democratic ideals among the Japanese people. However, General MacArthur also understood that the newspaper/baseball relationship could be treacherous: Shōriki Matsutarō, who remained the owner of Yomiuri Shinbun, was imprisoned for his wartime role in spreading militarist propaganda. Suzuki acknowledged this point and admitted that after the Pacific War, "baseball must be a democracy," arguing that baseball would lead Japanese people away from a "militant state" and towards "peacefulness" and "democracy."[42] It is worth quoting the article's conclusion at length, where Suzuki disavows imperialism and desires to develop in the model of the United States:

> So, the stage is set for baseball [in Japan], but the plan for democracy was born in America, a place where baseball has grown in prosperity and given greatness to all sports... for baseball in Japan, the amount of imperialism and militarism that existed in the past is to be detested... We must treat

---

40. Suzuki Sōtarō 鈴木惣太郎, "Yakyū demokurashii no mondai" 野球デモクラシイの問題 [The Question of Baseball Democracy] ベースボール・マガジン [*Baseball Magazine*] April 20, 1946, 12.

41. Suzuki Sōtarō, "Yakyū demokurashii no mondai," 12.

42. Suzuki Sōtarō, "Yakyū demokurashii no mondai," 13–15.

baseball and democracy as the same; if we don't create the atmosphere to cultivate democracy, then baseball democracy won't come to us.[43]

To receive General MacArthur's formal support for baseball, Suzuki appealed to the "American national game" to meet the early Occupation-era goals of democratization and demilitarization and created an image of Japan developing in the manner of the United States. Suzuki's argument further evidenced how the Japanese baseball community used overtures of "peace" and "democracy" to receive preferential treatment.

A June 1946 article challenges the authenticity of Suzuki's overtures. In the summer of 1946, Suzuki submitted an article to *Besuboru Magajin* titled, "On a Long-Term Championship Game," in which he used the metaphor of winning a baseball game as akin to winning at war, a trope which had appeared throughout English and Japanese publications since the turn of the twentieth century. Suzuki critiqued Japanese militarism during the Fifteen Years War by arguing that Japan relied on Carl von Clausewitz' theory of war, a model that required both material superiority and spiritual superiority for victory. He then discussed Japanese samurai as the embodiment of the "unscientific" and "traditional" Japan, describing pre-1945 Japan as a country that gave militarism "a favorable soil for flourishing."[44] Suzuki explained that the United States was "ever prepared to maintain an overwhelming physical power in a long term warfare, attack their opponents squarely, and never try to have recourse to a surprise attack... this is the kind of baseball Americans like."[45] GHQ censors deleted Suzuki's critique under the pretext of "militaristic propaganda" and prevented the original article's publication. The text that appeared in the final publication of *Besuboru Magajin* rehashed Suzuki's previous April article, "The Question of Baseball Democracy."[46] This intervention suggests that the GHQ wanted to control the precise path through which the Japanese baseball community expressed its remorse for militarization. The GHQ did not want to resurrect the image of the samurai and its connotations with *budō* martial arts, *bushidō* philosophy, and militarism.

---

43. Suzuki Sōtarō, "Yakyū demokurashii no mondai," 15.

44. Suzuki Sōtarō 鈴木惣太郎, "Chōki sōhasen ni tsuite" 長期争覇戦について [On a Long-Term Championship Game], ベースボール・マガジン *Besuboru Magajin* [Baseball Magazine], June 1946, 4–8. Quote is from unnumbered censorship document prepared by R. Matsumoto.

45. Suzuki Sōtarō, "Chōki sōhasen ni tsuite," 4–8. Quote is from unnumbered censorship document prepared by R. Matsumoto.

46. Suzuki Sōtarō, "Chōki sōhasen ni tsuite," 4.

Provisions of Equipment and Space

More than any other athletic community during the Occupation-era, the Japanese baseball community met the GHQ's expectations for spreading democracy and eradicating militarism. In response, GHQ created workarounds of rationed materials to provide equipment to the baseball community. There was a massive market for baseball goods, as evidenced by a 1946 survey conducted among Japanese males and females from elementary school to college. Of nearly 40,000 students surveyed, 50% indicated an interest in baseball; among boys, nearly 75% identified baseball as their favorite sport.[47] GHQ had distributed some athletic equipment for use by impoverished Japanese, but CIE and ESS officials struggled to consistently provide goods because of scarce raw material resources and rationing. Because sports equipment production had dwindled to zero by the end of the war, black market entrepreneurs hoarded the remaining equipment and re-sold the goods at inflated prices.

In order to advance the agenda of using athletics to teach democracy to the Japanese people, the GHQ organized to re-supply Japan with sporting goods, and most of the measures taken focused on revitalizing the baseball community. On September 12, 1946, representatives from the ESS, the CIE, the Japanese Ministry of Education, the Ministry of Commerce and Education, the Ministry of Forestry and Agriculture, the Hides and Leather and Control Union, the All Japan Sporting Goods Union and the Japan Athletic Association met to resolve the material shortage. Major John Norviel summarized GHQ's policy and provided his own opinion:

> The establishment of democracy begins rather than ends with political organizations and in the opinion of this Officer, there is no place where the practice of democratic activities can better be carried on than in the physical education program, therefore, production of the necessary amount of athletic equipment is in line with General Headquarters policy.[48]

In accordance with these goals, Norviel requested that GHQ authorities permit sporting goods manufacturers to reach their maximum production capacity as soon as possible.[49] The first and second production priorities were

47. "Student Sports Preferences," Supreme Commander for the Allied Powers: Civil Information and Education Division, Physical Education and Youth Affairs, Topical File 1945–1951, Box 05725, Folder 29, Sports Evaluation. Handwritten notes on the document indicate that the survey was widely released in January 1947.

48. Major John Norviel, "Production of Athletic Equipment," 2; Supreme Commander for the Allied Powers: Economic and Scientific Section, Industry Division, Box 07347, Folder 34.

49. Major John Norviel, "Production of Athletic Equipment," 1.

baseballs and softballs.[50] Norviel then reclassified athletic "shoes and clothing" (i.e. baseball cleats and uniforms) as necessities for Japanese people's welfare and therefore eligible for immediate distribution of raw materials. In Norviel's final report to SCAP authorities, he noted supporting physical education would "help to create an enthusiasm for wholesome peaceful activities, thereby providing an emotional outlet and reduce problems of the occupation."[51]

It was an onerous task for sporting goods manufacturers to reach these production levels. Production required over a half million pounds of imported leather, over 10,000 pounds of imported rubber and wool, and ancillary materials like cotton, hemp, paste, and felt.[52] To produce better equipment out of the preciously-acquired materials, sporting goods companies began to examine their products and quantify the results. By the end of 1946, four separate sporting goods companies combined — Daiichi Undō, Ayukawa, Mizuno, and Sanshin Kōgyō — reached SCAP's production goals of 10,000 baseball gloves.[53] However, the combined companies fell woefully short of meeting Norviel's request for 1.4 million softballs and 226,000 baseballs, producing only a combined total of 30,000 baseballs by mid-1947.[54]

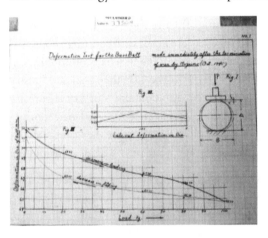

An example of the Mizuno Corporation's "deformation" testing of their baseball, which evaluated how a ball's material construction affected its usability.[55]

50. Major John Norviel, "Annex #1: Physical Education Equipment needed in Japan during 1946 and 1947," 1; Supreme Commander for the Allied Powers: Economic and Scientific Section, Industry Division, Box 07347, Folder 34.

51. Major John Norviel, "Production of Athletic Equipment," 1.

52. Major John Norviel, "Annex #1: Physical Education Equipment needed in Japan during 1946 and 1947," 3.

53. "Production Results." Supreme Commander for the Allied Powers: Economic and Scientific Section, Industry Division, Box 07347, Folder 34.

54. Major John Norviel, "Annex #1: Physical Education Equipment needed in Japan during 1946 and 1947," 2; and "Production Results."

55. Mizuno Sporting Goods Corporation, "Deformation Test for the Base-ball," Supreme Commander for the Allied Powers: Economic and Scientific Section, Industry Division, Box 07347, Folder 34. Image is declassified and in the public domain.

Due to the lack of equipment, sports organizations notified the GHQ that they could not meet its expectation of spreading democracy and individualism through sports. In March 1947, the Rubber Ball Baseball Association — which represented a kind of baseball played with a softer, all-rubber ball instead of a standard hard leather baseball with a rubber core — appealed to GHQ for support. Rubber ball baseball began in 1917 as a safer and less resource-intensive game than standard baseball, making it widely accessible and extremely popular game in Japan. However, because it was an informal "street-ball," with rules that morphed between regions and teams, eventually it became associated with a violent history that involved bribery, profiteering, and racketeering. After the Pacific War, rubber ball baseball fans formed their first official national organization and courted GHQ's desire to spread democracy through baseball. In 1946, there were 26,000 adult rubber ball baseball teams in the civilian sector. With a minimum of nine players per team, this number meant that at least 234,000 Japanese adults played rubber ball baseball. Elementary schools accounted for another 90,000 players.[56] The Rubber Ball Baseball Association's letter to GHQ demonstrated their organization's eagerness to spread peace:

> This association hopes people as many as possible to cultivate sportsmanship and strengthen their health while enjoying sports and to become such people as contributing to the construction of truly peaceful Japan and at the same time aims at the connection among local associations, negotiation with government authorities and smooth distribution of materials.

> Then Japanes [sic] people scarcely escaped from starvation thanks to kind release of food by the Allied Forces, but for construction of new Japan stir up of young generation is quite essential. However, regret to say, many young men who were demobilized after the war service found on the motherland no reliable thing spiritually and materially and, as you know, they are now in desperate condition to commit evil actions. This Association is really expecting such unhappy young men to awake as quick as possible to cooperate in the reconstruction of new Japan and at the same time to reward to your kind assistance.

> We are now endeavoring to popularize rubber baseball among young people and to attain the above mentioned aims, sweeping out the idea of war.[57]

---

56. All Japan Rubber Ball Association, "Rubber Ball Baseball," 5; Supreme Commander for the Allied Powers: Civil Information and Education Division, Physical Education and Youth Affairs, Topical File 1945–1951, Box 05725, Folder 17.

57. All Japan Rubber Ball Association, "Rubber Ball Baseball," 4.

The Rubber Ball Baseball Association appealed to the GHQ's interest in re-habilitating people away from "evil actions" by giving them a game to occupy their time. However, like other sporting communities, the Rubber Ball Baseball Association struggled to find equipment.

The association admitted to shopping on the black market because legitimate suppliers could not meet their needs. In 1946, two GHQ-initiated dispersals of equipment had provided only 1,500 gloves and 150 catcher mitts to nearly 20,000 civilian rubber-ball baseball players. Before the war, rubber ball baseball players used over 3.3 million rubber baseballs a year, which equaled about 126 balls per team. However, in 1946 most teams received a distribution of two or three balls, and one lucky team received ten balls.[58] With legitimate vendors undersupplying such a large market, the Rubber Ball Baseball Association admitted the black market fulfilled their rubber baseball demand. They calculated that 80% of rubber baseballs were made from "hidden materials," which meant rubber that had been smuggled, stolen, or obtained illegitimately from Americans; 15% were made from "leftover" rubber scraps from other companies; and 5% were legitimate rubber baseballs that had been stolen from the manufacturer.[59] Therefore, the association lamented that the lack of equipment drove them use the very markets that were antithetical to the cause of American democracy.

Conclusion

This chapter discussed how the Japanese baseball community advocated for the Occupation agenda of democratization and demilitarization from August 1945 until April 1947. The Japanese baseball community argued the sport helped rehabilitate Japanese men from the militarism of wartime Japan. In return for these gestures, the GHQ arranged for the production and distribution of baseball equipment and spaces to play baseball. The relationship between the Japanese baseball community and the SCAP and GHQ offices was characterized by dependency and subservience. The next chapter will discuss how the special treatment of the Japanese baseball community developed during the Reverse Course and the onset of the Cold War in the spring of 1947.

---

58. Numbers calculated by author based on statistics provided in All Japan Rubber Ball Association, "Rubber Ball Baseball," 7.

59. All Japan Rubber Ball Association, "Rubber Ball Baseball," 7.

CHAPTER EIGHT

The Cold War and the Reverse Course: Rearming Japan without Resurrecting *Bushidō* Philosophy

What about the homeless children at Ueno?...Let's have a social welfare program for them. You see so much vermin all around us...people are in distress...call upon the conscience of the nation. Newspapers are too cheerful [about sports], and I don't like it at all.[1]

— Opinion of a 45-year-old Japanese laborer provided to a GHQ investigator

Introduction

The previous chapter established how the Japanese athletic community made gestures of democratization and demilitarization and received GHQ support; this chapter addresses how these overtures translated into the post-1947 environment, where the GHQ reversed many of its early Occupation-era agendas and attempted to make Japan a partner in the Cold War. General MacArthur wanted Japanese athletes to participate in the Olympics, however, the lack of equipment and space prevented this from occurring in 1948. The GHQ supervised the re-emergence of athletic mega-events in Japan, yet the nascent National Athletic Meet bore a remarkable resemblance to the Imperial-era *Meiji Jingū Taikai*. Thus, the period spanning roughly from 1947 until 1950 is characterized as an attempt to build a new competitive athletic culture in Japan

---

1. "Some Reactions to the Victories of the Japanese Swimmers in the United States," 6. All but the first set of ellipses are in original text and indicate pauses in the man's speech instead of omissions.

without the resurrection of the familiar *bushidō*-inflected events that occurred in the Imperial era.

The Cold War

A series of chaotic events changed the political landscape of Japan and had drastic consequences for the demilitarizing and democratizing both the land-scape of athletics and Japanese society overall. On March 12, 1947, United States President Harry Truman requested 400 million dollars from Congress to bolster Greece and Turkey against the rising influence of socialism and com-munism; Greece was embroiled in civil war in which the military fought the Greek communist party.[2] This public statement of support for countries com-batting socialism and communism became known as the "Truman Doctrine" and marked the beginning of the Cold War between the United States and the Soviet Union. Then in April 1947, Japan held its first post-World War II dem-ocratic election. The results shocked GHQ authorities: the Japanese Socialist Party (JSP) won the popular vote, and Katayama Tetsu (片山哲), who opposed Occupation authorities and led the JSP, became the Prime Minister of Japan. In the Truman Doctrine's wake, SCAP commenced what historians now call the "reverse course" in Japan: GHQ released many politicians who had been jailed previously for wartime activities and began remilitarizing Japan as a bulwark of American capitalism in Asia.[3] Then, GHQ shifted from a policy of letting the Japanese economy largely run itself to a policy of government interven-tion; simultaneously, GHQ jailed socialists and communists.[4] By 1949, sur-veys revealed that the majority of Japanese people believed the United States' direction was "bad" for the country and that a military conflict loomed in the near future. This pessimistic outlook stood at odds with the pre-1947 agenda of demilitarization and ending the will to war.[5]

Prior to the reverse course, SCAP, GHQ authorities, and Japanese politi-cians and scholars had been working on a constitution for Japan. Focused on demilitarization and ending the Japanese will to war, General MacArthur in-

---

2. Harry Truman, "Recommendation for Assistance to Greece and Turkey," *Avalon Project: Yale Law School*, http://avalon.law.yale.edu/20th_century/trudoc.asp.

3. Gordon, *A Modern History of Japan*, 237.

4. Dower, *Embracing Defeat*, 546 and 526.

5. Dower, *Embracing Defeat*, 526.

sisted that Japan become permanently pacifist.[6] On May 3, 1947, two months into the Cold War and one month after the commencement of the Reverse Course, the Japanese Constitution went into effect. It contained the famous Article 9, the "Renunciation of War." Article 9 stated:

> Aspiring sincerely to an international peace based on justice and order, the Japanese people forever renounce war as a sovereign right of the nation and the threat or use of force as means of settling international disputes…land, sea, and air forces…will never be maintained. The right of belligerency of the state will not be recognized.[7]

Article 9 of the Constitution created a predicament within the context of the Cold War: how could Japan remilitarize while at the same time renouncing war and prohibiting Imperial-era mindsets of militarism?

GHQ did not have a clear answer to this problem. As the previous chapter established, GHQ controlled most athletic spaces in Japan and provisioned the Japanese baseball community with supplies and space due to their gestures of adopting the Occupation agenda. I argue that scholars can analyze SCAP's control of other athletic spaces to better understand how Japan's broader athletic community demonstrated a willingness to adopt the reverse course's goals without resuming Imperial-era militarist mindsets.

GHQ managed most of Japan's athletic space. According to a survey by the Japanese Ministry of Education, there were approximately 0.05 *tsubo* (one *tsubo* equals 3.31 square meters) of athletic space per capita in Tokyo; for a metropolis with over six million people, that equated to 1.12 million square meters.[8] The Meiji Jingū Outer Gardens contained nearly forty percent of this space was contained within GHQ had confiscated the Outer Garden properties because they symbolized imperial militarism and because they were some of the world's best athletic venues. By comparison, the combined athletic venues in the Meiji Jingū Outer Gardens — the National Athletic Stadium, *Meiji Jingū Baseball Stadium*, and several *sumō* rings — were six times larger than today's

---

6. Kenneth Port, *Transcending Law: The Unintended Life of Article 9 of the Japanese Constitution*, revised printing (Durham, NC: Carolina Academic Press, 2010), 44–45.

7. Prime Minister of Japan and His Cabinet, "The Constitution of Japan," (Official English Translation), http://japan.kantei.go.jp/constitution_and_government_of_japan/constitution_e.html.

8. Japanese Ministry of Education, "Result of Survey on Current Condition of Sport Equipment Throughout Japan," Supreme Commander for the Allied Powers, Civil Information and Education Section, Education Division, Special Projects Branch 1945–1952, Box 5727, Folder 29, 1–2.

largest stadium, the Rungrado May Day Stadium in North Korea.[9] SCAP officials renamed Japan's National Athletic Stadium (*Meiji Jingū Gaien Kyōgijō*)
to "Nile Kinnick Stadium" in honor of a deceased American marine, and they
renamed Meiji Jingū Stadium to "Stateside Park." Instead of being a space for
the promotion of Japanese athletics, the venues of the Meiji Jingū Outer Gardens often entertained United States servicemen with football and basketball
practices in the summer and ice skating and movies in the winter.[10]

While sporting goods manufacturers focused on meeting the massive Japanese baseball market, the GHQ opened an equally ambitious project of building baseball venues. Instead of permitting Japanese athletes to use the venues
in the shrine to the Meiji Emperor, the GHQ fronted money to local governments to build baseball stadiums. This New Deal-inspired program put people
to work and gave them the athletic spaces they desired. Funding began in 1947
and construction continued until 1952. Nine baseball stadiums with capacities
above 10,000 seats were built across Japan: Nagoya Stadium, Heiwadai Stadium
in Fukuoka, Toyama Stadium in Okinawa, Shimonoseki Stadium in Yamaguchi Prefecture, Nihon Seimei Stadium in Osaka, Okayama Stadium, Kawasaki
Stadium, and Nagasaki Stadium. The nine Occupation-era stadiums equaled
the number of stadiums built throughout Japan in the nineteen-year period
from 1922 through 1941, and equaled the number of stadiums built during
the twenty-five-year period from 1954 through 1979.[11] The Japanese baseball
community's acquiescence to being subservient to American demands gained
them an enormous amount of support for equipment and space not afforded
other sporting communities.

Olympic-Style Games during the Reverse Course

Much of SCAP and GHQ attention on sports during the Reverse Course focused on Olympic-style games. General MacArthur, the former President of
the United States International Olympic Committee, wanted the Japanese re-
admitted into the international sporting world as soon as possible, but he had

9. Information sourced from Stadium Database, http://stadiumdb.com/stadiums/pkr/run-
grado_may_day_stadium. Built in 1989, Rungrado has a seating capacity of 150,000 people and
is the location of the annual Arirang Festival (also known as the "Mass Games").

10. Ryōtarō Azuma, "Application for Approval on Our Use of Athletic Facilities Now Under
Administration by Allied Forces," 1; Supreme Commander for the Allied Powers: Civil Information and Education Division, Physical Education and Youth Affairs, Topical File 1945–1951, Box
05725, Folder 5.

11. Yōsensha, *Shōwa puro yakyū kyūjō taizen.*

concerns about the intentions of the Japanese Amateur Athletic Association (JAAA). In November 1946, the JAAA organized the "National Athletic Meet" (国民体育大会) in the Kyoto-Osaka region with 7,500 athletes participating and presented the "emperor's cup" to victorious athletes.[12] The GHQ immediately recognized that the National Athletic Meet was the revival of the Meiji Jingū Taikai. The GHQ did not halt the National Athletic Meet, but instead they restricted its access to athletic spaces.

Meanwhile, GHQ created a competitor event, "The MacArthur Cup." The initial spark of the event occurred when Japanese businessman Ikeda Masazō (池田政三) purchased three trophies engraved with General MacArthur's signature as a prize for a tennis competition. Ikeda's purchase was inspired by General MacArthur's use of an athletic competition named the "MacArthur Cup" during the Pacific War to encourage bonding among the servicemen aboard his ships.[13] The JAAA saw an opportunity to curry favor with SCAP, and it offered to host the first annual "General MacArthur Cup" (マッカーサー元帥枚) in August 1947.[14] This event birthed a tenuous relationship with General MacArthur's plan to have Japan re-enter the Olympics: on the one hand, the JAAA seemed eager to adopt the democratization agenda, while on the other hand, the National Athletic Meet was approaching levels of participation seen during the Imperial-era.

Advertisement for the 1951 MacArthur Cup Competition in Niigata Prefecture.[15]

---

12. Ryotaro Azuma, "Application for Approval on Our Use of Athletic Facilities now under Administration by Allied Forces," Supreme Commander for the Allied Powers: Civil Information and Education Division, Physical Education and Youth Affairs, Topical File 1945–1951, Box 05725, Folder 5.

13. Ōkubo Hideaki 大久保英明 and Yamagishi Kōji 山岸孝吏, "Makkasa Gensui mai supotsu kyōgikai no seiritsu to haishi" マッカーサー元帥枚スポーツ競技会の成立と廃止 [The General MacArthur Cup Competitions: Regarding their Establishment and Dissolution] (Kanazawa: Kanazawa University Education Department Bulletin, 2004), 92.

14. Ōkubo and Yamagishi, "Makkasa Gensui mai supotsu kyōgikai no seiritsu to haishi," 90–92.

15. Supreme Commander for the Allied Powers: Civil Information and Education Division, Physical Education and Youth Affairs, Topical File 1945–1951, Box 05725, Folder 3.

In 1948, General MacArthur enlisted a former Olympian, William Neufeld, to prepare Japan to re-enter the Olympics. In his first duty, Neufeld advocated for increased GHQ financial commitment Japanese school athletics. In 1948, the Physical Education Bureau of the Japanese Ministry of Education requested 347 million yen from GHQ in their budget. Initially, GHQ provided less than 6% of this request. Neufeld wrote a letter on the Physical Education Bureau's behalf, explaining that "to encourage better types of men and women as instructors, coaches, and leaders…it is suggested that some funds be allocated."[16] Neufeld argued that many Japanese schools continued to lack instructional handbooks and testing programs for sports. Due to Neufeld's letter, the Physical Education Bureau received 111 million yen, or about 30% of their initial request.[17] However, SCAP and GHQ officials interpreted this situation to mean that Japanese athletic infrastructure remained woefully unprepared for international athletic competition. When London managed to rebuild enough structures so that they could host the 1948 Summer Olympics, General MacArthur refused to relax the travel restrictions for Japanese athletes. Japanese athletes had to wait until 1952 to compete in the Olympics.

Undeterred by General MacArthur's decision, the Japanese Swimming Federation (日本水泳連盟) hosted a National Swim Meet in Tokyo. Held concomitantly to the London Olympics, event organizers posted the Japanese swimmers' results alongside their international competition in London. The event garnered international attention when two Japanese swimmers, Furuhashi Hironoshin (古橋廣之進) and Hashizume Shirō (橋爪四郎), unofficially beat the standing 1,500 meter freestyle world record by 21 seconds and bested the London gold medalist, Jimmy McLane of the United States, by nearly 40 seconds.[18] Two days later, Furuhashi swam a 4'34.4" 400-meter race; McLane took the London gold medal with a time a full ten seconds slower.[19]

16. William Neufeld, "Concerning the Revision of the Budget for Athletic Promotion Section;" Supreme Commander for the Allied Powers: Civil Information and Education Division, Physical Education and Youth Affairs, Topical File 1945–1951, Box 05725, Folder 28.

17. "Physical Education Bureau Budget for 1948–1949," 4; Supreme Commander for the Allied Powers: Civil Information and Education Division, Physical Education and Youth Affairs, Topical File 1945–1951, Box 05725, Folder 28.

18. "Furuhashi, Hashizume sengohyaku ni sekai shinkiroku," 古橋、橋爪千五百に世界新記録 [Furuhashi and Hashizume Set New World Record in the 1500] Yomiuri Shinbun, August 7, 1948, Morning Edition, 2. McLane's data provided by Sports Reference: Olympic Sports, http://www.sports-reference.com/olympics/athletes/mc/jimmy-mclane-1.html.

19. "Chōnin Furuhashi kyōi no igyō," 超人古橋驚異の偉業 [Superman Furuhashi: The Miracle of His Great Work] Yomiuri Shinbun, August 9, 1948, Morning Edition, 2. McLane's data pro-

After the Japanese swimmers' strong showing at the unofficial National Swim Meet, the American Amateur Athletic Union (AAU) made the unprecedented request that Japanese swimmers be allowed to participate in the 1949 National Men's AAU Swimming and Diving Championships in Los Angeles, California. General MacArthur permitted the Japanese swimmers to travel to the United States, making the swimmers the first Japanese athletes to travel abroad after World War II.

The American press excitedly promoted the swimming competition, as Dick Hyland of the *Los Angeles Times* wrote:

> The greatest group of swimmers and divers seen in one tank since the Olympic games in London last summer will strut their stuff. In some ways this meet will top the London affair. The lads wearing the Stars and Stripes shield on their suits swept every swimming and diving event in the [1948 London] Olympic Games. The Japanese did not compete.[20]

General MacArthur sent a personal message in Japanese encouraging the Japanese swim team:

> I've well known the activities of Japanese athletes since the Amsterdam Olympics. Now, in the role of athletes, you have the world's attention as the first delegates (*shisetsu* 使節) to travel to America after the war, but don't let this make you obstinate in your matches; instead, have the same pleasant feeling of giving your best as you did when you swam in Japan.[21]

On August 16, 1949, the Japanese swimmers competed in what amounted to a repeat of the 1948 London Olympics swimming event. The AAU Championships featured 168 participants, including the superstars of the 1948 Olympics in swimming: American Jimmy McLane (Gold, 1,500-meter freestyle) and Australian John Marshall (Silver, 1,500-meter freestyle). To start the day, Hashizume wowed the American crowd by finishing his 1,500-meter freestyle heat in 18'35.7", which destroyed the previous world record, set in 1938, by 21 seconds. In the next heat, Furuhashi obliterated Hashizume's minutes-old

---

vided by *Sports Reference: Olympic Sports,* http://www.sports-reference.com/olympics/athletes/mc/jimmy-mclane-1.html.

20. Dick Hyland, "Japan's Team in First U.S. Meet Since '41," *Los Angeles Times,* August 14, 1949, 32.

21. "Tobei senshu asu no shuppatsu mae ni mō renshū," 渡米選手あすの出発前に猛練習 [America-bound Swimmers Practice Hard Before Departure] *Yomiuri Shinbun,* August 11, 1949, Morning Edition, 2.

world record by finishing in 18'19", or 39.8 seconds better than the 1938 world record.[22] The *Los Angeles Times* admitted that the American swim team was humbled by the Japanese swimmers' record-breaking performance.

Following the Japanese athletes' triumphant success, the CIE was curious about the Japanese public's reaction: how did the average Japanese person feel about their countrymen returning to international athletics? The CIE sent interviewers to talk to people around their Tokyo headquarters, and also had employees covertly record public conversations on the street. While the CIE report admitted that its study was not scientific, they did receive information from a cross-section of nearly one hundred middle-class Tokyoites. The results were clear: 9 out of 10 respondents were interested in the AAU championships, and 75% had listened to the results of the swim meet on the radio. Most respondents (75%) were *not* sports fans. Instead, the CIE reported Japanese people were interested in the swimmers for two main reasons: 1) "the event represented Japan's first major bid since the war to participate in international affairs;" and 2) "the victory gained in swimming might provide a psychological 'shot in the arm' to the Japanese people."[23]

Despite the overwhelming support given to the Japanese swimmers, there were detractors. One self-avowed communist reported that he knew of the event only because somebody else had turned on the radio in his workplace; he would have ignored sports at any other time because they had nothing to do with helping society.[24] Other candid voices reflected the uncensored opinions of Japanese who found it ludicrous that GHQ officials prioritized constructing athletic spaces and funding of international swimming events while people were still homeless and hungry. With the Ministry of Education calculating the number of orphaned children at over 100,000 and many Japanese still reconstructing their homes, athletes who followed SCAP-prescribed agendas, such as preparing for the Olympics instead of the National Athletic Meet, received privileges not available the general population.

Meanwhile, the National Athletic Meet was growing quickly and needed a new home: The 1948 National Athletic Meet in Fukuoka — a prefecture on the island of Kyūshū with a population of about 3 million people — attract-

---

22. "Furuhashi Tops Record by 38.9s," *Los Angeles Times*, August 17, 1949, C1.

23. "Some Reactions to the Victories of the Japanese Swimmers in the United States," 2; Supreme Commander for the Allied Powers: Civil Information and Education Division, Physical Education and Youth Affairs, Topical File 1945–1951, Box 05724, Folder 28.

24. "Some Reactions to the Victories of the Japanese Swimmers in the United States," 3.

ed 23,657 athletes and an audience estimated at 830,000 people.[25] To capitalize upon this success, in December 1948, the director of the JAAA, Azuma Ryōtarō, requested GHQ permission to hold the 1949 National Athletic Meet in Tokyo and use the confiscated Nile Kinnick Stadium as the center of the festivities. With a larger stadium situated in a metropolis from which to draw spectators, Azuma expected an audience over a million people. However, the GHQ refused to permit the JAAA to use any of the venues in the Meiji Jingū Outer Garden complex.

On December 30, 1948, William Neufeld wrote to GHQ of his support for Azuma's plan:

> The people of Japan have always taken great pride in their international sports achievement. Since international competition is not feasible at present, the proposed national athletic meet is particularly significant as a morale builder. Consideration of means for accommodating the largest possible attendance is highly desirable.[26]

Neufeld agreed with Azuma that Tokyo was the best place to maximize attendance; Occupation personnel could even enjoy the games and bolster the attendance figures. Neufeld's bosses at the CIE agreed, stating on January 5, 1949, "CIE recommends approval of subject request on the grounds that athletics on a national basis should be encouraged as a potential contribution to democratic education."[27]

However, Neufeld's argument was undermined by historical imagery. Azuma's request to hold the reincarnation of the Meiji Jingū Taikai in the shrine to Emperor Meiji was unacceptable to the Headquarters and Services Section (HSS) of GHQ, which oversaw the stadiums. On March 16, 1949, the HSS denied the JAAA permission to use Nile Kinnick Stadium. The HSS defended its decision with a long list of inconveniences, none of which stated its actual fear that the event would reignite ultra-nationalism. The HSS argued that Nile

---

25. Ryotaro Azuma, "Application for Approval on Our Use of Athletic Facilities Now Under Administration by Allied Forces," 1; Supreme Commander for the Allied Powers: Civil Information and Education Division, Physical Education and Youth Affairs, Topical File 1945–1951, Box 05725, Folder 5.

26. William Neufeld, "Application for Use of Athletic Facilities Now Under Administration of Hq and Sv Group," 1; Supreme Commander for the Allied Powers: Civil Information and Education Division, Physical Education and Youth Affairs, Topical File 1945–1951, Box 05725, Folder 5.

27. "Check Sheet: Application for Use of Athletic Facilities Now Under Administration of Hq and SV Group," 2; Supreme Commander for the Allied Powers: Civil Information and Education Division, Physical Education and Youth Affairs, Topical File 1945–1951, Box 05725, Folder 5.

Kinnick Stadium could not be used for the National Athletic Meet because the army's six-man football team and basketball team would be unable to practice for a week; the army's ice skating rink would have to be removed, costing over of $1,700 (roughly $17,000 today); and weekend showings of movies for army officers would lose ticket revenue.[28] In response to this list of trivialities, on May 13, 1949, over 100 politicians from the Japanese National Diet wrote to the GHQ in favor of the National Athletic Meet receiving permission to use Nile Kinnick Stadium. They highlighted that the proposed competition dates included "Culture Day" on November 3, although they omitted that this national holiday had replaced "Physical Education Day," formerly held on Emperor Meiji's birthday.[29] Furthermore, they argued that because Nile Kinnick Stadium had been renovated for military recreational use, it would save the JAAA upwards of $30 million in finding or building another site.

Determined to succeed, the JAAA revised its request to use Nile Kinnick Stadium for only four days. This change prompted Lieutenant Colonel Donald Nugent, Chief of the CIE, to intervene on the JAAA's behalf on May 27. He argued that having the largest possible National Athletic Meet would prepare Japan "mentally, spiritually, and physically" to enter the 1952 Olympic Games. In addition, he derided the HSS' exaggerated list of excuses for denying the Japanese the use of their own stadium:

> This section [the CIE] realizes the importance of athletics for Occupation personnel. It has no desire to disrupt that program by encouraging unreasonable requests by the Japanese for use of athletic facilities now under control of Headquarters and Service Group. It is considered, however, that the use by the Japanese of the Nile Kinnick Stadium for a period of four days will not interfere unduly with the headquarters [sic] athletic program but will, on the other hand, afford a great stimulus to Japanese amateur sports and at the same time result in very favorable reactions from the Japanese public.[30]

28. "Check Sheet: Application for Use of Athletic Facilities Now Under Administration of Hq and SV Group," 6.

29. Federation of Sports Members of the National Diet, "Petition," 2; Supreme Commander for the Allied Powers: Civil Information and Education Division, Physical Education and Youth Affairs, Topical File 1945–1951, Box 05725, Folder 5.

30. Lieutenant Colonel Donald Nugent, "Application for Use of Nile Kinnick Stadium;" Supreme Commander for the Allied Powers: Civil Information and Education Division, Physical Education and Youth Affairs, Topical File 1945–1951, Box 05725, Folder 5.

Eventually, the Headquarters and Services Section permitted the JAAA to use Nile Kinnick Stadium but only to hold the opening ceremonies of the 1949 National Athletic Meet and for track and field events. The JAAA would finance additional renovations for press boxes and agree to cover any damages. The remaining athletic contests were spread throughout Japan wherever open facilities could be found; many events were located as far away as Osaka (500 kilometers from Tokyo).

Conclusion

This chapter illustrated how the Occupation authorities rebuilt the Japanese athletic world during first years of the Cold War. Athletics would be an important component of remilitarizing Japan, but they faced the problem of doing so without reviving Imperial-era militarism. General MacArthur wanted Japanese athletes to participate in the Olympics, so the GHQ enacted policies that aimed at bolstering Japanese athletes and their participation in international athletic events. However, the challenge caused by a continued lack of equipment and space was too much to surmount in a short time. The GHQ instead focused on controlling the re-emergence of athletic mega-events in Japan, events which recalled too much of Imperial-era Japan for GHQ tastes. In the next chapter, I will discuss how the Japanese baseball community reimagined itself in the context of the Cold War to gain favor with GHQ sponsors and build a powerful and enduring relationship with the United States.

CHAPTER NINE

Baseball's Cold Warriors

Our aim in "cold war" is not conquest of territory or subjugation by force. Our aim is more subtle, more pervasive, more complete. We are trying to get the world, by peaceful means, to believe the truth. That truth is that Americans want a world at peace, a world in which all peoples shall have opportunity for maximum individual development. The means we shall employ to spread this truth are often called... "psychological warfare"...[it] is the struggle for the minds and wills of men. Many people think "psychological warfare" means just propaganda...But propaganda is not the most important part in this struggle.[1]

— Dwight Eisenhower, campaign speech, 1952

Introduction

This chapter covers from the beginning of the Cold War in March 1947 until about 1955. I argue that GHQ-sponsored athletic initiatives created a mechanism for the United States' continued influence upon Japanese society after the formal end of Occupation in 1952. The United States relied upon the business and diplomacy skills of Shōriki Matsutarō to first rebuild professional baseball in Japan as a mimic of the American model, and then to implement nuclear power into Japan under the Atoms for Peace program. Throughout this chapter I discuss how the Japanese baseball community acquiesced, generally, to their recently-formed pro-American identities from 1947 until the mid-1950s. Because of the level of cooperation seen between Japanese and

---

1. Dwight Eisenhower, Speech delivered on 8 October, 1952. Quoted in Martin Medhurst, "Atoms for Peace and Nuclear Hegemony," 146.

American baseball communities during this period, many scholars interpret this period as a moment when Japanese baseball formed as a weak imitation of its superior American counterpart. Instead, I encourage readers to see this period through the light of Shōriki's attempts to create enduring bonds that would permit the resumption of baseball within the context of Japan's broader search to become a world power during the Cold War. Shōriki fervently believed that Japan should again become a world power, and by drawing nearer to the United States through baseball, Shōriki could make this dream possible.

The Collapse of the Japanese Baseball Federation and Creation of Nippon Professional Baseball

Simultaneous to the National Athletic Meet controversy, the Japanese Baseball Federation underwent a crisis that resulted in the disbanding of the league and the creation of a new league in the image of American Major League Baseball (MLB). This shift was enabled by the reverse course, which freed Shōriki Matsutarō from imprisonment on charges of being a war criminal and permitted him enough freedom to organize the new Nippon Professional Baseball League (日本プロ野球, *Nippon Puro Yakyū*, hereafter "NPB"). NPB mimicked MLB in every manner, from minor leagues to a championship series to an all-star game. Shōriki replaced his own creation, the Japanese Baseball Federation — a league which embraced multi-national and multi-ethnic players — with a league that restricted players based on their ethnicity, a practice prevalent in MLB at the time. Such a move demonstrated the degree to which Japan's baseball community was willing to rehabilitate Japanese men as collaborative with American culture. The next chapters will show the effects of how Japanese baseball players were affected by their willingness to adopt the ethnic restrictions seen in American baseball.

Shōriki spent the first two years of Occupation detained within Sugamo Prison, where he was charged as a Class A War Criminal and repeatedly interviewed about his role as Information Minister and member of the Imperial Rule Assistance Association during World War II. Despite Shōriki's close proximity to the emperor during the war, through shows of amiability and business acumen he convinced his interrogators that he had no interest in maintaining his ties to the militarist state and wanted to help rebuild of Japan.[2] Released from jail in late 1947, Shōriki promised GHQ that he would not hold positions

2. "House Arrest of Suspected War Criminals," Supreme Commander for the Allied Powers, Legal Section, Administrative Division, POW 201 File 1945–1952, Box 1203, Folder 201.

of significant influence in Japanese society. However, he immediately returned to his post as the president of the Japanese Baseball Federation. After much deliberation, GHQ officials determined Shōriki's employment as the president of professional baseball was a violation of his release conditions and they forced him to resign from the position in May 1949.[3] Undeterred, Shōriki assumed the newly-created position as "Chairman of the Joint Stock Company" for the Japanese Baseball Federation, after which GHQ officials gave him a "strict warning" to discontinue his attempts to control professional baseball in Japan. One GHQ officer described Shōriki's pattern thusly:

> The formation and dissolution of one organization after another composed of essentially the same members and with essentially the same purposes despite differences in names and stated objectives indicates that Shoriki is seeking loopholes in the ordinances to maintain himself in professional baseball activities. That despite the warning[s]...given in lieu of prosecution in court — Shoriki has never relinquished his influence in these [baseball] affairs.[4]

The GHQ was well-informed about Shōriki's complicity in the wartime militarization of professional baseball during the war. GHQ officials worried that the Japanese Baseball Federation would interpret Shōriki's resumption of the presidency as a movement toward baseball's wartime values.

Shōriki struggled to remain divested from baseball. Before the Pacific War, Shōriki built the Yomiuri Giants into the pinnacle of Japan's baseball world, and now he was forced to watch as the team continued to lack basic sporting equipment like hats, uniforms, and shoes.[5] Shōriki distracted himself by developing a business plan to build a television broadcasting station in Tokyo that would reach upwards of ten million people and assist in the modernization of Japan.[6] Without Shōriki at the helm, though, the Japanese Baseball Federation foundered when it clashed with a lingering problem of World War II and Imperial Japan: the repatriation of Japanese from the colonies.

---

3. "Memorandum for Col. Napier: Shoriki, Matsutaro," Supreme Commander for the Allied Powers, Government Section, Central Files Branch, Biographical File 1945–1952, Box 22750, Folder 17.

4. "Memorandum for Col. Napier: Shoriki, Matsutaro."

5. Hatano, *Nichibei yakyū no kakehashi*, 128.

6. Shōriki Masutarō, "Untitled Document from May 16,1950," Supreme Commander for the Allied Powers, Legal Section, Administrative Division, POW 201 File 1945–1952, Box 1203, Folder 201, "Shoriki, Matsutaro."

In the summer of 1949, a scandal involving Yomiuri Giants manager Mihara Osamu (三原修) ran afoul of the reverse course agenda at the same time as the GHQ dealt with JAAA's request to use Nile Kinnick Stadium. Earlier in the year, Mihara was involved in a dispute over the contract of pitcher Bessho Takehiko (別所毅彦). Bessho broke his arm in 1941 and was never drafted nor sent to the war front, instead pitching until the cessation of the league in 1944. Playing for the Nankai Great Ring and Nankai Hawks teams after the war, he became the league's most dominant pitcher. However, he felt mistreated by the Nankai Hawks management and started negotiating to play for the Yomiuri Giants, a violation of the Hawks management's rights to control fully a player's contract. Regardless, Bessho broke the rules and signed a contract with the Giants, hoping that the ill-feelings with the Nankai Hawks would dissipate over time. When Nankai and Yomiuri later played against each other, Yomiuri Giants' manager Mihara, spurred by the game's tension, became enraged and emerged from the dugout to argue with an umpire.[7] Mihara was indefinitely suspended for this action.

Mihara's permanent replacement as manager of the Yomiuri Giants was Mizuhara Shigeo (水原茂), who had been recently freed from a Siberian gulag and had just returned to Japan. Embroiled in a crackdown on socialism, SCAP took notice that a returnee from the Siberian internment assumed a high-ranking position on Japan's most symbolic professional baseball team. As a soldier, Mizuhara had been captured in Siberia in 1942 and interned in the Soviet Union's gulag prison camp system for the next seven years, one among millions of Japanese subjects who survived the early famines of the Siberian interment and to partake in what historian Andrew Barshay described as a long phase of Soviet socialist re-education.[8] As the re-education process reached its peak intensity in early 1949, GHQ worried about the return of these millions of Japanese nationals more than the local Japanese Socialist Party because the returnees had lived and navigated in socialist society. In Barshay's words:

> The efforts of Soviet administrators and Japanese [internment] camp activists to reeducate the internees meshed with those of the Communist Party in Japan to gain a million members. For the internees themselves, ideological concerns were inseparable from — but not entirely reducible to — their universal desire to return to Japan even one day sooner. If they thought it necessary to show enthusiasm in [re-education] activities, enthusiasm they

---

7. Yamamuro Hiroyuki, *Puro yakyū fukkōshi*, 68.

8. Barshay, *The Gods Left First*, 43.

would show… The obverse of the hope of return was the fear of being kept back. The question for each internee was how far one was willing to go to gain a taste of certainty that *domoi* [the Russian word for "release"] would actually happen.[9]

At the same time as the GHQ fielded the JAAA's request to hand out the Emperor's Cup in the shrine to Emperor Meiji, GHQ officials watched Mizuhara, who had spent years undergoing Soviet socialist indoctrination and embodied the losing war effort, become the manager of Japan's most iconic baseball team.

As GHQ noticed the Japanese Baseball Federation's struggles, they warmed up to the idea of Shōriki resuming his role as the commissioner of Japanese professional baseball. Shōriki himself seemed insouciant to the fact that he had angered GHQ officials on several occasions, and ultimately American intelligence agencies realized that they benefitted from Shōriki's desire to rejoin the baseball community. Instead of the GHQ forcing the American model of baseball onto Japanese society, they let Shōriki become the vanguard of rebuilding professional baseball in Japan. Shōriki had earlier approached GHQ with a three-stage plan to revitalize professional baseball in Japan, and GHQ now acquiesced to the plan: 1) inviting the San Francisco Seals — a AAA minor league team managed by Lefty O'Doul who had visited Japan twice before — to Japan; 2) creating a professional baseball league in Japan modeled after MLB; and 3) guaranteeing the Yomiuri Giants exclusive use of Kōrakuen Stadium.[10] Satisfied with Shōriki's plan, GHQ permitted Shōriki to implement it. The Seals' tour occurred in late 1949 and heralded the formation of a new professional baseball organization in Japan. In the winter of 1949 and continuing until the spring of 1950, the GHQ allowed Shōriki to reorganize Japanese Baseball Federation as the Nippon Professional Baseball League (NPB). Given a second chance to create a baseball league, Shōriki organized it so that "his" team, the Yomiuri Giants, had enduring connections to the United States and would benefit from this relationship both in terms of finances and media attention.[11] Shōriki dreamed of having a "true world series" in which the United States and Japan competed for the global baseball championship, a competition that could demonstrate Japanese baseball's maturity.

---

9. Barshay, *The Gods Left First*, 82.

10. Yamamuro Hiroyuki, *Puro yakyū fukkōshi*, 73.

11. Besuboru Magajin Sha, *Nippon Puro Yakyū 50 nen shi* 日本プロ野球50年史 [Fifty Year History of Japanese Professional Baseball] (Tokyo: Besuboru Magajin Sha, 1984), 88.

Although Shōriki remained a vocal proponent for the Americanization of baseball in Japan, GHQ prevented him from assuming any position of power in the baseball league. For a short time in 1950, Shōriki acted as commissioner of NPB in title only, with the actual position going to Fukui Morita, a lawyer and former attorney general of Japan, from 1951 until 1954. Although the new American-style league saved professional baseball in Japan, it created unexpected opportunities for the dependent relationship created by GHQ authorities to reinvent Japan's baseball community increasingly in the mold of American culture.

Baseball Takes Occupation into Extra Innings

Japan's baseball community offered several pathways for the United States to continue influencing Japanese economics, society, and politics well beyond the formal end of Occupation in Spring 1952. The first process occurred less than three months into the first NPB season in 1950, when the Korean War disrupted the SCAP-led narrative of baseball in Japan. Whereas one of the purposes of baseball in the late 1940s had been to distract Japanese men from war, after the Korean War, baseball in Japan shifted to producing allies in the United States' Cold War in Asia.

The Korean War extended the United States' influence into Japanese politics, economics, and society by means of its drastic boost to the Japanese economy. On June 25, 1950, the Soviet-supported North Korean force of 135,000 personnel advanced quickly past the 38th parallel into South Korea, reminding some United States officials stationed in Japan of the Soviet Union's 1945 intention to create, as Andrew Barshay quipped, the "People's Republic of Hokkaido."[12] In accordance with the Truman Doctrine to prevent the spread of communist influence, the United States diverted the 24th Infantry Division in Japan from its Occupation duties and deployed them to halt the North Korean advance. Supported by conservative Prime Minister Yoshida Shigeru, SCAP created the National Police Reserve (NPR) for domestic defense and circumvented the Peace Constitution by allowing the NPR to operate military vehicles designated as "special vehicles."[13] Although Japan's Constitution forbade the state to engage in belligerent actions in the Korean War, the Japanese Coast Guard secretly participated in United Na-

---

12. Barshay, *The Gods Left First*, 21.
13. Port, *Transcending Law*, 43.

tions-sanctioned minesweeping in Korean waters.[14] Japanese manufacturers provided massive quantities of armaments for the United States, comprising sixty percent of Japanese exports from 1951–1953 and leading to an economic revitalization. Although Prime Minister Yoshida called the war a "gift of the gods" because of the boon to the Japanese economy, it is important to recognize the degree of devastation of the Korean War.[15] In a span of three years, nearly one in ten Koreans became a casualty, with 2.5 million Koreans either killed, injured, abducted, or disappeared.[16]

Japanese baseball players felt that they had incurred a debt to the United States military for the existence of the NPB league and created a fundraiser to support United States' ground troops in Korea. Amid the preparation for the NPB's first-ever championship series in September 1950, the Pacific and Central Leagues hosted an all-star exhibition game, giving ticket proceeds and volunteer donations to support United States troops wounded in the defense of South Korea. With United States military officials present in the stands, in a single day the NPB raised three million yen (the equivalent of $83,000 dollars at the time of writing) for the medical care of wounded United States soldiers.[17]

The Baseball Exchange Students

Six months after the NPB fundraiser, in March 1951 NPB intensified its relationship with United States professional baseball in the form of the "foreign exchange student," or *ryūgakusei* (留学生). NPB officials explained that they wanted Japanese players to be trained first in the American way of life (*amerika no seikatsu*) and second in baseball. At a time when Japanese nationals were generally prohibited from traveling abroad — and in the middle of the Korean War — GHQ approved four Japanese baseball players to travel to the United States: Kawakami Tetsuharu (川上哲治), Sugishita Shigeru (杉下茂), Kozuru

---

14. Port, *Transcending Law*, 64.

15. John Dower, *Empire and Aftermath: Yoshida Shigeru and the Japanese Experience* (Cambridge: Harvard Council on East Asian Studies, 1980), 316.

16. Institute for Military History, "Let's Learn! History of the 6.25 War" 알아봅시다!6·25전쟁사(제3권고지쟁탈전과휴전협정) (Armistice Agreement, Book 3)], 144. Thanks to Soo Hyun Jackelen for the Korean translation.

17. "296 man en okuru ryō rigu imon kikin" 296万円贈る　両リーグ慰問基金 [2.96 Million Yen Awarded From Both Leagues' Condolence Fund], *Yomiuri Shinbun*, September 26, 1950, Morning Edition, 2.3 million yen was about $8,300 dollars in 1950. In 2019 dollars, that is about $83,000. Data calculated by the author using historical exchange rates and the Consumer Price Index Calculator, available: https://data.bls.gov/cgi-bin/cpicalc.pl?cost1=8300&year1=1950&-year2=2016.

Makoto (小鶴誠), and Fujimura Fumio (藤村富美男). They traveled to San Francisco to spend spring training as "exchange students" with the familiar minor-league affiliate of the San Francisco Giants, the San Francisco Seals.[18]

There were two notable aspects about this trip that were not reported in the media. First, each Japanese player was already quite successful and needed very little training in baseball skills with the Seals. The Seals were chosen for their familiarity with Japan and its players, but they were the worst team in their minor-league division in 1951.[19] Sugishita, the youngest of the group at 25 years old, led all NPB pitchers in strikeouts in 1950. Twenty-eight-year-old Kozuru was the NPB's homerun king in 1950, knocking an unprecedented 51 balls out of the park. Fujimura was renowned as the face of the Osaka Tigers team and affectionately called "Mr. Tiger." Meanwhile, Kawakami was already a Japanese baseball legend. As a teenager in the imperial Kōshien tournament, Kawakami took a handful of Kōshien Stadium's famous dirt infield and put it in his pocket to take home, starting a tradition that continues to this day of high school players collecting Kōshien's soil. As a professional baseball player, Kawakami earned the nickname the "God of Hitting," a play on the Japanese homonym for *kami*, which could also mean God (神). The second aspect not reported was that each player served in the Japanese military during World War II: Sugishita served as a hand-grenade thrower, Kozuru served as an army regular infantryman, Fujimura had been in multiple battles throughout the South Pacific, and Kawakami served as a lieutenant in the Air Force Maintenance division on Japan's mainland and did not see battle. The *Los Angeles Times*, which was the lead newspaper covering the tour of America, made no mention that the "Four Jap Stars," as they introduced them to the American public, had engaged in combat against America during World War II.[20] Instead, the Japanese players were supposedly in the United States to learn baseball from a minor league team that ranked at the bottom of their division.

Kawakami, who was familiar with media expectations due to his fame, acted as the group's spokesperson during phone and in-person interviews. After participating in spring training in the United States, Kawakami explained to a Japanese reporter that the most important aspect of the tour was learning

---

18. "Kawakami senshura kito e 26hi sōkō wo shuppatsu" 川上選手ら帰途へ・26日桑港を出発 [Kawakami and Other Players on their Way Home, Will Leave San Francisco on the 26th], *Yomiuri Shinbun*, Morning Edition, March 23, 1951, 3.

19. Statistics in this section derived from www.baseball-reference.com.

20. Associated Press, "Four Jap Stars Train with Seals," *Los Angeles Times*, February 27, 1951, C2.

the "American lifestyle" (*Amerika no seikatsu*, アメリカの生活) and that he would teach it to Japanese players in the NPB.[21] He described the "American way of life" as "practice" (*renshū*, 練習), emphasizing that Americans prepared for their games not with mental or philosophical consideration but with time shared running, pitching, hitting, and watching baseball.

After a month in the United States, the four players flew to Hawai'i to participate in a baseball game in Honolulu with a *nikkei* team (descendants of ethnic Japanese who were no longer living in Japan).[22] The Japanese all-stars formed a team with other *nikkei* players and ultimately lost to the Hawaiian team. On one level, the game symbolically joined Japanese soldiers and residents of America in the same city that housed the Pearl Harbor naval base. However, because of United States immigration policy from 1924 onward, many *nikkei* were not citizens. As another level of symbolism, the collective group of Japanese and *nikkei* players represented racial and ethnic groups that were excluded from joining Major League Baseball.

By demonstrating that Japanese baseball players could travel to America safely, these four players, called "foreign exchange students" by the Japanese media, eased the way for future groups of sports "exchange students" and deepened the connections between America and Japan. In 1953, two years after the first baseball "foreign exchange" and a year after the formal end of Occupation, Kawakami Tetsuharu led a second tour of younger and inexperienced Yomiuri Giants "foreign exchange student" players to America for a month of spring training in San Francisco. On February 20, 1953, Columbia Broadcasting distributed television footage and radio coverage of the Japanese players practicing with Americans throughout the United States.[23] For the first time after World War II, this television broadcast allowed the American public to see Japanese baseball players alongside Americans. Over the next decade, Kawakami and the Yomiuri Giants team regularly sent their entire team to the United States to participate in spring training with MLB teams.

21. "Sayonara Amerika kanpu yosōgai no hyōban ni odoroku 4 senshu kyō kikoku no to e" さよならアメリカ・キャンプ　予想外の評判に驚く　4選手きょう帰国の途へ [Goodbye American Camp, 4 Players will Return to Japan Surprised at their Unexpected Fame], *Yomiuri Shinbun*, Morning Edition, March 27, 1951, 2.

22. "Pa senbatsugun daihai se 4senshu fukumu AJA ni /Honoruru" パ選抜軍大敗　セ4選手含むＡＪＡに／ホノルル [Pacific League All Stars Take a Big Loss] *Yomiuri Shinbun*, March 30, 1951, 2.

23. "Zenbei e terebi hōsō kyojingun no renshū buri wo" 全米へテレビ放送　巨人軍の練習ぶりを [The Giants Broadcast Practice to Entirety of American Television], *Yomiuri Shinbun*, Morning Edition, February 20, 1953, 4.

These Japanese baseball players became some of the earliest symbols of "re-habilitated Japanese" to travel within the Cold War America. During the Pacific War, the United States government cleared the entire West coast of ethnic Japanese, with citizens and non-citizens alike uprooted from their homes and relocated into the deserts of Arizona and Oklahoma.[24] After the conclusion of the Pacific War, ethnic Japanese were allowed to resettle on the West Coast, and the tour of the Japanese baseball players permitted the formerly-interred people a chance to see some of their ethnic countrymen on American soil playing an American game against Americans. Such a display promoted the narrative that the Japanese baseball community with its immature professional baseball league was now dependent upon learning from the superior and experienced American baseball community.

Baseball in the Physical Culture Project and *Seinendan* Youth

In the 1950s, baseball further ingrained itself into Japanese youth through a United States-sponsored program to keep boys and girls busy with athletics. In summer 1951, shortly after the return of Kawakami and his colleagues from their United States tour and one full year after the start of the Korean War, SCAP authorities implemented a massive nationwide effort to improve both Japanese youth's athletic ability and social discipline. This effort was called in English the "Physical Culture Project" and in Japanese the *Sei Shōnen Taiiku Shidō Keikaku* (青少年体育指導計画, "Youth Physical Education Leadership Program"). Overseen by William Neufeld, the civilian representative who oversaw Japan's re-entry to the 1952 Olympics, the program's goal was to use youth groups, called *seinendan* (青年団), to teach all boys *and* girls how to play baseball in addition to other sports and then evaluate their success. The Physical Culture Program was an expansion of the Social Physical Education (*shakai taiiku*, 社会体育), and the Japanese Ministry of Education thus described the motivation for program:

> Physique, scholarship, and morality of the youth and juvenile [sic] have remarkably declined having been affected by bad conditions during and after the War. Statistical figures indicate surprising increase [sic] of criminal and bad acts. Such evils will not be remedied unless adequate and effective measures are taken immediately. It is no exaggeration to say that if such

---

24. Greg Robinson, *A Tragedy of Democracy: Japanese Confinement in North America*, (New York: Columbia University Press, 2009), Chapter 2: The Decision to Remove Ethnic Japanese from the West Coast.

situation is neglected there will be a risk of the fundamental collapse of the national reconstruction. It is necessary to establish a fundamental policy without a moment's delay and execute strong concrete measures based on the policy.[25]

Beginning on June 1, 1951, the program used physical education to "promote a closer bond between the children and youth of the community" and "prevent juvenile delinquency and anti-social behavior by providing constructive leaders and make a greater contribution to the community life," a process which would reduce police officers' workload.[26] The CIE tasked the *seinen* [youth] leaders to develop their local communities through regulated sports examinations, effectively creating large-scale after-school groups where boys and girls engaged in continuous athletic training for the purposes of community building. As one of the recruitment letters for the youth leaders explained:

> If young men and women of the Seinen Dan are capable of and willing to accept the responsibility of undertaking the project described in this letter, they will be making an invaluable contribution to the future of Japan at a time when the best effort of every Japanese person is desperately needed if the general culture of Japan is not to retrogress and possibly disintegrate.[27]

Therefore, the Physical Culture Project had a future-oriented vision: it wanted to overcome past militarism and instead prepare youth — both in terms of behavior and physical capacity — to be the leaders of the new Japan. Ultimately, GHQ officials hoped that the Physical Culture Project would defend the United States' vision of Japan as a stable society that would also "assure Japan of a continuing supply of the champions she needs to represent her in International competition."[28]

The Physical Culture Project had high standards for its examinations. In addition to the Olympic-style events of running and jumping, the project included games like ping pong, volleyball, and baseball. Baseball was the most challenging sport on the examination: for teenage boys to earn a top grade, they had to throw a baseball eighty meters, which is roughly the distance from

---

25. "Sei Shonen Taiiku Shido Keikaku," 2, Supreme Commander for the Allied Powers, Record Group 331, Box 05951, Folder 2.

26. "Physical Culture Project," 1, Supreme Commander for the Allied Powers, Record Group 331, Box 05951, Folder 2.

27. "General Instruction," 2; Supreme Commander for the Allied Powers, Record Group 331, Box 05951, Folder 2.

28. "Physical Culture Project," 1.

shallow center field to the catcher on an adult professional baseball field.[29] There was also a category for throwing a baseball accurately, requiring boys to hit a one-foot by two-foot mark from fifteen meters away (the distance from a pitcher's mound to the catcher on a modern Little League field).[30] The base running test was perhaps the most grueling: for boys to earn a top grade, they needed to run the bases of a standard adult baseball diamond in 17 seconds (they were allowed a 10 second rest at second base).[31] On these examinations, girls were given slightly more lenient expectations: girls earned top scores by throwing a ball 60 meters, making accurate pitches from twelve meters, and running the bases in 18.5 seconds. Through these examinations, boys and girls developed both a familiarity with baseball and, even by contemporary standards, advanced skills.

The Physical Culture Project operated at the municipal level and had varying levels of commitment from prefecture to prefecture, although documents indicate that it was highly successful throughout Japan. In January 1952, Kanaboshi Toyoji, President of the Nippon Seinendan National Council, contacted new SCAP Commander-in-Chief General Matthew Ridgeway. Kanaboshi asked that William Neufeld, the civilian representative tasked with developing Japan's Olympic program, remain in Japan after the end of Occupation to continue advising the Physical Culture Program.[32] Kanaboshi argued that as of January 1952, over 20,000 *seinendan* groups existed and had ingrained themselves into Japanese society so intensely that he emphasized the program had become essential to the Japanese state's stability in three ways: "1) To promote cultural standard of youth [sic], 2) To render community service as core of its activities, 3) To train themselves as good citizens through real experiences."[33] Kanaboshi's invitation for the American advisors' presence beyond the Occu-

---

29. "Physical Education Projects," 2, Supreme Commander for the Allied Powers, Record Group 331, Box 05951, Folder 2.

30. "Physical Education Projects," 2, Supreme Commander for the Allied Powers, Record Group 331, Box 05951, Folder 2.

31. "Physical Education Projects," 2, Supreme Commander for the Allied Powers, Record Group 331, Box 05951, Folder 2. By contemporary standards, top-tier high school athletes who run the bases in 17 seconds are considered "above average" for speed.

32. Toyoji Kanaboshi, "Untitled Letter to General Matthew Ridgeway," Supreme Commander for the Allied Powers, Record Group 331, Box 05628, Folder 22. General MacArthur had been removed from command for voicing his dissent over the Korean War. William Neufeld's arrival is discussed in the Occupation Era chapter.

33. Toyoji Kanaboshi, "Untitled Letter to William Neufeld," Supreme Commander for the Allied Powers, Record Group 331, Box 05628, Folder 22.

pation underscored GHQ's creation of Japanese athletic dependence on United States expertise. Neufeld, however, opted to return to the United States after Occupation ended.

Within the context of the Korean War and the Cold War, the dependency of Japan's athletic communities upon American athletic expertise was a gift to President Harry Truman, who wanted the United States to influence Japan as long as possible.[34] The San Francisco Peace Treaty and the United States-Japan Security Treaty ended the Allied Occupation of Japan and framed relations between the two countries throughout the Cold War. United States military bases and personnel remained in Japan, effectively incorporating it within the United States' broader policy of containment policy against communism.[35] Prime Minister Yoshida Shigeru embraced continuing a policy of "subordinate independence," known as the Yoshida Doctrine, in which Japan focused on economic growth while under the United States' nuclear umbrella.[36] The Japanese baseball community, however, forged social connections that permitted the United States to influence Japan beyond the Occupation.

How Does One Pitch an Atom? Baseball's Role in Atoms for Peace

The enduring connections created through baseball and athletics gave the United States leeway within Japan that researchers have often underestimated, such as Japan's unexpectedly quick transition to atomic energy power. Beginning with the Eisenhower administration, the United States used atomic energy's allure to entice nation-states under its umbrella of nuclear security. President Dwight Eisenhower proposed the Atoms for Peace Program to provide allied states with atomic energy and to fulfill his desire to "wage peace" by portraying the atom's power as a "boon to humankind."[37]

Marketing Atoms for Peace to Japan should have been difficult given Japan's unique experience as the victims of atomic weapons. Hiroshima and Nagasaki were destroyed by atomic bombs at the end of World War II. In 1954, the United States hydrogen bomb test covered a Japanese fishing boat, the *Lucky Dragon No. 5*, with radioactive fallout and became the inspiration behind the movie

---

34. Gallicchio, *The Scramble for Asia*, 127.

35. Gordon, *A Modern History of Japan*, 240.

36. Port, *Transcending Law*, 57.

37. Martin Medhurst, "Atoms for Peace and Nuclear Hegemony: The Rhetorical Structure of a Cold War Campaign," *The Cold War: National Security Policy Planning from Truman to Reagan and from Stalin to Gorbachev*, Vol. 2, Ed. Lori Lyn Bogle (New York: Routledge, 2001), 149.

monster Godzilla (*Gojira*, ゴジラ).[38] Less than six months after this incident, a group of housewives drafted the Suginami Appeal and collected over 32 million signatures — about half of the Japanese voting population — opposing nuclear weapons.[39] Despite popular contempt for atomic energy, Japan became an early adopter of the Atoms for Peace program under the direction of none other than the former wartime Information Minister and baseball magnate, Shōriki Matsutarō.

Because GHQ prevented Shōriki from continuing as NPB commissioner and from assuming other public roles, he waited until the end of Occupation to become President of the Japanese Television Network (日本テレビ) where he became keenly interested in importing American technology into Japan.[40] In December 1954 Shōriki pre-emptively contacted the United States and invited atomic energy experts to visit Japan. Officials at the Central Intelligence Agency (CIA) noted Shōriki's offer and recognized that he was "ready to extend his facilities to the utmost in carryout out an enlightenment propaganda program through the facilities of his [news]paper and his TV network."[41] Over the next month, the CIA and Shōriki created a plan where Shōriki would "hit the streets" to support the Atoms for Peace Program masked as an atomic energy program produced by his own media outlets. The CIA reported that:

> [Shōriki's] basic plan is to use Japanese artists, make up men and printers who would rework CIA furnished material to 1) play down or conceal original source of this material, 2) fit [the] current attitude [of the] Japanese public and general Japanese psychology.[42]

---

38. Shunichi Takekawa, "Drawing a Line Between Peaceful and Military Uses of Nuclear Power: The Japanese Press, 1945–1955," *The Asia-Pacific Journal: Japan Focus* 10, 37, no. 2 (September 9, 2012), http://apjjf.org/2012/10/37/Shunichi-TAKEKAWA/3823/article.html.

39. Anthony DiFilippo, *Japan's Nuclear Disarmament Policy and the U.S. Security Umbrella* (New York: Palgrave MacMillan, 2006), 70.

40. Peter Kuznick, "Japan's Nuclear History in Perspective: Eisenhower and Atoms for War and Peace," *Bulletin of Atomic Scientists*, 13 April 2011, http://thebulletin.org/japans-nuclear-history-perspective-eisenhower-and-atoms-war-and-peace-0.

41. Central Intelligence Agency Memorandum, December 31, 1954, Central Intelligence Agency, Second Release of Name Files Under the Nazi War Crimes and Japanese Imperial Government Disclosure Acts, 1936–2002, Box 119, Record Group 263, National Archives Building, College Park, MD.

42. Central Intelligence Agency Memorandum, "Exploitation of Atoms for Peace Program in Japan," January 28, 1955, Second Release of Name Files Under the Nazi War Crimes and Japanese Imperial Government Disclosure Acts, 1936–2002, Box 119, Record Group 263, National Archives Building, College Park, MD.

Ultimately, the cooperation between the CIA and Shōriki worked. In 1956, Shōriki became the president of the Japanese Atomic Energy Commission (原子力委員会); Japan began its first test reactor in 1963, and in 1966, Japan imported its first commercial reactor from the United Kingdom.[43]

Conclusion

This chapter explained how Nippon Professional Baseball came into being as a league complicit in copying American baseball customs and traditions, eschewing the Imperial-era agenda of multi-ethnicity and instead placing restrictions upon ethnicities. The relationship created between Japanese and American baseball communities at this time permitted the United States to influence Japanese society long after the formal end of Occupation, which had been a wish of President Truman and President Eisenhower. Although the relationship between Japanese and American baseball communities seemed pleasant, the cordiality did not last long. The next chapter will discuss how the two communities severed formal relations from 1965 until the late 1990s as a result of American over-extension into Japanese affairs.

---

43. "Nuclear Power in Japan," *World Nuclear Association*, http://www.world-nuclear.org/information-library/country-profiles/countries-g-n/japan-nuclear-power.aspx.

CHAPTER TEN

The Severance of Baseball Communities

We have trouble because we have so many Negro and Spanish speaking players on this team. They're just not able to perform up to the white players when it comes to mental alertness.[1]

— Alvin Dark, San Francisco Giants Manager, 1964

Introduction

Although NPB had created several pathways for the United States to continue influencing Japan in the 1950s, these pathways ultimately brought historical memories of unequal treatment to the minds of Japanese. Most of NPB's commissioners, managers and players had been trained in their youth by imperial Japanese education that sought to remediate Japan's unequal position in global affairs. Throughout the 1950s and early 1960s, NPB officials realized that MLB was attempting to control the Japanese league and Japanese players, a process which MLB had done to Latino players and leagues throughout the 1940s and 1950s. This chapter discusses two "problems," as they are phrased in the Japanese language, that emboldened the NPB to step away from its cordial relationship with MLB. The outcome of these events was the complete severance of official baseball relations between NPB and MLB from 1965 until the end of the Cold War.

---

1. "Dark Reported on Way Out as Pilot: Quotes on Negroes by Giants' Skipper Dismissed as Reason," Los Angeles Times, August 5, 1964, B1.

Major League Baseball Surveys Nippon Professional Baseball

Starting in 1947, MLB turned its interests toward monopolizing the global market for baseball labor, seeking to re-narrate its history of racial exclusion into one of racial inclusion. As a result, MLB eventually eliminated or controlled every professional league in the Western hemisphere. Although six black Latinos had played for the Washington Senators team in the period from 1911–1946, in 1947, Jackie Robinson became the first black American to play on an MLB team, the Brooklyn Dodgers.[2] The integration of black Americans into MLB advanced the cause of desegregation throughout the United States, but within ten years, all Negro League teams became defunct and their associated communities were devastated.[3] By means of integration, the MLB eliminated its strongest domestic competition for cheap baseball talent, the Negro Leagues.

MLB also extended its reach to the Cuban Leagues, which was its strongest international competition. In 1947, MLB signed a pact with the Cuban Leagues that had two consequences: first, it restricted MLB's activity in Cuba by forcing the organization to respect any previously existing contract on a Cuban player; second, and more importantly, American baseball teams had the right to insert American players arbitrarily into Cuban teams for the purposes of training and development.[4] This pact led to profitable relations between Cuban and American baseball leagues during the Fulgencio Batista regime of the 1950s. However, when Fidel Castro took power in 1959, he used the pact to justify Cuban leagues' elimination on the grounds of removing foreign influence from Cuba.[5] Castro, a lifelong baseball fan, then sponsored the creation of a new league for Cuban nationals only, which shifted MLB's efforts to recruit cheap baseball talent to the Dominican Republic, Panama, and Venezuela.

Because of MLB's actions, from the 1960s until the 1990s, only two established professional baseball leagues remained in the world: American Organized Baseball (OB, which was Major League Baseball and its associated Minor Leagues), and Nippon Professional Baseball (NPB). The disappearance of com-

---

2. Bjarkman, *Baseball with a Latin Beat*, 200–205.

3. Japeth Knopp, "Negro League Baseball, Black Community, and the Socio-Economic Impact of Integration," *The Baseball Research Journal* (Phoenix, AZ: Society for American Baseball Research, 2016), 73.

4. Echevarría, *The Pride of Havana*, 48.

5. Echevarría, *The Pride of Havana*, 303–304.

petitor baseball leagues on the international level was a momentous boon for OB; it now controlled the pathways by which men, regardless of nationality, could become professional baseball players.

MLB turned its attention to the NPB in the hopes of expanding its control of global baseball. Ford Frick, the new MLB commissioner, had previously been the President of the National League since 1934. He remembered Shōriki Matsutarō's efforts throughout the early 1930s to have a group of American All-Star baseball players visit Japan.[6] Following the armistice of the Korean War, in 1954 Frick organized a world tour so that he could become familiar with baseball in other countries. He began the tour in Japan, where he attended several NPB games and participated in goodwill events. After returning to the United States, Frick told the *New York Times* that he greatly enjoyed watching the matches in Japan, noting that Japanese players had an "enthusiasm [that] surpasses belief and they'll try anything."[7] In addition to Frick developing an emotional bond with Japanese baseball players, he met with Shōriki Matsutarō, who at the time was planning to court American nuclear power. Shōriki gave Frick a gift intended for President Dwight Eisenhower: a suit of ceremonial samurai armor reported to be 700 years old.[8]

I argue that the gift of ceremonial samurai armor was a gesture of Japan's "subordinate independence" to America.[9] President Eisenhower was the European Theater's equivalent of General MacArthur in World War II. The samurai was the symbolic figure that the Japanese had supposedly — under the threat of American punishment — overcome and placed securely in their past. In short, a defeated Japanese ambassador handed over his culture's ancestral defense garment to a victorious general that had assisted in the end the Japanese empire. Ford Frick served not only as the messenger of this symbolic defeat, but also as the ambassador who sought to bring Japanese baseball under the control of the United States, thus further intensifying American control of Japanese society in the Cold War.

---

6. See Fitts, *Banzai Babe Ruth*.

7. John Drebinger, "Frick Emphasizes 'Urgent' Need for Expansion of Major Leagues," *New York Times*, November 8, 1953, S9.

8. Associated Press, "Japan's Fans Send Gift to Eisenhower," *New York Times*, February 7, 1954, S1.

9. Gordon, *A Modern History of Japan*, 240.

Ford Frick (rear) gives President Dwight Eisenhower (left) a gift of ceremonial samurai armor from Shōriki Matsutarō.[10]

Ford Frick was so impressed by his 1954 Japan tour that he agreed to send the entire New York Yankees team to Japan in 1955, where they would play a total of twenty games against various NPB teams. The symbolism of sending the *entire* New York Yankees squad to the bulwark of democracy and capitalism in Asia should not be underestimated. After World War II, the Yankees' rich spending on players led to nearly two decades of uninterrupted success on the field and established their cultural status as "America's team."[11] The Yankees had just lost the 1954 World Series to the Brooklyn Dodgers, and Frick permitted the players to bring their families and stay in Japan after the competition, which was the first time any traveling MLB baseball player was allowed to spend extended time in post-Occupation Japan.[12] Frick continued to visit Japan throughout the 1950s, simultaneously encouraging the Yomiuri Giants to spend a month each year during spring training with MLB teams. This exchange validated Shōriki's dream that the Yomiuri Giants would be the vanguard of meeting the United States' benchmarks of development and therefore receiving special attention.

NPB Breaks Its Bond With MLB: The "Stanka Problem"

NPB's severance of official relations with MLB began with a contract dispute over American player Joe Stanka in the late 1950s. Throughout the first two decades of the NPB's existence, the Yomiuri Giants' chief rival were the Osaka-based Nankai Hawks. Indeed, it was a quarrel between the two teams led to the Japanese Baseball Federation's dissolution in 1949. In the twelve-year

---

10. Associated Press, "Japan's Fans Send Gift to Eisenhower," *New York Times*, February 7, 1954, S1. No publication testifies to this armor's provenance or how Shōriki came to acquire it.

11. David Surdam, *The Postwar Yankees: Baseball's Golden Age Revisited* (Lincoln, NE: University of Nebraska Press, 2008), 4.

12. "Yankees Will Make Exhibition Tour of Japan This Fall," *New York Times*, August 23, 1955, 29.

span from 1950 until 1962, the Giants and the Hawks squared off six times in the NPB Championship series, with the Hawks winning only one championship in 1959. Like the Giants, the Hawks sent Japanese players to train with American players during spring training. Unlike the Giants, the Hawks tried to attract American talent to NPB. Joe Stanka, a pitcher, had been in the MLB minor leagues for nine years when the Chicago White Sox promoted him to the majors in 1959; however, the White Sox used him in only two MLB games that year because of his inexperience.[13] Pitching in a mere five innings, Stanka walked more batters than he struck out. Frustrated by his lack of playing time with the White Sox, that winter Stanka independently sought out and signed a contract to play with the Nankai Hawks in 1960.

This contract presented a problem because of the nature of baseball contracts in the United States and Japan. Beginning in the 1880s and continuing until the mid-1970s, MLB followed the "Reserve Clause," a practice that the Supreme Court had upheld in the 1920s, which declared that players were their teams' property and ineligible to seek their own contracts, even after the terms of the contract ended. Therefore, Stanka did not have the authority to seek his own contract.[14] When Stanka signed a contract with the Hawks, the White Sox filed a complaint with MLB, citing their existing contract with Stanka as the legal reason that NPB must negotiate with their team for the right to employ Stanka.[15]

While MLB officials deliberated the White Sox' complaint, Stanka thrived with the Hawks and became the team's second-best pitcher with 17 wins and 240 innings pitched. In the winter of 1960, MLB officials demanded Stanka return to the United States, and he obeyed. The *Chicago Daily Tribune* reported that Stanka was "Oriented" by the Japanese and the newspaper refused to report his NPB statistics because, as the White Sox publicity director said, "I can't read Japanese."[16] Bullied by MLB and the Chicago media, in the spring of 1961 Stanka refused to report for White Sox team activities and left his MLB contract unsigned in his house. Instead, Stanka returned to Japan and signed another contract with the Nankai Hawks.

---

13. Joe Stanka's statistics and transaction history are available at https://www.baseball-reference.com/players/s/stankjo01.shtml.

14. The Reserve Clause was eventually removed from MLB in the mid-1970s after a series of events that began when black American Curtis Flood petitioned the Supreme Court. The Reserve Clause persisted in NPB until the early 1990s, when Ochiai Hiromitsu (落合博光) became the NPB's first free agent.

15. "Article 11," *New York Times*, February 2, 1961, 33.

16. "Honorable Joe Stanka Rejoins Sox; Was 'Oriented'," *Chicago Daily Tribune*, December 24, 1960, B2. NPB statistics often used the same English terminology (e.g., ERA, Wins, Losses, etc.).

This time, MLB commissioner Ford Frick immediately supported the White Sox, explaining that, "Stanka told the Japanese he was a free agent. He wasn't and I have written to the Nankai club telling it [that] he remains White Sox property."[17] Although the NPB was outside his jurisdiction, Frick ordered the Nankai Hawks to bench Stanka until the contract dispute was resolved. The Hawks refused to negotiate with Frick, inflaming the situation by giving Stanka the symbolic honor of pitching the team's season opener despite his status as the team's second-best pitcher behind Sugiura Tadashi, who was arguably the NPB's best pitcher in 1960.[18]

In 1962, the contract dispute finally resolved with the creation of a "gentlemen's agreement" between MLB and NPB, which declared all player contracts between Japan and America must be made through the respective commissioner's offices of the MLB and NPB.[19] Most notably, the resolution to the "Stanka problem" (in Japanese, *Sutanka mondai*, スタンカ問題) closely mirrored MLB's 1947 pact with the Cuban Leagues, demonstrating MLB's continued intent to control NPB. Stanka finished his career in Japan and never again played in MLB. He won the NPB championship with the Hawks in 1964 and becoming the first foreigner to win NPB's Most Valuable Player award.[20] After the agreement was reached regarding Stanka's playing status, Japanese-American baseball relations were relatively calm until tempers flared again in 1964 over a young pitcher named Murakami Masanori (村上雅則).

The "Murakami Problem"

Joe Stanka helped reinvigorate the Nankai Hawks, but another championship continued to elude the team. In 1961, the Hawks lost the championship to the Giants, and then placed second in their division for two consecutive years. Entering the 1964 season, Hawks management wanted to keep a year-round "pennant race" attitude that aimed to minimize mistakes on the playing field. In a trail-blazing move in February 1964, Hawks' management sent three young baseball players — Tanaka Tatsuhiro, Takahashi Hiroshi, and Murakami Masanori — to the San Francisco Giants not just for the usual stint at spring

---

17. Edward Prell, "Stanka Pitches Sox Into Global Feud," *Chicago Daily Tribune*, February 1, 1961, B1.

18. "Japan Nine Defied Frick by Pitching Joe Stanka," *New York Times*, April 11, 1961, 44.

19. "U.S., Japan O.K. Trading Pact — In Baseball," *Chicago Daily Tribune*, October 29, 1962, C4.

20. C. Paul Rogers III, "Joe Stanka," *Society for American Baseball Research Biography Project*, http://sabr.org/bioproj/person/d3043c8c#_edn25.

training, but for the entire season.[21] The Hawks valued the twenty-year-old Murakami but recognized that he had no experience playing professionally and feared he would make mistakes.

Murakami had no particular interest in the United States outside of the chance at a higher salary and to have some fun.[22] When Murakami arrived in the United States, Harada "Cappy" Tsuneo, the former soldier who raised SCAP awareness of Japanese professional baseball in 1945, took Murakami to Disneyland before sending the young player to his assignment with the San Francisco Giants' rookie team in the Arizona Instructional League. Murakami soon realized American baseball was very different from Japanese baseball: his team was filled with Latino players with whom his translator could not communicate, and his salary was so low that he could only afford one hamburger per day and drink water thereafter.[23] Murakami played well against his minor-league competition, pitching over one-hundred innings by August. The San Francisco Giants continued promoting Murakami through the ranks of their minor league system to face increasing challenges, much like they would any regular player under their control.

The San Francisco Giants were well-known for using non-white players on their major-league roster. Six of the eight starting position players in 1964 were Latino or black Americans: there were future Hall of Fame black American players Willie Mays and Willie McCovey; the famed brothers from the Dominican Republic, Matty and Jesus Alou; and Orlando Cepeda from Puerto Rico.[24] Toward the end of the year, the team fell into disarray when reports emerged that manager Alvin Dark blamed non-White players for poor team performance. The Los Angeles Times reported Dark as saying, "We have trouble because we have so many Negro and Spanish speaking players on this team. They're just not able to perform up to the white players when it comes to mental alertness."[25] When his opinions became known publicly, Dark backpedaled from his remark and pointed out that Willie Mays, a black American, was

21. "Giants Sign Three Japanese Baseball Players for Farm Club," *New York Times*, February 23, 1964, S4.

22. Murakami, Masanori 村上雅則, *Tatta hitori no dai-riga*たった一人の大リーガ [The Only Major Leaguer] (Tokyo: Kōbunsha, 1985), 74–75.

23. Murakami, *Tatta hitori no dai-riga*, 77.

24. The full roster of the 1964 Giants is available at http://www.baseball-reference.com/teams/SFG/1964.shtml

25. "Dark Reported on Way Out as Pilot: Quotes on Negroes by Giants' Skipper Dismissed as Reason," *Los Angeles Times*, August 5, 1964, B1.

his team captain. However, the damage had been done and it seemed likely that Dark would be fired at the end of the season. With nothing left to lose, Dark saw little harm in promoting the Japanese pitcher Murakami to the Major League level, which at least advanced the club's multi-racial image. Whereas the integration of Jackie Robinson in 1947 took months of preparation, the integration of Murakami — the first Japanese citizen in MLB — occurred with almost no planning.

Murakami's first game in the Major Leagues was on September 1, 1964 in New York's Shea Stadium, the newest baseball stadium in the United States. As Murakami walked on the field for warm-ups, the Vice President of the San Francisco Giants frantically chased him down to sign a contract.[26] Murakami took the mound in the 8th inning in front of an announced crowd of 39,000 people.[27] Somebody working the stadium loudspeakers thought it would be appropriate to play "Sukiyaki," a Japanese pop song that had taken the number one spot on the American Billboard Hot 100 chart in June 1963.[28] While the intention was to welcome Murakami with a Japanese song, perhaps no worse song could have been played. When the song was brought to the United States, it was renamed "Sukiyaki" after a Japanese beef dish that was familiar among GIs; the actual song, *Ue wo Muite Arukou* (上を向いて歩こう, "Look Up as You Walk") was a mournful song. Sung in Japanese, Murakami would be the only person on the field (and because his translator did not accompany him, probably the entire stadium) who understood the final refrain: "Look up as you walk / So that the tears won't fall / I cry as I walk / All alone at night."[29] Murakami felt the gravity of being alone — the only Japanese player in MLB. Even the Japanese media seemed to overlook Murakami's integration into MLB; his promotion received only a tiny footnote in the Yomiuri Shinbun that described him as just another "exchange student" (留学生).[30] However, the contract that Murakami signed without the presence of a translator or representative caused another clash between NPB and MLB as they fought over the rights to Murakami.

Through his skilled pitching, Murakami gave the San Francisco Giants hope. Murakami performed well in the final month of 1964: he struck out

---

26. Joseph Durso, "Japanese Hurler Appears in Relief," *New York Times*, September 2, 1964, 42.

27. Attendance figures from http://www.retrosheet.org/boxesetc/1964/PKL_NYC171964.htm.

28. Murakami, *Tatta hitori no dai-riga*, 10.

29. Japanese language lyrics available from http://j-lyric.net/artist/a000c56/l007472.html.

30. "Yomiuri sunpyō" よみうり寸評 [Yomiuri Review], *Yomiuri Shinbun*, Evening Edition, September 3, 1964, 1.

nearly 30% of the hitters he faced while walking only a single batter, finishing with a spectacular 1.80 ERA.[31] Although the San Francisco Giants ended 1964 in emotional disarray because of their manager's comments, the outlook for 1965 seemed favorable: the roster held four future Hall of Fame players, and the team was excited to play for their new player-friendly manager, Herman Franks.

After the Nankai Hawks' "exchange students" returned home to Japan in December 1964, Murakami announced that he had already signed a contract to return to the San Francisco Giants in 1965. The Nankai Hawks insisted that Murakami did not have the right to negotiate his own contract with MLB; according to the 1962 gentlemen's agreement, the negotiation of a contract was a matter to be resolved between NPB and MLB commissioners. The Hawks contended that they had invested more in Murakami than the $10,000 they had received from the Giants for Murakami's contract and therefore had the right to control a player that was, under NPB rules, still their "property."[32]

The "Murakami problem" (Murakami mondai, 村上問題), as it became known in the Japanese media, brought together the American and Japanese baseball commissioners to attempt a resolution to the contract dispute but resulted in deadlock. The NPB commissioner, Uchimura Yūshi, had extensive familiarity in working with Americans. Uchimura had been trained as a medical doctor and spent the Occupation years performing psychiatric evaluations on Class-A War Criminals on behalf of the American Occupation Forces. Meanwhile, Ford Frick represented MLB's interests. Frick stated in the media that "a contract is a contract" and fought for Murakami to return to the team that had integrated the first Japanese baseball player into MLB, the San Francisco Giants.[33] By February 1965, negotiations over Murakami's contract had become so contentious that Frick severed business ties between MLB and NPB.[34] The Hawks reluctantly agreed that Murakami could return to America for the 1965 season.

While the drama over his contract unfurled, Murakami showed great poise for a twenty-one-year-old and performed well. The new Giants' General Man-

---

31. Murakami's statistics are available online: http://www.baseball-reference.com/players/split.cgi?id=murakma01&year=1964&t=p.

32. "Murakami tōshu ga kikoku" 村上投手が帰国 [Murakami Returns Home], Yomiuri Shinbun, Morning Edition, December 17, 1964, 9 and Robert Trumbull, "Giants Portrayed as Bad Yanks As Murakami Case Stirs Japan," New York Times, March 28, 1965, S2.

33. Trumbull, "Giants Portrayed as Bad Yanks as Murakami Case Stirs Japan."

34. "U.S.-Japanese Relations Are Severed in Baseball," New York Times, February 18, 1965, 39.

ager, Chub Feeney, wanted to keep Murakami in America for the 1966 season, but Ford Frick wanted Murakami to make his own decision.[35] The Giants sweetened their offer by asking Murakami to be a starting pitcher in 1966, which was effectively a promotion from his current position as a relief pitcher.[36] However, in November 1965, Murakami decided to return to Japan to be near friends and family. Although Murakami had yet to play a single game in Japan, he agreed to a new contract with the Nankai Hawks in December 1965, signing for $83,000, or eight times what the San Francisco Giants paid him in 1964.[37] Murakami's baseball career in the United States lasted slightly over one year but ended formal baseball relations between Japan and the United States, stopping Japanese players from working in MLB for the next thirty years.

The importance of Murakami's story is not only that he was the first Japanese player to play professional baseball in America, but also that he was the last Japanese baseball "exchange student" and marked the symbolic end of Japan's dependence upon United States athletic expertise. Shōriki Matsutarō had once imagined a "true World Series," in which NPB and MLB baseball organizations would compete for a global championship and celebrate Japanese players as equal in skill and culture to the United States.[38] However, after Murakami's contract dispute, Ford Frick dismissed the possibility of a global World Series and prohibited ethnic Japanese players from appearing on MLB rosters. Of the countries that produced baseball players from the 1950s through the 2000s, no other state was absent from representation in MLB longer than Japan; MLB went thirty years without employing a single ethnic Japanese player. Even during the height of the United States embargo on Cuba in the 1980s, there were, at minimum, three Cuban nationals in MLB.[39] Murakami was the last ethnic Japanese player to appear in MLB until 1995, when Nomo Hideo used a loophole in his NPB contract that enabled him to retire in Japan, move to the United States, and then sign a free agent contract to play with the Los Angeles Dodgers.

With Japanese nationals excluded from MLB rosters, the NPB responded by tightening restrictions against players from the United States and the Caribbean.

---

35. "Rainen ha Murakami no sentaku ni makasu" 来年は村上の選択にまかす [Murakami to Make His Own Decision Next Year] *Yomiuri Shinbun,* Morning Edition, October 8, 1965, 10.

36. "Murakami, raiki mo kiyō" 村上, 来季も起用 [Murakami's Next Season and Use] *Yomiuri Shinbun*, Morning Edition, October 25, 1965, 10.

37. "Japanese Club Gets Murakami for $83,333," *Los Angeles Times*, December 15, 1965, C4.

38. "Japanese Challenge U.S. to 'Real' World Series," *Washington Post,* January 4, 1965, A14.

39. Data aggregated from http://www.baseball-reference.com/friv/placeofbirth.shtml.

When Shōriki formed the NPB in 1950, he included a clause in the NPB constitution that each team was limited to three foreign players; the terms used to describe "foreign" are both the common colloquial word, *gaikokujin* (外国人) and a specific statement of "non-Japanese" (*nihonjin denai,* 日本人でない). Because United States servicemen and citizens were not permitted to play professional baseball in Japan during the Occupation, this rule initially applied to players hailing from Japan's former colonies. At the formal end of Occupation in 1952, the NPB amended the foreign player restriction to exempt any "non-Japanese" (日本人でない) player who was already under NPB contract.[40] This rule change gave existing "foreigners" in the NPB—who were almost entirely ethnic Taiwanese—the right to continue playing in the NPB while simultaneously opening roster spots for other foreign-born players.[41] The rule was further relaxed in 1959 to allow exemptions for players who became Japanese citizens prior to 1959. Further provisions were added throughout the 1950s–1970s to exempt players who had spent time in Japanese secondary schools, which was effectively a Japanese residency requirement. The players most affected by these exemptions were those of Taiwanese, Korean, and Chinese heritage, many of whom lived in Japan but were not technically citizens.

Following the Murakami incident in 1966, NPB reduced the number of "foreign" roster spots to two per team, and this rule remained in place until 1991.[42] Because so many players from Asia were exempt from the restriction, the 1966 amendment clearly targeted players from the Americas, specifically United States citizens, but it also applied to players from the Caribbean. More than a simple retribution against MLB's cessation of business relations, the amendment also provided a concrete metric to understand how the NPB implemented measures that made the league monoethnic Japanese. From 1966 to 1991, there were 24 available active roster spots annually for "foreign" players in the NPB (12 teams and 2 spots per team). About 300 distinct players appeared annually in the NPB, which allowed at most 8% of NPB roster spots to be allotted for non-exempt foreign players.[43] Although the NPB allotment may seem strict, it was comparable to MLB's use of non-American talent throughout the 1960s: MLB used no more than 12% of non-American players, most

40. Besuboru Magajin Sha, *Puro yakyū 70 nen shi,* 561.

41. Data on nationality compiled from www.baseball-reference.com.

42. Besuboru Magajin Sha, *Puro yakyū 70 nen shi,* 561. Of minor note, in 1981 NPB permitted teams to have three "foreign" players under contract, although only two "foreign" players could be active at a time, essentially keeping in place the two player limit.

43. Data compiled from www.baseball-reference.com.

of whom were poached from the now defunct Cuban Leagues.[44] Ironically, whereas MLB had set the standard for racial exclusion for most of the twentieth century, from the 1960s onward many MLB teams openly advertised their use of foreign-born or minority talent, such as the 1965 San Francisco Giants' employment of non-white players. Meanwhile, NPB teams in the 1930s had been founded on the acceptance of the multi-ethnic empire, yet in the 1960s they flaunted sourcing their talent from Japan. In the 1960s, the Yomiuri Giants regularly advertised their refusal to use the foreign-born roster limit, despite rostering the most famous ethnic Taiwanese baseball player in history, Oh Sadaharu.[45]

Conclusion

The Stanka and Murakami problems led to the severance of official relations between NPB and MLB for the remainder of the Cold War and caused NPB to restrict who could play professional baseball in Japan. By recognizing and resisting American encroachment, the Japanese baseball community forged its own path in the global baseball community that would last until the 1990s. On this path the Japanese baseball community began to transform the concept of who was Japanese and who was not. The next chapter discusses how ethnic minorities in Japan became symbolic of a burgeoning Japanese nationalism in the 1960s and 1970s.

---

44. Data compiled from "Place of Birth" database on www.baseball-reference.com.
45. "Baseball No.1 in Land of Rising Sun," *Los Angeles Times*, September 3, 1968, E6A.

CHAPTER ELEVEN

Nihonjinron and The Power of Minorities in NPB in the 1960s–1970s

I clearly remember the night after the atomic bomb fell. Truly, it looked like the picture of hell. The screams and groans leap out of my memory...I can't remember if my sister lived for one more night or two. She kept groaning, "it burns, it hurts."...As was the custom of Korean culture, my mother violently cried and then carried the hurt within her chest, not talking about it again...In Japan, we are left with the opinions of the event of people who are culturally important, but the opinions of people like my mother are completely discarded.[1]

— Harimoto Isao, NPB Hall of Fame baseball player and Korean national

Introduction

Harimoto Isao, a South Korean citizen and survivor of the Hiroshima atomic bomb, had been considered an outsider in Japanese society. In his autobiography, he recalled that on the morning of August 6, 1945, his parents, originally named Chan (張) but living under the Japanese name Harimoto (張本), sent their children to school on the train. At 8:15 AM, an American B-29 bomber dropped an atomic bomb on Hiroshima, killing tens of thousands of people within minutes and reducing the city center to rubble. As subjects of Imperial Japan, hundreds of thousands of Koreans had moved to Japan proper, and about 40,000 Korean imperial subjects died in the atomic bombings in Hiro-

---

1. Harimoto Isao 張本勲, *Mō hitotsu no jinsei: Genbakusha toshite, hito toshite* もう一つの人生：原爆者として、人として [Another Life: As an Atomic Bomb Survivor, As a Person] (Tokyo: Shin Nihon, 2010), 22–26.

shima and Nagasaki alongside their Japanese masters. As Harimoto indicated, the Korean lives lost in the bombing were considered unimportant. However, Harimoto later had the privilege to tell his family's story because he became one of NPB's most popular and successful baseball players. To do so, he needed to display a Japanese identity that downplayed his true heritage as a South Korean who lacked Japanese citizenship.

This chapter illustrates how professional baseball in Japan in the 1960s and 1970s became characterized by the success of minority players who showcased — often in a grandiose fashion — characteristics deemed to be ethnically "Japanese." This period of celebrity minority baseball players in the NPB occurred at the same time as a national discussion of *nihonjinron*, or "theories of Japaneseness," swept Japanese mainstream culture. *Nihonjinron* — a new form of nationalism — reaffirmed the image of a homogeneous Japanese culture and obviated the minorities who lived in Japan, who created Japanese culture, and who contributed to the economic success of Japan. By exploring these tensions between ethnicity, nationality, philosophy, and baseball, I reveal how the Japanese baseball community transformed the notion of who was included in the concept of "Japanese" and who was excluded from cultural citizenship. The best example of *nihonjinron*'s power to include and exclude minorities from Japanese society is Oh Sadaharu, the most famous NPB player in history and the global homerun champion.

The Homerun Gap: Batting Power and Ethnic Identity in Cold War Japan

Understanding ethnic minorities' important role in the Japanese baseball community in the 1960s and 1970s requires an understanding of the home run. The top homerun hitters in the United States *and* Japan have been disproportionately ethnic minorities or non-citizens of their respective leagues: 8 out of 10 of the top global homerun leaders are ethnic minorities of their leagues; 4 of the top 10 NPB homerun hitters are non-ethnic Japanese.

Top 10 All-Time Global Homerun Leaders[2]

Rank	Name	Career Homeruns	Race/Ethnicity	Place of Birth
1	Oh Sadaharu	868	Taiwanese	Japan
2	Barry Bonds	762	Black	USA
3	Hank Aaron	755	Black	USA
4	Babe Ruth	714	Caucasian	USA
5	Alex Rodriguez	696	Latino	USA
6	Albert Pujols	662	Latino	Dominican Republic
7	Willie Mays	660	Black	USA
8	Nomura Katsuya	657	Japanese	Japan
9	Ken Griffey, Jr	630	Black	USA
10	Jim Thome	612	Caucasian	USA

Top 10 All-Time NPB Homerun Leaders[3]

Rank	Name	Career Homeruns	Race/Ethnicity	Place of Birth
1	Oh Sadaharu	868	Taiwanese	Japan
2	Nomura Katsuya	657	Japanese	Japan
3	Kadota Hiromitsu	567	Japanese	Japan
4	Yamamoto Kōji	536	Japanese	Japan
5	Kiyohara Kazuhiro	525	Japanese	Japan
6	Ochiai Hiromitsu	510	Japanese	Japan
7	Harimoto Isao	504	Korean	Japan
7	Kinugasa Sachio	504	Black American / Japanese	Japan
9	Osugi Katsuo	486	Japanese	Japan
10	Kanemoto Tomoaki	476	Korean	Japan

English-language authors frequently believe that MLB players monopolize homeruns—and by association, physical strength. Correspondingly, these authors think that NPB players lack the strength to hit homeruns and there-

---

2. Chart made by the author from data compiled from www.baseball-reference.com. It is worth pointing out that while Alex Rodriguez was born in New York, he regularly identifies with his ethnic Latino heritage and played for the Dominican Republic national team in the 2009 World Baseball Classic.

3. Chart made by the author from data compiled from www.baseball-reference.com.

fore rely on stolen bases and sacrifice hits. This conflation of Japanese baseball with "small ball" — a term used to indicate the preference for single base
hits, sacrifice hits, and quick base running — began in Robert Whiting's 1977
popular journalism work *The Chrysanthemum and the Bat*. He repeated it in
his successful 1989 book, *You Gotta Have Wa* (which became the basis of the
modestly successful 1992 Tom Selleck film, *Mr. Baseball*), and his 2004 book,
The Meaning of Ichiro. For Whiting, "small ball" was the result of Japanese
"national character," which encouraged the entire team to work in unques-
tioning harmony and unison to succeed with precision plays. Whiting used
examples from the 1960s and 1970s to claim that the entirety of Japanese baseball was characterized by "small ball," and he outlined his own "Samurai Code
of Conduct" to explain how NPB players followed a "national character" both
on and off the field.[4] Because Robert Whiting is the world's most powerful and
well-known author about Japanese baseball, the "small ball" narrative about
Japanese baseball has been repeated in most modern academic works about
Japanese baseball, such as Joseph Reaves' 2004 book *Taking in a Game: A History of Baseball in Asia*; George Gmelch's 2006 book, *Baseball without Borders*;
Alan Klein's 2006 book *Growing the Game: The Globalization of Major League
Baseball*; and Robert Lewis' 2010 book *Smart Ball: Marketing the Myth and
Managing the Reality of Major League Baseball*.[5]

The "small ball" narrative does not accurately describe the reality of baseball
in Japan. Instead, it is the long-term result of the American narrative concocted during the Occupation-era and continuing throughout the Cold War to
portray Japan as weak, immature, and perpetually in a state of development.
Those authors who adopt the position that NPB is characterized by "small ball"
and transcendent samurai-inspired "national character" have adopted a false
narrative instead of using evidence or historical documentation. From the inception of NPB in 1950 through 1985, homeruns per game surged upward, stolen bases per game declined by 25%, and sacrifice hits remained mostly stable.
Put simply, in the NPB from 1965–1985, homeruns occurred about 30–50%
more frequently than stolen bases or sacrifice hits.[6]

---

4. Robert Whiting, *You Gotta Have Wa* (New York: Vintage Books, 1989), 49.

5. Robert Whiting, *The Chrysanthemum and the Bat*; George Gmelch, ed., *Baseball without
Borders*, 36; Alan Klein, *Growing the Game*, 125; Joseph Reaves, *Taking in A Game*, 4; Robert
Lewis, *Smart Ball*, 124.

6. Graph created by the author from data compiled from www.baseball-reference.com.

NPB Batting Trends, 1950–1985

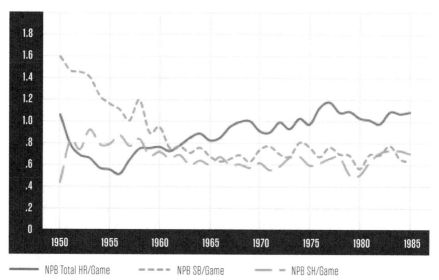

———— NPB Total HR/Game   - - - - NPB SB/Game   — - NPB SH/Game

HR=Homeruns, SB=Stolen Bases, SH=Sacrifice Hits.

After 1965, the NPB no longer had a formal relationship with MLB, and I argue that the popular sentiment of Japanese national strength became renewed in the context of baseball through the homerun hitting prowess of Oh Sadaharu (王貞治). Unlike many Japanese baseball players of the 1950s, Oh's success as a player did not stem from his participation in spring training sessions with MLB players. Instead, Oh began as a proficient hitter and refined his *personal* virtues through a unique combination of *budō* martial arts and philosophical readings stemming from *bushidō* philosophy. As Oh approached homerun records held by American men, his success fed into narratives of Japanese uniqueness that flourished throughout the 1970s and 1980s, obviating the fact that Oh was neither an ethnic Japanese nor a Japanese citizen.

Oh Sadaharu

It is not hyperbolic to say that the homerun made Oh Sadaharu the icon of "Japanese baseball." Although Babe Ruth's MLB homerun record of 714 (set at his retirement in 1936) has since been undone by Hank Aaron (755 in 1976) and Barry Bonds (762 in 2007), Oh's 868-homerun total, hit in a career spanning from 1959–1980, has been the global record for nearly forty years. Oh surpassed then-global homerun leader Hank Aaron's career homerun total (755) on September 3, 1977; Aaron traveled to Japan two weeks later to acknowledge and congratulate Oh on the accomplishment.[7] At the end of 1977, the Japanese government bestowed upon Oh the first National Honor Award (国民栄誉賞), which exalts one's achievements as a model for Japanese society.[8] After retiring from playing at the end of the 1980 season, Oh spent nearly two decades successfully managing for several teams, and in 2006, he managed the inaugural Japanese World Baseball Classic team to a championship against all-star teams from across the world. Now retired from coaching, he continues to act as a spokesperson for the return of baseball and softball to the 2020 Tokyo Olympics.[9]

Oh was born in 1940, the weaker half of a pair of twins. He recalled his youth as being one of "hunger," mostly for food and baseball. Although his hunger was managed because his parents owned a successful soba shop in Tokyo, his appetite for baseball became insatiable after his older brother took him to see the first American minor league baseball team to tour post-war Japan, the San Francisco Seals. Oh spent the next decade working on his baseball skills, appearing as a star pitcher for Waseda Commercial High School in the 1956 and 1957 Kōshien Tournaments. Based on this success, Waseda Commercial High School was invited to the annual National Athletic Meet (国民体育大会) in the fall of 1957. Oh was excited by the invitation, but then learned that he was not permitted to play because of his Taiwanese citizenship.[10] In his autobiography, Oh said of this moment:

> Waseda High School was invited to the National Athletic Meet in Shizuoka Prefecture, but I didn't appear because of my Taiwanese citizenship. It really was too bad, but the only thing I could do, honestly, was to be sad... With apologies to the people of the National Athletic Meet, it was never my goal to appear at their event. My goal was to play at Kōshien. I'm Taiwanese. If you think about the actual name of the [National Athletic Meet] — an ath-

7. "Aaron Congratulates Oh For Passing Homerun Total," *New York Times*, September 18, 1977, 63.

8. Cabinet Office, Government of Japan, *Kokumineiyoshō* 国民栄誉賞 [National Honor Award], http://www.cao.go.jp/others/jinji/kokumineiyosho.

9. "WBSC Makes Official Presentation to add Baseball, Softball to Tokyo 2020 Olympics," *World Baseball Softball Confederation*, August 10, 2015, http://www.wbsc.org/news/wbsc-makes-official-presentation-to-add-baseball-softball-to-tokyo-2020-olympics-2.

10. Oh Sadaharu 王貞治, *Yakyū ni tokimeite* 野球にときめいて [Prospering in Baseball] (Tokyo: Chūoronsha, 2011), 51–53.

letic event for the "Japanese citizen" — then I don't really see any prejudice in not making me the first Taiwanese citizen to appear at the event.[11]

Not only was Oh ineligible to play in the National Athletic Meet, Oh was effectively stateless, neither a recognized citizen of Japan nor Taiwan. Following the creation of the People's Republic of China (PRC) and the Republic of China (ROC, or Taiwan) in 1949, Taiwan sought to be recognized as an independent and sovereign state and created its own laws and government. Anthropologist Sara Friedman wrote that the Taiwanese Nationality Law:

> [A]ffirmed that [Taiwanese] nationals were not automatically citizens. The status of citizen with its attendant rights and responsibilities was granted only to those nationals who had established official household residence in Taiwan. And the ability to establish official household residence was tightly controlled, limited primarily to nationals whose immediate relatives were themselves ROC citizens.[12]

Oh's parents moved to Japan in the 1920s, meaning Oh did not meet the Cold War era residency requirements of Taiwan to have the rights and responsibilities of a true Taiwanese citizen.

After his high school graduation in 1959, Oh entered NPB as a pitcher with the Tokyo Giants. Oh was not counted as a "foreigner" because the NPB had just exempted non-Japanese who had attended a Japanese high school from the "non-Japanese" roster spots allotted to each team. The Giants team was managed by none other than Mizuhara Shigeo (水原茂), the fiery manager whose 1949 release from a Siberian internment camp precipitated the end of the Japanese Baseball Federation. Mizuhara and Oh got off to a rocky start. The Giants had signed Oh out of high school based on his prowess as a pitcher, but after Mizuhara watched Oh in spring training, Mizuhara decided that Oh was unfit to pitch in any capacity in the NPB.[13] Mizuhara instructed Oh to play first base, ostensibly to replace the aging Wally Yonamine, a *nisei* Japanese born in Hawai'i. Playing out of position and far younger than anybody else on the elite Giants team, Oh's first year in professional baseball as a 19-year-old was miserable: playing in about 2/3 of the Giants' games, he managed a paltry .161

---

11. Oh Sadaharu, *Yakyū ni tokimeite*, 53.

12. Sara Friedman, *Exceptional States: Chinese Immigrants and Taiwanese Sovereignty* (Oakland, CA: University of California Press, 2015), 11.

13. Oh Sadaharu, *Yakyū ni tokimeite*, 67.

batting average and struck out about 32% of the time.[14] Hecklers in the crowd jeered "O, O, Oh the strikeout king!", a play on Oh's family name, 王, which can mean "king" in Japanese.[15]

After his first season, Oh seemed would be a good candidate to gain playing experience with an MLB team during spring training. However, Giants team officials were convinced that Oh's struggles derived not from his lack of baseball skills, but because he was a "bad boy" who smoked cigarettes, chased after girls, drank relentlessly, got angry at his manager, and "stayed out all night regularly."[16] After the 1961 season, Tokyo Giants officials gave Oh a choice to either fix his behavior or leave, and at this moment, fate intervened. The Giants had just hired a recently-retired baseball player, Arakawa Hiroshi (荒川博), as their batting coach. Arakawa and Oh had a chance meeting nearly a decade earlier that set Oh's career in motion. One day, Arakawa, then a player on the Mainichi Orions professional baseball team, stopped by his alma mater, Waseda Commercial High School, to watch baseball practice. Seeing fourteen-year-old Oh struggling at the plate as a right-handed hitter, Arakawa advised that him to try batting left-handed.[17] The advice worked and turned Oh into a successful high school player. Oh remembered the advice that Arakawa had given him as a teenager and he agreed to attend what became famously as "Arakawa's Dōjō" (荒川道場), a decision which molded him into the world's most prolific homerun hitter.[18]

It is ironic that Arakawa is remembered almost entirely for his work in reinventing Oh as a power hitter because Arakawa was a poor hitter during his NPB career. Arakawa spent most of his nine seasons in the NPB as a backup, with an acceptable but unimpressive career batting average of .251 and a meager 17 career homeruns. Oh hit the same number of homeruns in his second year alone, when he was considered an immature 20-year-old who could not

---

14. Data and team roster available at http://www.baseball-reference.com/register/team. cgi?id=68465a6c.

15. Oh Sadaharu, *Yakyū ni tokimeite*, 68.

16. Oh Sadaharu, *Yakyū ni tokimeite*, 84.

17. Oh Sadaharu, *Yakyū ni tokimeite*, 7.

18. Arakawa died in December 2016. Several obituaries appeared across Japanese newspapers, and almost without exception they recount Oh's time spent in Arakawa's Dojo. See "Ippon ashi dahō shidō, kyojingen ko-chi Arakawa-san no tsuya" 一本足打法指導 巨人元コーチ 荒川さんの通夜 [The Wake of the Former Giants Coach Arakawa, Adviser to the "Flamingo Stance"], *NHK News Web*, December 10, 2016, http://www3.nhk.or.jp/news/html/20161210/ k10010802401000.html.

maintain focus on the field.[19] However, Arakawa's job was not to teach his "disciple" how to hit, but how to live. Oh himself said that "Arakawa's Dōjō" began with the cessation of his vices like smoking and chasing girls.[20] To end these distractions, Arakawa forced Oh to participate in a number of *budō* martial arts, like *iaidō* (居合道, the art of drawing one's sword), *aikidō* (合気道, a martial art), study *kabuki* theater, and meditate in the Zen Buddhist method.[21] In the process of correcting Oh's personal behavior, Arakawa amended Oh's batting posture to include an exaggerated leg lift modeled after the dramatic actions seen in *kabuki* theater, such as pauses followed by sudden bursts of powerful expression. Although Oh's personal reinvention came through his moral training and discipline, his batting transformation came through his new extravagant batting form, derisively called the "flamingo stance" by many but more accurately called the "One-legged stance" (一本足打法). Oh's teammates, the majority who were ethnic Japanese, did not undertake similar training, did not ascribe to any samurai aesthetic, and did not train in *budō* martial arts.

By citing modern statistics, I oppose the viewpoint that *budō* martial arts and *bushidō*-inspired philosophy were responsible for Oh's rebirth as a hitter.[22] Advanced statistics reveal that Oh was only a "strikeout king" for the first year of his career in 1959; Oh was a proficient if not exceptional hitter before he ever stepped foot in Arakawa's Dōjō in late 1961. Oh had sought help from his teammates well before his stint with Arakawa. In 1960, Oh consulted the team's best hitter, Nagashima Shigeo (長嶋茂雄), and in spring 1961, Kawakami Tetsuharu (川上哲治), "the God of Hitting" who had taken dozens of Japanese players to the United States, became the Giants' manager and further helped Oh in fixing his batting technique. In his autobiography, Oh refers to these two as the "unforgettable advisors" (忘れがたき先輩たち), and says of Kawakami, "I owe him everything."[23] In Oh's 1960 sophomore campaign, his strikeout rate plummeted from 32% to 20% and he posted

---

19. Statistics available from www.baseball-reference.com.

20. Oh Sadaharu, *Yakyū ni tokimeite*, 86.

21. Oh Sadaharu, *Yakyū ni tokimeite*, 88.

22. "SABR-metrics" is a kind of statistics popularized by the Society of American Baseball Research (SABR). Put simply, SABR-metrics uses statistical analysis to present player performance as described in percentages and ratios instead of raw numbers. Such an approach permits the comparison of player performance regardless of playing era. Although it began in the 1970s with Bill James, only in the late 2000s did advanced metrics become the norm for player evaluation in the United States and the Caribbean. As of the time of writing in 2020, very few Japanese writers and statisticians use SABR-metrics.

23. Oh Sadaharu, *Yakyū ni tokimeite*, 70–71.

the fourth-highest OPS (.823) in the NPB.[24] Oh followed up in 1961 with the sixth-best OPS (.802) in the NPB. Had the 21-year-old Oh been on any of eight other NPB teams when he entered Arakawa's Dōjō, he would have been the team's best hitter. He was still four years younger than the average NPB player.[25]

Therefore, Arakawa was not the man who "fixed" Oh's hitting with *budō* martial arts, but he tinkered with it to improve an already good product. What Oh needed "improving" were his "bad boy" ways. Recall that Kawakami, who became the Tokyo Giants' new manager in 1961, had been the vanguard of taking young baseball players to the United States for both physical and cultural training. When Kawakami brought the Giants team to the United States in 1961 to participate in spring training against some of the Los Angeles Dodgers' best minor league players, Oh was included on the roster.[26] Howev-

er, training in the "American way of life" did not manage Oh's off-the-field behavior. Instead, Arakawa's *dōjō* sufficiently managed Oh's vices and had the unintended side effect of turning him from a good hitter to a great hitter. In the 1960s, most fans were unconcerned with Oh's idiosyncratic training regimen; that fascination did not occur until nationalist discourse intensified in the 1970s and Robert Whiting published *The Chrysanthemum and the Bat*, which portrayed Oh as a modern samurai.

Oh Sadaharu demonstrating his sword training, as prominently featured in Robert Whiting's 1977 book, *The Chrysanthemum and the Bat.* It opens the chapter titled, "Baseball Samurai Style."

---

24. Statistics available at www.baseball-reference.com. "OPS" combines On-Base Percentage with Slugging Percentage. On-Base Percentage is the percent of the time a batter gets on base (Hits+Walks+Hit By Pitch/Plate Appearances). Slugging Percentage is a metric of power hitting (Total Bases/Plate Appearances). OPS is considered to be a metric that allows statisticians to see the overall quality of a hitter, with higher numbers being considered better. In terms of global leaders in OPS, Oh is behind only Babe Ruth and Ted Williams.

25. Data compiled from statistics available at www.baseballreference.com.

26. "Kyojin, dai 2 sen mo katsu" 巨人、第 2 戦も勝つ [Giants Win 2 More Games], *Yomiuri Shinbun*, March 13, 1961, Morning Edition, 7.

Baseball and *Nihonjinron* Discourse in the 1960s and 1970s

Beginning in the 1960s and peaking in the 1970s and 1980s, *nihonjinron* (日本人論, literally, "theory of Japaneseness") discourse propagated through Japanese popular culture and echoed many of the sentiments of Imperial-era *bushidō* discourse. Anthropologist Befu Harumi defines *nihonjinron* as a "reservoir of knowledge on characteristics of Japanese culture, people, society, and history" that often appealed to essentialist definitions of Japanese culture based upon the so-called "traditional" conceptions of indebtedness, collective thinking, and the soul (*kokoro*, 心) of Japan.[27] *Nihonjinron* discourse appeared in literature — both academic and popular — music, television, and governmental policies. *Nihonjinron* shared several ideas in common with its predecessor philosophy, *bushidō*, because they were both ideologies that rewrote or reorganized the past to serve modern political agendas. Befu identifies the most salient trends among *nihonjinron* discourse: the uniqueness of Japanese identity; ethnocentrism that privileged mainland Japanese identity and discriminated against non-ethnic Japanese within the state; and a transcendent ethnic homogeneity of the Japanese nation-state.[28] Befu argues that the claims of ethnic homogeneity posited by *nihonjinron* discourse became a "civil religion," inscribed in the beliefs of Japanese society and embodied in the language and laws of the government.[29] In other words, as people consumed *nihonjinron* media, they believed that the messages and morals transmitted through the media confirmed the character traits that made them Japanese.

The most notable baseball-themed *nihonjinron* media to appear in the late 1960s was *Kyojin no Hoshi* (巨人の星, "Star of the Giants"), which first appeared in *manga* (comic book) form in 1966 and then as an animated television show (*anime*) in 1968. The series capitalized on the success of the Yomiuri Giants team, although it notably used the team's militarized alter-ego name from the 1940s, *Kyojin* (巨人). The animated television show was broadcast on Nihon Television (日本テレビ), the broadcast network that Shōriki Matsutarō presided over until his death in 1969, and was designed as part of a block of "sports dramas" that appealed to young audiences.[30] The series fo-

---

27. Harumi Befu, *Hegemony of Homogeneity: An Anthropological Analysis of Nihonjinron* (Melbourne, Australia: Trans Pacific Press, 2001), 2.

28. Befu, *Hegemony of Homogeneity,* 66–71.

29. Befu, *Hegemony of Homogeneity,* chapter 6: Civil Religion.

30. Yamaguchi Tomohisa山口智久, "Terebijyon jidai to supōtsu" テレビジョン時代とスポーツ [The Television Era and Sports], *Hitotsubashi University Departmental Report,* August, 1994: 7.

cused on the Hoshi family (星, the kanji for a celestial star). Sports dramas like
Kyojin no Hoshi helped maintain the television viewership of professional and
high-school baseball throughout the 1970s, when other sports experienced a
marked decline in viewership.[31]

Kyojin no Hoshi resurrected images of practices made popular at Ichikō and
Kanō High Schools during the Imperial-era, such as practicing until one bled.
The first episode opens with the father of the Hoshi family, Ittetsu, forcing his
son, Hyūma, to practice pitching during a blizzard. Hyūma coughs and deliv-
ers his 291st pitch, struggling to stay upright. Ittetsu goads him on, demanding
Hyūma to channel his "spirit" (*seishin,* 精神) to finish his practice session.
Hyūma throws another pitch and then collapses in the snow. Without making a gesture of aid, Ittetsu, a former baseball player, berates his son to throw
eight more pitches or he'll never be a baseball star. Hyūma struggles to stand
and finishes his regimen. They return home, where Ittetsu repeatedly slaps
his son — the mother looking on helplessly — to drive him to practice harder.
The episode advances to springtime, when Hyūma travels to see the real-life
baseball player Nagashima Shigeo of the Yomiuri Giants. Hyūma attracts the
attention of the *Kyojin* team manager with an impromptu display of his near
supernatural pitching ability. Thus, the "Star of the Giants" had a path out of his
small town to the big leagues, and the next 130 episodes document the sweat,
tears, blisters on his hands, and *heart* required to be a baseball star.[32]

A 1971 episode of *Kyojin no Hoshi* demonstrated the combination of *nihonjinron* discourse and samurai imagery. One night, Ittetsu kneels at the family
memorial to his deceased ancestors, and his son Hyūma peeks through a door
and secretly watches his father's prayers. Ittetsu laments to his ancestors that
he cannot motivate his son to be a "perfect" (*kanzen,* 完全) "baseball person"
(*yakyūjin,* 野球人). In using the term "baseball person" instead of "baseball
player" (野球選手), Ittetsu highlights how baseball should be the defining
condition of one's identity. Ittetsu clutches his own baseball jersey from his
youth, numbered 84, and exclaims that when combined with his son's uniform,
numbered 16, it creates the "perfect" number: 100. This numerology convinces
Ittetsu that his son is destined to become a flawless baseball person. Emphasizing the word "battle" (*tatakai,* 戦い), the episode cuts to an imaginary world
where the father and son are samurai warriors in a duel on a grassy plain.

---

31. Yamaguchi, "Terebijyon jidai to supōtsu," 9–10.

32. Kajiwara Ikki 梶原一騎, *Kyojin no Hoshi*巨人の星 ["Star of the Giants"], episode 1 (1968),
Nihon Terebi Corporation.

Hyūma draws his sword and bests his father, symbolizing the son's ascension as the family's premier warrior. Back in the real world, Hyūma, who has been eavesdropping on his father's lament, reels backwards with tears in his eyes and exclaims that perfection is impossible (*Muri da!* 無理だ!). Distraught from the experience yet recognizing the inescapability of the situation, Hyūma leaves his house and runs through town, shouting of his father's "lunacy" (*baka da!* バカだ!).

Befu and Iwabuchi both argued that non-Japanese media contributed to *nihonjinron* discourse and in many cases provided outside legitimization of the myths of homogeneity and uniqueness. Befu and Iwabuchi used as an example of foreigner *nihonjinron* discourse Ruth Benedict's 1946 book, *The Chrysanthemum and the Sword*.[33] Trained as an anthropologist of the Americas, Benedict had never been to Japan, had no formal training in Japanese cultures, and did not speak Japanese. Her study of the Japanese psyche, called an "ethnography at a distance," was conducted via English translations of Japanese literature, reading secondary accounts of Japanese culture and history, and conducting interviews with interred Japanese-Americans during World War II (many of whom had been living in the United States for decades).[34] Benedict's results claimed Japanese society had deep roots in self-sacrifice, groupthink, and co-operation. For Anglophone scholars and laypeople alike, Benedict's text dominated the field of Japan studies throughout the Cold War.

I argue Robert Whiting's 1977 work, *The Chrysanthemum and the Bat*, a clear homage to Benedict's work, should be considered as a work of foreigner *nihonjinron*. Whiting relies on Oh Sadaharu and his *budō*-inspired training regimen to extrapolate a "Samurai Code of Conduct" that spoke to the entirety of baseball in Japan throughout the course of its history. From 1965–1973, the Yomiuri Giants team won nine consecutive championships, but during this period, the Japanese media paid almost no attention to Oh's *budō*-inspired training regimen. The first article about Oh's training regimen in the Yomiuri Shinbun — a conservative-learning newspaper associated with the Yomiuri Giants team — appeared in 1971; no articles appear again until 1975. Only when Oh approached and then surpassed the career homerun record of Hank Aaron in 1977 — which coincided with the publication of *The Chrysanthemum and the Bat* — did Oh's *budō*-inspired training regimen become of interest to the me-

---

33. Befu, *Hegemony of Homogeneity*, 57.

34. Christopher Shannon, "A World Made Safe for Differences: Ruth Benedict's 'The Chrysanthemum and the Sword,'" *American Quarterly* 47, no. 4 (Dec. 1995): 659–680.

dia. From 1977 until 1982, the Yomiuri Shinbun published a dozen articles on Oh's training regimen.[35] In 1974, Oh and ethnic Korean player Harimoto Isao made up the heart of the Yomiuri Giants batting order, forming the "OH-canon," the military symbolism of Oh-Harimoto hitting a barrage of homeruns. As the media became increasingly interested in the use of "traditional" Japanese training methods by baseball superstars, neither member of the most prolific homerun-hitting duo in the NPB were Japanese citizens.

The cases of minority baseball players like Harimoto and Oh underscored the reality of post-colonial life in Cold War Japan. Their citizenship status reflected the broader relationship Japan had with its geographical neighbors and the problematic issues of citizenship and sovereignty in Cold War Asia. Like Oh, Harimoto went to high school in Japan and was excluded from the foreign-born roster limits on NPB teams, meaning that for most his playing career, he downplayed his status as a foreign-resident and instead emphasized motifs of Japanese tradition. These non-Japanese living in Japan had few if any formal channels to survive in the instability wracking their ethnic homelands. Although at times Harimoto and Oh each experienced ostracism in Japan, the protection offered by the baseball community far outweighed the dangers of returning to Taiwan

or Korea. Those minorities in the Japanese baseball community who championed the "traditional" values of Japanese culture were no longer identified by the precariousness of their ethnicity, but instead vaulted into a privileged position within the emerging *nihonjinron* discourse.

Harimoto Isao playing the shamisen.[36]

---

35. Data sourced from *Yomiuri Shinbun* digital archive. The first article on Oh's training regimen in 1971 is an article about how Arakawa devised the famed flamingo stance by combining *kendō* sword techniques with the drama techniques of Kabuki actors. "Kendō masshigura" 剣道まっしぐら [Kendō at Full Speed], *Yomiuri Shinbun*, January 15, 1971, 21.

36. Harimoto Aki 張本有希, available: https://twitter.com/AkiHarry0829/status/712662902281375744. Aki Harimoto is Isao's daughter.

The Power of Minorities in the NPB

By highlighting images of imperial-era strength and national culture, players like Oh transcended their non-Japanese status and became cultural icons at a time when the general Japanese population turned a blind eye to ethnic minorities and non-citizens. Befu Harumi noted that during the 1960s and 1970s, the Japanese public education curriculum portrayed the Japanese culture as homogeneous and removed the narratives of the Imperial-era multi-ethnic empire.[37] Sociologist Eiji Oguma argued that from the late 1960s through the millennium the majority of ethnic Japanese and their government chose to overlook the presence of indigenous Ainu and Ryūkyū peoples while also making little effort to recognize the economic, cultural, and political contributions of Korean, Taiwanese, Chinese, Filipino, Russian, and American inhabitants of Japan.[38] Sociologist John Lie noted that many of these ethnic minorities, immigrants, and marginalized communities participated in what became known as the "3K" careers: *kitsui* (きつい, difficult), *kitanai* (汚い, dirty), and *kiken* (危険, dangerous), which were most commonly sex work and construction industries run by the *yakuza* gangs and motorcycle *bōsōzoku* gangs as labor brokers.[39] In short, the case of Oh and Harimoto using images of Japanese strength offered them a path to economic and cultural success unavailable to the majority of other non-Japanese during the Cold War. Therefore, the baseball community transformed the precarity of the post-colonial ethnicity into the certainty of Japanese identity.

Oh's adoption of nationalist symbols elevated him above ethnic Japanese who did not openly engage with nationalist discourse. By comparison, Oh's emergence as a power-hitter occurred simultaneously to the playing career of Nomura Katsuya (野村克也), the second all-time homerun hitter in NPB history and seventh all-time globally. Nomura, an ethnic Japanese who played three years longer than Oh, from 1956–1980, also had a successful two-decade career as a manager upon completing of his playing career. Although Nomura was a well-liked public figure, he was never given a "National Honor Award," was never asked to manage the Japanese National Team in the Olympics or

---

37. Harumi Befu, "Internationalization of Japan and Nihon Bunkaron" in *The Challenge of Japan's Internationalization: Organization and Culture,* eds. Hiroshi Mannari and Harumi Befu (Hyogo, Japan: Kodansha International, 1983), 232–266.

38. Eiji Oguma, *A Genealogy of 'Japanese' Self-Images,* trans. David Askew (Melbourne, Australia: Trans Pacific Press, 2002), Chapter 17: The Myth Takes Root.

39. John Lie, *Multiethnic Japan* (Cambridge, MA: Harvard University Press, 2001), Chapter 1: The Second Opening of Japan.

World Baseball Classic, and was not asked to support the return of baseball and softball to the Tokyo 2020 Olympics. Nomura never explained his prowess as a hitter by appealing to any kind of *budō* practice, martial arts, or Japanese "tradition." Instead, at a time when cultural *nihonjinron* swept Japan, Nomura developed a style known as "ID *Yakyū*" (ID野球, "Important Data Baseball"), which made informed judgements based on statistical data and analysis.[40] Nomura's ID *Yakyū* resonated closely with contemporary MLB trends to use advanced metrics to understand player performance and determine a player's worth, which was popularized in the United States by Michael Lewis' 2004 book *Moneyball: The Art of Winning an Unfair Game* (an eponymous movie starring Brad Pitt was made in 2011). Whereas Nomura's style of play and management closely resonates with modern conceptions of professional baseball, Oh's status as an enduring cultural icon is directly linked with Japanese nationalism.

It is worth pointing out that Oh was not the only ethnic minority superstar in the 1960s and 1970s who operated within the context of Japanese nationalism. In fact, the most prominent NPB players are almost entirely ethnic minorities. Behind Babe Ruth's homerun record, Lou Gehrig's "Iron Man" record of 2,130 consecutive games played was arguably the second-most heralded baseball accomplishment in the early twentieth century. In 1987, Kinugasa Sachio (衣笠祥雄), a half-black American/half-Japanese man, broke Gehrig's record and finished his career with 2,215 consecutive games played; Kinugasa is also tied for seventh on NPB's all-time homerun list. Upon retirement in 1987, Kinugasa was awarded the sixth National Honor Award (国民栄誉賞).[41] Kinugasa is tied on the all-time NPB homerun list with the Korean player, Harimoto Isao. Another ethnic Korean, Kaneda Masaichi (金田正一), who became a naturalized Japanese citizen after marrying a Japanese woman in 1960, set almost every NPB pitching record during his twenty-year career from 1950–1969 and continues to hold the career record for pitching wins (400). Because of NPB's expanded roster exemptions in the 1950s for "non-Japanese" who went to Japanese high school or became naturalized citizens, none of these players occupied the restricted "foreigner" roster spot throughout the 1960s or 1970s.

---

40. "Nomura Katsuya no "ID Yakyū" kankeisha no hanashi kara mieta igai na shinjitsu ha" 野村克也の『ID野球』 関係者の話から見えた意外な真実は [The Surprising Truth as Seen From the Stories of Those Who Follow Nomura Katsuya's "Important Data Baseball"], *Ameba News*, March 4, 2015, http://news.ameba.jp/20150304-267/.

41. Data compiled from www.baseballreference.com and Cabinet Office, Government of Japan, *Kokumineiyoshō* 国民栄誉賞 [National Honor Award], http://www.cao.go.jp/others/jinji/kokumineiyosho.

The artificial limit on the number of foreigners who could play baseball in Japan allowed the NPB to promote and enforce social ideals within Japanese popular culture. This gave the illusion that these were not ethnic minorities who were achieving the heights of baseball stardom, but Japanese nationals. In 2004, *Besuboru Magajin* (Baseball Magazine, now NPB's official media outlet) published a list of notable "foreigners" — now rendered with the euphemism "helpers" (*sukketo*, 助っ人) — who had played in the NPB. Although other Taiwanese and Korean citizens were included in the list, notably absent were Oh, Kinugasa, Harimoto, and Kaneda.[42] The Japanese baseball community had transformed these ethnic minorities into icons of "Japaneseness."

Conclusion

Nihonjinron discourse powered a new age of Japanese nationalism in the 1960s and 1970s, which gave minorities in the Japanese baseball community the ability to transform their ethnic and national heritage into the new standard of Japanese homogeneity. Ethnic minorities who displayed both their powerful prowess with a bat and the power of traditional Japanese imagery characterized NPB superstardom in the 1960s and 1970s. By masking their true ethnic identity, these players escaped the indignities lumped upon the thousands of other ethnic minorities who toiled in dangerous jobs and received no recognition from the Japanese government or society. The next chapter will discuss how an unintended consequence of free agency in MLB, coupled with the end of the Cold War, shifted the global baseball communities again.

---

42. Besuboru Magajin Sha, *Puro yakyū 70 nen shi*, 555–561, 634–639.

CHAPTER TWELVE

The Japanese Baseball Community in the Post-Cold War Context

[I] sometimes wonder if Japan is not becoming a nation of ETs, that charming visitor from outer space with an oversized head and spindly arms and legs. If that is the course of evolution, ET-like human beings will first appear in Japan. That would explain why we did so poorly at the Seoul Olympics, winning only a handful of gold medals. Maybe that miserable performance indicates that we are acquiring an unconventional, sophisticated temperament and life-style. As a nation, however, we would be better off if our Olympic athletes won a basket of medals and the younger generation did strenuous work.[1]

— Ishihara Shintarō, "The Japan that Can Say 'NO!'"

Introduction

How did the Japanese baseball community advance images of national strength at times of national uncertainty, such as the end of the Cold War? This chapter covers from 1980 through 2008, a period which juxtaposes the end of the Cold War and Japan's participation in the War on Terror. This period illustrates an interesting tension between the Olympic and baseball communities within Japan; when South Korea, which had openly engaged in human rights violations, was awarded the 1988 Olympics over Japan, it set off discussions spearheaded by conservative politician Ishihara Shintarō about the disappearance of physical strength from the Japanese population. After the formal end of the Cold War in 1992, the Japanese baseball community watched in frustration as their

---

1. Ishihara Shintarō, *The Japan that Can Say NO*, trans. Frank Baldwin (New York: Simon and Schuster, 1991), 18–19.

professional baseball players began retiring from their NPB contracts to move to MLB. This trend accelerated in the 2000s, leaving many Japanese feeling that the United States was purchasing Japanese people. In response, Prime Minister Koizumi Junichirō built a relationship with United States President George W. Bush based upon baseball. By treating the baseball community similarly to Japan's broader policies of direct investment in foreign markets, Koizumi deployed a new Japanese nationalism — *kokusaika* — as a defensive internationalism that projected Japanese influence among the global baseball community. In this way, the Japanese baseball community worked to remedy the unequal treatment they received from the United States.

The Long Reach of the 1988 Seoul Olympics

The context for how Japanese baseball communities acted in the post-Cold War world was shaped by South Korea's success in hosting the 1988 Olympics. In September 1981, the International Olympic Committee (IOC) selected Seoul, South Korea, to host the 1988 Summer Olympics over its only competitor: Nagoya, Japan. Japan had famously received the rights to host the 1964 Summer Olympics as a means of showcasing its post-World War II economic and democratic development, and the northern Japanese city of Hokkaido had hosted the 1972 Winter Olympics. The continuing Japanese economic success throughout the 1970s pushed Japanese officials to pursue hosting yet another athletic mega-event in the 1980s. However, the Japanese sporting community's hopes were dashed when Japan's former colony, South Korea, became the second Asian nation-state to host the Summer Olympics.[2]

Granting the Summer Olympics — which continued to advertise itself as an apolitical sporting event that celebrated the heritage of Western civilization — to Seoul made the international sporting community's complicit in state-sponsored violence. South Korea had yet to enter the United Nations and had been ruled by autocratic dictators from the 1960s onwards. In October 1979, South Korean President Park Chung-Hee (who had been in power since 1963) advanced his military elite's idea to use athletic mega-events as a political distraction, and he began the application process to host the 1988 Summer

---

2. It is a fair criticism to say that Australia, which has held two Summer Olympic Games (1956 and 2000) should count as an "Asian Olympics." I recognize such a claim can be made, but instead will adhere to the consensus among historians of sport that the Olympics held in Japan, South Korea, and the People's Republic of China are the "Asian Olympics." The People's Republic of China became the third Asian state to host the Summer Olympics in Beijing in 2008.

Olympics in Seoul.[3] Park was assassinated later that month before the Olympic proposal progressed significantly. In the resulting power vacuum, Army General Chun Doo-Hwan placed himself in charge of state intelligence agencies and became acting president. Chun brutally cracked down on pro-democracy demonstrations and attacked his regime's critics, making the authoritarian Park "look like a moderate" by comparison.[4] The Olympic application begun by Park slowly advanced under the Chun regime while he consolidated power and violently quelled dissent.

Chun engaged in numerous human rights violations in the year between his seizure of power and his formal ascendency to the Presidency. On May 18, 1980 Chun implemented martial law throughout South Korea. When the citizens of Gwangju, a city about 270km south of Seoul, protested the appearance of soldiers in their city, Chun ordered state security forces to suppress the protestors with violence, resulting in the massacre of over 600 citizens with an additional 2,000 civilian casualties.[5] Although Chun used forces under his command and not those under the "Combined Forces" associated with the United States military, many Koreans felt that the Americans' idleness during the Gwangju Massacre made them "complicit and guilty of a 'moral failure.'"[6] In August 1980, Chun forced nearly sixty-thousand Korean citizens to enter military "re-education camps" for "purification." The prisoners at the camp in Samcheong were required to sign an affirmation that they supported the government while soldiers held them at gunpoint.[7] Later that month, Chun dissolved the Korean parliament and, under the direction of a military junta, formally assumed the Presidency of South Korea in what became known as the "Fifth Republic." Most records of President Chun's attacks on his own population were struck from the press, coming to renewed attention only after

---

3. J.A. Mangan and Gwang Ok, "Seoul '88 — Media, Politicians, Public: Confrontation, Cooperation and Democratic Consequences," *The International Journal of the History of Sport* 29, no. 16 (October 2012), 2278.

4. Emmanuel Pastreich, "The Balancer: Rooh Moo-hyun's Vision of Korean Politics and the Future of Northeast Asia," *The Asia-Pacific Journal: Japan Focus* 3, no. 8 (August 3, 2005), http://apjjf.org/-Emanuel-Pastreich/2041/article.html.

5. Jonson N. Porteaux, "Reactive Nationalism and its Effect on South Korea's Public Policy and Foreign Affairs," *The Asia-Pacific Journal: Japan Focus* 14, 9, no. 5 (May 1, 2016), http://apjjf.org/2016/09/Porteux.html.

6. Porteaux, "Reactive Nationalism and its Effect on South Korea's Public Policy and Foreign Affairs."

7. Henry Scott Stokes, "Seoul Said to Hold 15,000 in Camps Without Trial," *New York Times*, September 20, 1981, http://www.nytimes.com/1981/09/20/world/seoul-said-to-hold-15000-in-camps-without-trial.html.

the 2005 creation of a "Truth and Reconciliation Commission" that sought to investigate the Chun regime.[8]

Despite Chun's track record of violent suppression of dissent, many South Koreans voiced disapproval about continuing the application to host the 1988 Summer Olympics. Throughout the second half of the twentieth century, the Summer Olympics had become well-known for placing a massive debt burden on host cities.[9] City officials in Seoul told the Korean Ministry of Education that they could not meet the demand to build the necessary athletic facilities.[10] Undeterred, Chun advanced the Olympic application and in spring 1981, the Korean Olympic Committee discovered it was in a direct competition with Nagoya, Japan, to host the games. Realizing the gravity of the situation, the Korean Olympic Committee admitted that they had underestimated the cost of the games by a factor of three and would have to raise over 400 billion won (over 600 billion US dollars) to build nearly twenty venues within seven years for the events.[11] The infrastructure construction facing the Korean Olympic Committee was more daunting than Japan's construction of nine massive baseball stadiums between 1947 and 1952. Although Nagoya's Olympic bid was supported by a favorable popular vote, the South Korean public was deeply against continuing the application to host the games.[12] A South Korean student organization argued that Chun sought the Olympics as a form of political distraction designed to create a coerced sense of national unity while simultaneously justifying enormous tax increases.[13]

President Chun, undeterred in his desire to triumph over South Korea's former colonizers, began a two-pronged effort to overcome Korea's infrastructure and human rights shortcomings. The Korean Olympic Committee made enthusiastic overtures — celebrations, parties, and Korean shows of attendance — to

8. Gavan McCormack and Kim Dong-choon, "Grappling with Cold War History: Korea's Embattled Truth and Reconciliation Commission," *The Asia-Pacific Journal: Japan Focus* 7, 8, no. 6 (February 17, 2009), http://apjjf.org/-Gavan-McCormack/3056/article.html.

9. Mangan and Ok, "Seoul '88 — Media, Politicians, Public: Confrontation, Cooperation and Democratic Consequences," 2279.

10. Seoul Olympic Organizing Committee, *Official Report: Organization and Planning, Volume 1* (Seoul: Korea Textbook Co., Ltd., 1989), 34.

11. Seoul Olympic Organizing Committee, *Official Report: Organization and Planning, Volume 1*, 35.

12. Mangan and Ok, "Seoul '88 — Media, Politicians, Public: Confrontation, Cooperation and Democratic Consequences," 2279.

13. Mangan and Ok, "Seoul '88 — Media, Politicians, Public: Confrontation, Cooperation and Democratic Consequences," 2280.

appease the International Olympic Committee. Meanwhile Chun cozied up to the Reagan administration in the United States to be seen as "approachable" in showing remorse their previous human rights violations.[14] A setback occurred when President Chun requested and was denied a six billion-dollar (US) loan from Japan — a mere hundredth of the Olympics' expected cost — which further evidenced Korea's inadequate infrastructure.[15] Nonetheless, the International Olympic Committee found Nagoya had too many "rural touches" for their liking, which was a justification that ignored the fact that Nagoya was a metropolis of over two million people that was nearly as large as Los Angeles, which had hosted the 1984 Summer Olympics.[16] What appealed to committee members most about Seoul was its comparative lack of infrastructure, meaning that sports venues would be custom-built to the Olympic Committee's desires. By a two-to-one margin, the IOC selected Seoul over Nagoya to host the 1988 Summer Olympics. North Korea tried unsuccessfully to petition South Korea to hold some Olympic events in North Korean territory. When South Korea rejected this plan, North Korea "began a campaign of terror" to disrupt the Seoul Olympics.[17] In November 1987, two North Korean spies working under orders from Kim Jong-Il planted a bomb on Korean Air Flight 858 in the hope of derailing the Olympics. The bomb detonated as the flight approached a stop-over in Thailand, killing all 115 passengers.[18]

Despite the immense financial burdens, intolerance of dissent, and terrorism, the 1988 Seoul Olympics occurred. By the time the Games began, Chun Doo-Hwan had given South Korea the appearance of a legitimate democracy when he relinquished his Presidency to the popularly-elected Roh Tae-Woo, the general who in 1981 ordered his troops to massacre 600 civilians in Gwangju. After the Olympics, South Korean citizens were both surprised and pleased to hear that the Seoul Olympics left the world's developed countries with a favorable image of South Korea as a "conduit of peace" in Cold War

14. Robert Wampler, "Seeing Human Rights in the 'Proper Manner:' The Reagan-Chun Summit of February 1981," *The National Security Archive*, Book no. 306, February 2, 2010, http://nsarchive.gwu.edu/NSAEBB/NSAEBB306/.

15. Seoul Olympic Organizing Committee, *Official Report: Organization and Planning, Volume 1*, 40.

16. Seoul Olympic Organizing Committee, *Official Report: Organization and Planning, Volume 1*, 36.

17. Mangan and Ok, "Seoul '88 — Media, Politicians, Public: Confrontation, Cooperation and Democratic Consequences," 2282.

18. Chico Harlan, "She Killed 115 People before the last Korean Olympics. Now she wonders: 'Can my sins be pardoned?'" *Washington Post*, February 5, 2018.

Asia.[19] In other words, hosting the Olympics had remade South Korea's image from a human rights violator into a peaceful and productive member of the Western capitalist community. The Olympics' momentum advanced the image of South Korea as a key member of the global community, and South Korea entered the United Nations in 1991.[20]

Japanese Internationalist Nationalism and Sports

Japan's defeat in hosting the 1988 Olympic games generated a sense of athletic inferiority that supported different types of Japanese nationalist discourse. Japan's strength in the Asian and American markets in the 1980s was a product of Prime Minister Nakasone Yasuhiro's *kokusaika* (国際化) policy, a term which directly translated to "internationalization" but had a different connotation than was often used in the West. As Marilyn Ivy explains:

> While internationalization elsewhere implies a cosmopolitan expansiveness (even while retaining the national frame), the Japanese state-sponsored version tends toward the domestication of the foreign. Schemes to internationalize the communications industry, education, and the citizenry index the pressures on the state to give the appearance, at least, of openness, while carefully circumscribing the problem of identity and difference. As many observers, both domestic and foreign, have noted, kokusaika is a conservative policy that reflects the other side of a renewed sense of Japanese national pride, if not nationalism. It has thus been remarked that instead of opening up Japan to the struggle of different nationalities and ethnicities, the policy of internationalization implies the opposite: the thorough domestication of the foreign and the dissemination of Japanese culture throughout the world.[21]

Befu Harumi argued that the *kokusaika* policy in Prime Minister Nakasone's Japan was an evolution of *nihonjinron* philosophy, one which was simultaneously internationalist and culturally nationalist.[22] Many programs begun under

---

19. Mangan and Ok, "Seoul '88 — Media, Politicians, Public: Confrontation, Cooperation and Democratic Consequences," 2284.

20. Mangan and Ok, "Seoul '88 — Media, Politicians, Public: Confrontation, Cooperation and Democratic Consequences," 2283.

21. Marilyn Ivy, *Discourses of the Vanishing: Modernity, Phantasm, Japan* (Chicago: University of Chicago Press, 1995), 3.

22. Chris Burgess, "Maintaining Identities: Discourses of Homogeneity in a Rapidly Globalizing Japan," *Electronic Journal of Contemporary Japanese Studies* (May 2012), 6.

the *kokusaika* policies continue at the time of writing this book's publication, including the popular Japan Exchange and Teaching (JET) Program (of which I was once a member). Within the context of state-sponsored *kokusaika* discourse and its emphasis on Japanese cultural homogeneity, sports re-emerged as a field for discussing national strength (indeed, the JET Program includes formal positions for professional athletes to become supervisors of Japanese athletic education).

Throughout the 1980s, the Japanese economy boomed with corporations using significant capital to update their technological infrastructure, making property purchases and trade goods the manifestation of Japanese economic power. Japanese businessmen purchased notable properties in the United States, such as Rockefeller Center and Pebble Beach Golf Course.[23] Symbolic of Japan's prowess in technology, the Nintendo Entertainment System (NES) and Sega Master System video game consoles — each developed and sold by Tokyo-based companies — raked in billions of dollars in revenue from the American market by 1990.[24] A more significant impact of the Japanese economy under the *kokusaika* policy was Japan's increased Foreign Direct Investment (FDI). The Japanese government took the extra revenue from its successful economy and re-invested it into its geographical neighbors, becoming the largest contributor of Official Development Aid (ODA) in the world.[25] Many researchers preferred to describe this development aid as Japan contributing to world welfare, but in contrast, Japan often used ODA to improve relations with a nation-states where it wanted to acquire strategic resources.[26] Japanese manufacturing shifted to avoid exporting goods and instead produce goods domestically in foreign markets: Toyota, Nissan, Honda, Mitsubishi, Sony, NEC, Fujitsu, and Nintendo had production plants based in the United States by the mid-1990s.[27]

Despite this domestic and international economic success, the IOC had favored South Korea in hosting the 1988 Summer Olympics because it was less-economically advanced and therefore more malleable to meeting the

---

23. Gordon, *A Modern History of Japan*, 292-293.

24. Andrew Pollack, "Market Place; Nintendo's Dominance in Games May be Waning," *New York Times*, April 23, 1993, http://www.nytimes.com/1993/04/23/business/market-place-nintendo-s-dominance-in-games-may-be-waning.html.

25. Gordon, *A Modern History of Japan*, 295.

26. Young-Kwan Yoon, "The Political Economy of Transition: Japanese Foreign Direct Investments in the 1980s," *World Politics* 43, no. 1 (October 1990), 8.

27. Yoon, "The Political Economy of Transition," 10.

IOC's desired image. The United States and the People's Republic of China continued to call for Japan to apologize to its geographical neighbors for war crimes committed during World War II, while South Korea was rewarded the Olympics less than a year after a military dictatorship had massacred its own civilians and instituted violent re-education camps. The specter of the unequal treatment of Japan by the West seemed renewed, and this contributed to a revived relationship between athletics and nationalist discourses.

Shortly after the Seoul Olympics ended in fall 1989, Ishihara Shintarō (石原慎太郎) published the popular book, *The Japan that Can Say NO* (「NO」と言える日本). Ishihara represented Tokyo in Japan's House of Representatives and later became governor of Tokyo. Ishihara gained international recognition in 1991 when he stated his belief that the Nanjing Massacre, a war atrocity committed by Japanese soldiers at the beginning of the Second Sino-Japanese War in 1937, was a lie fabricated by the Chinese.[28] Ishihara remained a strong conservative presence in Tokyo for the next thirty years and regularly pushed for the Summer Olympic to return to Japan. In 2005 he led Tokyo's unsuccessful bid to host the 2016 Summer Olympics, and then in 2012 he led its successful bid to host the 2020 Summer Olympics.[29] In 1989, however, Ishihara was best-known for his popular book that admonished Japan's continuing subservience to the United States and advocated a homogeneous identity among the Japanese nation.

In *The Japan that Can Say NO*, Ishihara lamented that Japan's economic prowess in high-tech industries weakened the Japanese physical body, which was a trope that borrowed from Japan's Imperial-era equation of physically-strong individuals as symbolic of national strength. Ishihara used the Seoul Olympics to portray Japanese national strength as lacking. In his first chapter titled, "A New National Consciousness," Ishihara writes:

> In human terms, if we heard that a tall, muscular man was going to be "re-sized," it would be cause for alarm. Nevertheless, today, everybody…is saying that Japanese industry must be restructured and the economy led by the knowledge intensive sector. Is that good for Japan? Will we be able to sustain our prosperity? People will no longer do hard physical labor. They

---

28. Ishihara Shintarō 石原慎太郎, "Nihon wo otoshireta jōhō kūkan no kai" 日本を陥れた情報空間の怪 [The Mystery of Japan Falling into the Information Gap] *Bungei shūjun* 69, no. 2 (1991): 94–110, http://dl.ndl.go.jp/info:ndljp/pid/3380863.

29. "Tokyo Makes Shortlist for 2020 Games," *The Japan Times*, May 25, 2012, http://www.japantimes.co.jp/news/2012/05/25/national/tokyo-makes-shortlist-for-2020-games/.

will not make things in factories and machine shops, get their hands dirty on assembly lines, or sweat in front of blast furnaces...[All] brain and no brawn cannot be good for the country. Everyone an egghead? History is not encouraging; no such nation has ever flourished...

[I] sometimes wonder if Japan is not becoming a nation of ETs, that charming visitor from outer space with an oversized head and spindly arms and legs. If that is the course of evolution, ET-like human beings will first appear in Japan. That would explain why we did so poorly at the Seoul Olympics, winning only a handful of gold medals. Maybe that miserable performance indicates that we are acquiring an unconventional, sophisticated temperament and life-style. As a nation, however, we would be better off if our Olympic athletes won a basket of medals and the younger generation did strenuous work.[30]

However, Ishihara's hope for a strong Japanese athletic performance after the Seoul Olympics did not immediately come to fruition because of the Cold War's end and a subsequent shift in the global market for baseball labor. The Berlin Wall fell in November 1989, and the Soviet Union collapsed in 1991. After a meeting between United States President George H.W. Bush and Soviet President Boris Yeltsin, the formal end of the Cold War was announced on February 1, 1992.[31] Japan, being the Cold War bulwark of capitalism in East Asia, was no longer the forefront of American policy in Asia and needed to relocate itself among the shifting post-Cold War alliances. Additionally, despite Japan's powerful economy, Japanese baseball players continued to make poor wages compared to their American counterparts. Thus, new markets were opened both by the post-Cold War environment and the shift in how baseball laborers earned wages.

Major League Baseball's Internationalist Nationalism

Within the context of *kokusaika*, FDI, and ODA, the NPB's maneuvers in the 1990s and beyond become easier to understand as attempts to create an internationalist nationalism. Coinciding with the decline of the Cold War, NPB

---

30. Ishihara Shintarō, *The Japan that Can Say NO*, trans. Frank Baldwin (New York: Simon and Schuster, 1991), 18-19.

31. Michael Wine, "Bush and Yeltsin Declare Formal End to Cold War; Agree to Exchange Visits," *New York Times*, February 2, 1992, http://www.nytimes.com/1992/02/02/world/bush-and-yeltsin-declare-formal-end-to-cold-war-agree-to-exchange-visits.html?pagewanted=all.

made several business decisions to compete with the MLB and secure a market for cheap Caribbean labor. Since the early twentieth century, MLB had placed scouts and camps located in Cuba. After Fidel Castro took power in 1960 and ended these camps, MLB teams scouted for talent and built baseball training camps in the Dominican Republic, Puerto Rico, Panama, Venezuela, and Mexico. The introduction of free agency (a player's ability to determine their own labor contract) to MLB in December 1975, after a lengthy Supreme Court battle by black American player Curtis Flood and a subsequent labor dispute with white player Andy Messersmith, hugely inflated player salaries.[32] Prior to the 1975 decision, MLB owners operated with a sense of certainty about their future teams because, via the Reserve Clause, they controlled access to a player even after the original contract expired. Free agency upended this system by giving players and their agents the rights to negotiate their own salaries; this had a side-effect of teams recruiting cheaper and younger players from the Caribbean islands.

Free agency immediately affected MLB salaries. In the first full year of free agency, the highest salary in the MLB doubled from $240,000 to $560,000. By 1980, the highest salary in the MLB increased to $1 million.[33] By comparison, in the NPB (where free agency did not yet exist), wages did not grow at the pace of MLB salaries. From 1975–1980, Oh Sadaharu had the NPB's highest salary. In 1975, Oh earned the equivalent of US $180,000, or about 75% the salary of MLB's leading player (Hank Aaron). By 1980, Oh's NPB salary was the equivalent of US $359,000, or 30% that of the leading MLB salary (Nolan Ryan).[34] The salary gap between the top players in the NPB and MLB increased in the 1980s. In 1985, NPB's top-earning player, Yamamoto Kōji (山本浩二), made 25% of the wages of MLB's top earner, Mike Schmidt.[35] Although the yen-dollar exchange rate improved in the late 1980s, NPB's top earner in 1990, Ochiai Hiromitsu, earned only 40% as much as MLB's top earner, Robin Yount.

---

32. *Flood v. Kuhn*, 407 U.S. 258 (1972). https://supreme.justia.com/cases/federal/us/407/258/case.html.

33. Michael Haupert, "MLB's Annual Salary Leaders since 1874," *Society of American Baseball Research* (Fall 2012), http://sabr.org/research/mlbs-annual-salary-leaders-1874-2012.

34. Oh's salary from *Oh Sadaharu senshū (intai) no nenpō jōhō* 王貞治選手（引退）の年俸情報 [Oh Sadaharu (Retired) Salary Information], http://www.baseball-money.net/retire/retire_players.php?id=2. Yen to dollar conversion rate in 1980 available from the US Federal Reserve: https://fred.stlouisfed.org/data/EXJPUS.txt.

35. "Puro yakyū senshu no rekidai nenpō nendo betsu 1bai wa kono hito da! 70 Nendai~90 Nendai," プロ野球の歴代年俸別１倍はこの人だ！70年代～90年代, *Middle Edge,* November 25, 2016, https://middle-edge.jp/articles/CZKKf.

Although the Japanese economy grew faster than the United States' economy at times, the comparatively low salaries in NPB created unease among the players.

However, MLB free agency caused such a massive increase in salaries that MLB teams sought new ways to lower their costs. American teams intensified their efforts to recruit young and cheap talent, locating baseball academies in the Dominican Republic to enlist teenage boys — some as young as 13 or 14 years old, often from abject poor backgrounds — and offered them schooling, housing, food, and baseball training.[36] In return, the boys signed long-term, low-value contracts with their parent baseball club. The Los Angeles Dodgers operated the cleanest and best-organized academy in Las Palmas. Constructed in 1986, it featured modern dorms and educational facilities that gave them access to the top Dominican talent. However, the Dodgers were the exception, and many other Dominican academies lacked medical facilities to treat injuries. Most facilities more closely resembled ad-hoc establishments that guaranteed only marginal improvement over the boys' original situations.[37] However, the allure of landing a lucrative MLB contract proved to be worth the risk, and the Dominican academies dramatically changed MLB's ethnic composition. By 1990, the number of Dominican baseball players appearing in MLB doubled, reaching a total of 6% of all players and by the 2000s nearly 10% of all players.[38] These academies made the Dominican Republic — which had a total population smaller than the city of Tokyo — MLB's largest talent producer outside of the United States.

NPB officials recognized MLB's new tactic in pursuing cheap labor and began to follow suit in a manner that matched *kokusaika* policy and FDI trends. Throughout the 1980s, Japan had heavily funded Foreign Direct Investment in Latin America and the Caribbean because it saw both opportunities for market growth and access to strategic resources like oil.[39] However, Japanese FDI never extended to the Dominican Republic because it lacked these strategic resources. The Dominican Republic was, however, home to the world's best training grounds for cheap baseball labor, so it quickly became a target of investment by Japanese baseball clubs. In 1990, the Hiroshima Carp NPB team opened its first baseball academy in the Dominican Republic; in 1994, Robinson Checo

---

36. Major League Baseball, "Academies," *MLB.com*, http://mlb.mlb.com/dr/academies.jsp.

37. Alan Klein, "Latinizing the 'National Pastime,'" in *America's Game: A Critical Anthropology of Sport*, eds. Benjamin Eastman, Michael Ralph, and Sean Brown (New York: Routledge, 2008), 163–164.

38. Data from Place of Birth Report, http://www.baseball-reference.com/friv/placeofbirth.cgi.

39. John Tuman and Craig Emmert, "Explaining Japanese Foreign Direct Investment in Latin America, 1979–1992," *Social Science Quarterly* 80, no. 3 (September 1999): 541–542.

became the first player to emerge from this academy and join the Carp.[40] To accommodate the expected increase in foreign-born players, in 1991 NPB relaxed its roster restrictions on foreign-born players. Although NPB maintained its existing maximum of two *active* foreign-born players on rosters, they added a third foreign-born contracted player under team control.[41] Although adding one player under team control might seem to be a minor change, it increased the number of foreign-born players in NPB by 33% and was the first significant change in the roster limit since 1966. Because NPB academies in the Dominican Republic were not a true minor league system, the teenage boys located there did not count toward roster limits. There was no regulation on how many boys the academies could train, just a regulation on how many foreign-born players could appear on an NPB team at one time. An NPB team could keep their academy students engaged in the Dominican indefinitely or sell their contracts to other teams if desired.

NPB Free Agency as Protectionism

Although MLB free agency was introduced in December 1975, NPB team owners remained in control of player salaries throughout the 1980s, a practice which it used to control incoming baseball players from the United States. A notable example occurred in 1982, when the Minnesota Twins sold the contract of Greg "Boomer" Wells, a black American, to the NPB Hankyū Braves team. The transaction was of questionable legality because of the boycott in relations between NPB and MLB, but Minnesota's ownership framed it as Wells' terminating his MLB contract to move to Japan. In 2004, Wells recounted his experience to anthropologist Rob Fitts, saying:

> Why did I go to Japan? Because I was sold like a slave! I was with the [Minnesota] Twins, playing ball in Puerto Rico when my agent called and said, 'You've just been sold to Japan.' I was like, 'Wait a minute — they can do that without my permission?'...I said, 'No Way! I'm not going over there'...Finally, Calvin Griffith, the Twins' owner, called me directly and said, 'Look, we've already sold your contract, and you're going...If you don't go to Japan, there's no telling where I'll send you next year!'[42]

---

40. Alan Klein, "Sport and Culture as Contested Terrain: Americanization in the Caribbean," *Sociology of Sport Journal* 8 (1991): 82.

41. Besuboru Magajin Sha, *Puro yakyū 70 nen shi*, 561.

42. Robert K. Fitts, *Remembering Japanese Baseball: An Oral History of the Game* (Carbondale, IL: Southern Illinois University Press, 2005), 152.

Twins president Calvin Griffith hinted that he would sell Wells to a baseball league in South Korea — which had fallen under President Chun's authoritarian control — if he did not acquiesce to playing in Japan. Reluctantly, Wells signed a contract with the Hankyū Braves that was significantly below his MLB salary. In one quick move, the Hankyū Braves acquired a talented power-hitter for below-market value, and the Minnesota Twins removed an expensive contract.

The NPB introduced free agency after the 1993 season. Ochiai Hiromitsu (落合博満), a well-known slugger for the Nagoya-based Chunichi Dragons, became the first free agent in NPB history when he dictated his own contract with the Yomiuri Giants. Ochiai had been the highest paid player in NPB since 1987; signing to play with the Giants in 1994 resulted in an additional sixty-five percent raise in salary.[43] However, there is a protectionist angle to the story of the free agent baseball market in Japan. Only players who had played in the NPB for at least ten years could be eligible for free agency. Players drafted out of high school, players coming from a foreign country, or players from a Dominican academy remained under team control for the first ten years of their NPB career.[44] NPB's introduction of free agency gave the illusion that it was forging a global identity by including more international players, including the highly-prized Caribbean players who were scouted by MLB.[45] However, only Japanese players would receive the highest paying contracts determined by free agency market. Most Japanese players cared little about switching teams because it was so rare: only twenty-nine NPB players switched teams through the free agent market from 1993–2012.[46]

---

43. "Puro yakyū senshu no rekidai nenpō nendo betsu 1bai wa kono hito da!", https://middle-edge.jp/articles/CZKKf.

44. Keiji Kawai and Matt Nichol, "Labor in Nippon Professional Baseball and the Future of Player Transfers to Major League Baseball," *Marquette Sports Law Review* 25, no. 2 (2015): 497. The number of years of service has lessened gradually, and currently sits at seven years to earn free agency.

45. Keiji Kawai and Brent McDonald, "Globalisation, Individualism and Scandal: New Directions in Japanese Baseball," *The International Journal of the History of Sport* 29, no. 17 (November 2012), 2451.

46. Kawai and Nichol, "Labor in Nippon Professional Baseball and the Future of Player Transfers to Major League Baseball," 498. Most players eligible for NPB free agency used the leverage of the market to make their original team pay them more money. Only in 2017 did foreign-born players — Ernesto Mejia and Dennis Sarfate — become the top salary earners in the NPB. Source: "Top 100 Salaries of NPB (Japan Professional Baseball) Players in 2017," http://nbakki.hatenablog.com/entry/Top_100_Salaries_of_NPB_Players_in_2017.

Despite the protectionism that promoted Japanese-born baseball players in the mid-1990s, many Japanese players remained concerned about NPB's level of competition and desired to move to MLB. Additionally, MLB player salaries continued to skyrocket: between 1990 and 1995, the top MLB salary nearly tripled, rising from $3.2 million to $9.2 million.[47] Although NPB salaries had also tripled within two years, Ochiai Hiromitsu, the highest paid NPB player in 1995, earned the equivalent of US $3 million, or 30% of the MLB's leading player.[48] However, NPB players could not leave their professional league because the cessation of business relations between MLB and NPB — which began in 1965 after the fiasco with Murakami Masanori's contract fiasco — remained intact.

The return of Japanese players to MLB occurred when Nomura Don (野村団), a half-Japanese, half-American baseball agent, sought to "liberate" NPB players from their restrictive contracts and enter the lucrative MLB market.[49] In 1995, Nomura enlisted pitcher Nomo Hideo (野茂英雄) to circumvent NPB contract restrictions. Entering the NPB with the Kintetsu Buffaloes in 1990, Nomo had played only four professional seasons and was still six years from becoming a free agent. Nomura recognized a loophole that would allow Nomo to voluntarily retire from his NPB contract, which formally ended the Kintetsu Buffaloes' control of Nomo's NPB contract yet permitted him the possibility of a future return. Instead of returning to the NPB, Nomo applied as an independent Free Agent for MLB, and the Los Angeles Dodgers signed him to a contract exceeding two million dollars in 1995.[50]

In context, Nomo — who had only three years of effective pitching on his record — signed a MLB contract that, on the surface, was worth nearly as much as Ochiai Hiromitsu's NPB-leading contract; Ochiai had been in the NPB for nearly twenty years, was a ten-time all-star and held numerous league records. Nomo debuted for the Dodgers on April 27, 1995 and became the first ethnic Japanese player in MLB since Murakami Masanori in 1965. For authors like Robert Whiting, Nomo's arrival in MLB signified Japanese baseball players' liberation and the NPB "catching up" to global labor standards.[51] However, I

---

47. Michael Haupert, "MLB's Annual Salary Leaders since 1874," *Society of American Baseball Research* (Fall 2012), http://sabr.org/research/mlbs-annual-salary-leaders-1874-2012.

48. Data compiled from salary data at https://middle-edge.jp/articles/CZKKf and historical exchange rates from the US Federal Reserve, available: https://fred.stlouisfed.org/data/EXJPUS.txt.

49. Kikkawa and Nara, *Fan kara mita puro yakyū no rekishi*, 221.

50. Contract information available on Nomo's player page at http://www.baseball-reference.com/players/n/nomohi01.shtml.

51. Whiting, *The Meaning of Ichiro*, 147.

contend that Nomo's signing with the Dodgers can be viewed from the opposite angle: Nomo was yet another minority player signed to an MLB team with an affordable, team-friendly contract. The two-million-dollar contract that Nomo signed with the Dodgers was heavily loaded with a "signing bonus," which is a one-time payment to a player; Nomo's actual salary in 1995 was the league-minimum $109,000. That year, Nomo won MLB rookie of the year honors, and in 1996, Nomo finished fourth in the voting for the Cy Young Award, which was given to the league's best pitcher. Using the SABRmetric of Wins Above Replacement (WAR), which measures how good a player's performance is compared to the league average, Nomo was a top-ten pitcher in the first two years of his MLB career, yet he earned less than half of the average MLB salary.[52] Nomo may have been "liberated" from team control in NPB, but over the length of his first MLB contract, in terms of monetary compensation, he earned less in the United States than he would have earned had he remained in the NPB.

The Unsettling of Japan's Global Position in the 1990s

After decades of near-continual economic growth, the Japanese economy halted and then recessed after 1991, seemingly reinforcing Ishihara's 1989 warning that Japan could not depend upon brain power alone. The end of the Cold War and the Japanese economic recession resulted in the end of fifty years of continuous conservative political control in Japan when the Japanese Socialist Party won the majority vote in 1994. In that election, Murayama Tomiichi became the first non-conservative Prime Minister since Katayama Tetsu in 1947. 1995 was the fiftieth anniversary of the end of World War II hostilities, and Prime Minister Murayama emphasized that his administration would make amends with the People's Republic of China for Japanese aggression in World War II.

In May 1995, Maruyama met with Chinese President Jiang Zemin to express Japanese regret for atrocities committed in World War II and re-state Japan's commitment to peace in Asia.[53] Murayama rejected Ishihara's denial of the Nanjing Massacre and publicly stated to the People's Republic of China his regret for the atrocity. After Jiang accepted Murayama's statement, the two continued negotiations to create an East Asian Economic Community,

---

52. Data compiled from www.baseball-reference.com. In particular, Nomo Hideo's personal page (https://www.baseball-reference.com/players/n/nomohi01.shtml) and yearly pitching statistics (https://www.baseball-reference.com/leagues/NL/1995-value-pitching.shtml).

53. "Maruyama Rues Japanese Aggression," *Beijing Review*, May 22–28, 5.

an idea which originated under the Nakasone administration and was effectively an expansion of the ASEAN (Association of South East Asian Nations) trade bloc. Many of Japan's geographical neighbors felt uneasy about Japan's renewed interest in political and economic relations in the post-Cold War era. The East Asian Economic Community never developed in the 1990s because the proposed community seemed eerily close to a re-creation of Japan's imperial sphere.[54] Many Japanese conservatives felt that Murayama was being pushed around by Chinese demands for apologies and being rebuffed by the same Southeast Asian nations that benefitted from Japan's development assistance.

Simultaneous to Murayama's reconciliation visits, several additional NPB players followed Nomo's lead and retired from their Japanese contracts to move to the United States. To reassemble a sense of control over Japanese baseball labor, NPB created the "posting system" that required MLB teams wishing to employ NPB players prior to their free agency eligibility to pay a sum of money to the owning team. The first player to be "posted" to the MLB was Alejandro Quejada, a product of the Hiroshima Carp's Dominican Republic academy. The Cincinnati Reds paid the Carp $400,000 to sign Quejada to a contract, demonstrating the possibility of that NPB could profit from the system.[55] However, in 2000, the NPB's best hitter and highest-paid player, Suzuki Ichirō (hereafter referred to by his well-known moniker, "Ichiro") used the posting system to move to the Seattle Mariners. The Orix Blue Wave received the sum of $13 million in return for releasing Ichiro, but many NPB fans and managers quickly realized that the money was a pittance because Ichiro became one of the best hitters and fielders in MLB history.[56] Following Ichiro's departure to MLB, Matsui Hideki, NPB's best contemporary power hitter, joined the New York Yankees via free agency in 2003. The highest posting fee for a Japanese baseball player occurred in 2007, when the Boston Red Sox paid $51 million to acquire pitcher Matsuzaka Daisuke.[57] For the most part, the posting system did not provide adequate financial returns to many NPB teams because many Japanese players had long and successful careers in MLB. Matsuzaka is the best example of an NPB team profiting from the posting system. Matsuzaka, who in

54. Wilfrido V. Villacorta, "Japan's Asian Identity: Concerns for ASEAN-Japan Relations," *ASEAN Economic Bulletin* 11, no. 1 (July 1994): 79.

55. Information from Alejandro Quezada's page at http://www.baseball-reference.com/bullpen/Alejandro_Quezada.

56. Ichiro continues to play in MLB baseball at the time of writing.

57. "Matsuzaka, Red Sox Reach Agreement on Six-Year Deal," *ESPN*, February 23, 2007, http://www.espn.com/mlb/news/story?id=2696321.

his youth was famed for his pitching endurance, succumbed to arm fatigue and injury shortly after his introduction to MLB and had a relatively unproductive career thereafter.

The protectionism offered by NPB was simply not powerful enough to compete with the massive sums of money that MLB owners spent on celebrity players. Although NPB received monetary compensation for losing players to MLB, many Japanese baseball fans felt that the NPB was losing its cultural identity. Whereas many Americans worried about Japan purchasing of American properties in the 1980s, the tables had turned by the year 2000, and Japanese fans worried that the MLB was purchasing iconic Japanese *people*. Despite trying to assert a form of control in the guise of the posting system, the Japanese baseball community felt the Americans treated them unequally.

Turning a Weakness into a Strength: Baseball Diplomacy in the 2000s

Prime Minister Koizumi Junichirō served three consecutive terms from 2001–2006 and was one of the most powerful politicians in post-Cold War Japan. Koizumi made a spectacle of performing official state visits to the Yasukuni Shrine in Tokyo, a site where the spirits of soldiers who died in Japan's imperialist wars — including war criminals from World War II — had been symbolically enshrined.[58] Although many sitting Japanese Prime Ministers had visited Yasukuni Shrine previously, Koizumi emphasized the political and nationalist nature of his visits. In response, Chinese Premier Wen Jiabao ended formal relations with Japan until Koizumi left office in 2006. Meanwhile, United States President George W. Bush sought support for the global War on Terror, and Koizumi diverted from the previous anti-American rhetoric of nationalist conservatives like Ishihara and instead curried favor with the United States. Outside of politics, Koizumi was internationally renowned for his two passions popular among Americans: Elvis Presley and baseball. President George W. Bush had formerly owned the Texas Rangers MLB team. Sharing a love both for baseball and conservative politics, Bush and Koizumi became fast friends and were regularly seen playing or watching baseball throughout the 2000s.

Despite the long history of baseball in Japan serving as a catalyst against American intrusion into Japanese affairs, Prime Minister Koizumi used baseball to forge a relationship with President Bush that promised to renew Japan's

---

58. Akiko Takenaka, "Mobilizing Death in Imperial Japan: War and the Origins of the Myth of Yasukuni," *The Asia-Pacific Journal: Japan Focus*, 13, 38, no. 1 (September 21, 2015), http://apjjf. org/-Akiko-TAKENAKA/4377.a.

image as a powerful ally. Although Japan was constitutionally prohibited from participating in aggressive wars, in January 2004, the Japanese Ground Self Defense Force arrived in Iraq to participate in Operation Iraqi Freedom in the role of "humanitarian and reconstructive assistance."[59] This was the Self Defense Force's first official participation in an overseas military mission outside United Nations' peacekeeping operations. In September 2004, Koizumi traveled to New York, where he threw out the first pitch at a Yankees game and then visited the September 11 Ground Zero site for the third time in three years.[60] Yankees fans were thrilled to see Japan's Prime Minister throwing the first pitch to their prized free agent acquisition, Matsui Hideki.

Matsui, a prodigious homerun hitter playing for the New York Yankees — "America's Team" — symbolized the new cultural power of Japan by means of the baseball community. At the end of the 2000s, Japanese politicians entered American public life and built the images of a strong Japan-U.S. alliance. Although decades of Japanese conservative politicians had passively tolerated the unequal relationship between the United States and Japan, Prime Minister Koizumi threw out first pitches at Yankees games with semi-regularity. Similar to the Yasukuni Shrine visits, Koizumi made a yearly visit to Ground Zero, the near-sacred site where the spirits of those who died in the first attack of the War on Terror rested. From 2003 to 2008, nearly 10,000 members of the Japanese Self Defense Force contributed to security operations in Iraq. Although Koizumi had promised that these troops would be in strictly non-combat operations in accordance with the Japanese Constitution's Renunciation of War, documents released in 2018 revealed that many of the troops were subjected to military aggression from Iraqi fighters.[61] Like Nissan, Toyota, Sony, and so many other Japanese manufacturers, the Japanese baseball community had adapted to the unequal treatment it experienced when competing against the world's most powerful capitalist country. That is, the Japanese baseball community had integrated itself with American culture so seamlessly that the two nations would be considered allies — both in protecting democratic capitalism and in baseball — for the foreseeable future.

---

59. David Fouse, "Japan's Dispatch of the Ground Self Defense Force to Iraq: Lessons Learned," *Asia-Pacific Center for Security Studies* (July 2007): 1.

60. "Koizumi's Yankee-Sox Pitch a No-Hitter," *The Japan Times*, September 21, 2004, http://search.japantimes.co.jp/cgi-bin/nn20040921a4.html.

61. Masaya Kato, "SDF Logs Cast Doubt Over Legality of Japan's Iraq Mission," *Nikkei Asian Review*, April 17, 2018, https://asia.nikkei.com/Politics/SDF-logs-cast-doubt-over-legality-of-Japan-s-Iraq-mission.

Conclusion

In this chapter, I argued that Japan's loss in hosting the 1988 Summer Olympics renewed a sense of nationalism. In the context of *kokusaika* in the 1980s and the early 1990s, the Japanese baseball community first demonstrated an increased sense of internationalism while simultaneously protecting Japanese baseball labor. However, the unsettling of Japan's regional and global position at the end of the Cold War coupled with global shifts in baseball labor led to the weakening of NPB as its most iconic players left Japan to play for massive amounts of money in the United States. This coincided with the slowing of the Japanese economy and the unsettling of Japan's place of Asia following the end of the Cold War. Rebuffed by China, Prime Minister Koizumi Junichirō broke with the former tactics of conservative politicians and used baseball to get closer to the United States and participate in an unconstitutional overseas military engagement. Here, the Japanese national game took spun in a new direction: no longer did the baseball community seek to produce characteristics of Japanese identity at home, but in accordance with *kokusaika* policy, the baseball community sought to domesticate the foreign and bring Japanese culture into the world.

Conclusion

In 2006, the inaugural World Baseball Classic (WBC) tournament promoted baseball goodwill throughout the world and featured baseball teams from sixteen countries and territories. The WBC began only after President George W. Bush restructured the United States' forty-five-year-old embargo on Cuba so as to permit Cuban nationals to play on United States soil.[1] Using teams comprised of professional players, this round-robin tournament determined, unofficially and for the first time, the "world champion" of baseball. With national pride on the line, the WBC exposed tensions lingering from Cold War politics and heightened nationalism stemming from the current War on Terror.

When the South Korean team defeated the Japanese team in a semi-final round, South Korean pitcher Jae Seo planted a miniature South Korean flag on the pitcher's mound of San Diego's Petco Park, protesting Japanese team and Japan's re-emergence in international wartime affairs. Seo explained that his actions reflected South Korean disapproval of Japan's historical colonization and interference in his home country. He told reporters, "It goes back to our history and tradition. It stems from our parents' generation and us. I'm sure that our next generation will probably feel the same."[2] At the end of the World Baseball Classic, Japan rallied from its semi-final loss and became the WBC champion by defeating the Cuban team before an announced crowd of 42,696 people in San Diego.[3] For the first time in history, Japan had become the global champion of baseball.

---

1. "Treasury Department Allows Cuba into WBC," *ESPN.com News Services*, January 23, 2006, http://www.espn.com/mlb/worldclassic2006/news/story?id=2299485.

2. Kevin Baxter, "South Korea-Japan Rivalry Shows no Sign of Cooling," *Los Angeles Times*, March 20, 2009, http://articles.latimes.com/2009/mar/20/sports/sp-wbc-asia20.

3. Box Score available: http://mlb.mlb.com/wbc/2009/stats/boxscore.jsp?gid=2006_03_20_jpnint_cubint_1.

Officially named "Samurai Japan" (侍ジャパン) and managed by the all-time global homerun champion, Oh Sadaharu, the victorious Japanese WBC team symbolized national strength on an international stage. "Samurai Japan" deployed the moniker of the premodern Japanese aristocratic class, the *samurai*. By equating Japan's ancient military and aristocratic class with modern baseball success, the "Samurai Japan" team crafted a distinctly Japanese history for both itself and its country on the global stage. However, this historical continuity was tenuous: samurai had been mythologized throughout the twentieth century, and moreover, the man managing the team, Oh Sadaharu, was not a Japanese citizen. The moniker "Samurai Japan" used the samurai's image as warriors to narrate a distinctly Japanese genealogy of baseball.

Thus, the transformative power of the Japanese baseball community was also cyclical: many in the community have come to identify with the *bushidō*-inflected origins of the sport. Remembering back to Murakami Haruki — the café owner-turned-author whose inspirational day at the ballpark started this book — what are we to think of his transformation? As a baseball fan feeling liberated by the sound of a bat hitting a ball during the height of Japanese *nihonjinron* nationalism in the 1970s, did he set out to write novels that were distinctly pro-Japanese and iconographic of samurai virtues? I would argue that he did not. Murakami's novels are vociferously critical of Japanese imperialism. In *The Wind-up Bird Chronicle*, perhaps Murakami's most well-known book, he uses several subplots about atrocities committed in the puppet-state of Manchūkuo during the Fifteen Years War to provide backstory for the contemporary actions of his characters. Because Japanese public education curriculum and conservative politicians have either downplayed or denied Japanese wartime atrocities, Murakami's use of such imagery is a strong statement against the post-war narrative of a guiltless or innocent Japan.

Thus, the transformative power sparked by baseball is not homogeneous. The path I followed in this book linked three forms of nationalism — *bushidō*, *nihonjinron*, and *kokusaika* — to connect the story of baseball as it became the Japanese national game. In many cases, the Japanese baseball community was transformative through its unity of purpose, at times to promote domestic multiculturalism, or at other times to oppose unequal treatment. However, it did not spark change in the same way every time. People like Murakami demonstrate the multitudes of ways that baseball can inspire transformation. Because the "national game" is influenced by what constitutes "the nation," the majority of the ways baseball and its community operates are dominated by the prevalent ideologies of any given time period. Thus, the nationalist ideologies of Inoue Testujirō and Ishihara Shintarō have as much mark on the Japanese baseball community as do subjects like Free Agency.

The early chapters of this book began with the illustration of the how the Japanese baseball community transformed national and international characteristics of the emerging Japanese society. *Bushidō* baseball evolved alongside philosopher Inoue Tetsujirō's account of Imperial *Bushidō* in the late nineteenth century. This initial step took the "American pastime" and realigned baseball with narratives of Japanese national identity. As Imperial *Bushidō* discourse boomed alongside the expansion of the Japanese empire during the early twentieth century, baseball exploded in popularity and became a stage for the discussion of Japanese national and imperial identity. After the introduction of the Kōshien Tournament in 1915, high school baseball in Japan became the largest athletic mega-event in the world by the mid-1920s. However, baseball was not the only athletic mega-event to increase in popularity; the *Meiji Jingū Taikai*, which was run by multiple government ministries, surpassed the Kōshien Tournament in participation and inculcated Japanese subjects with loyalty towards the emperor. While the political parties of Japan's government pursued increasingly fascistic policies during the 1930s, professional baseball appeared for the first time in Japan and rebuked the exclusionary model that existed in the United States. Both amateur and professional baseball fell under the direction of the Japanese government during the war and became symbolic of enduring Japanese militarism and strength during times of hardship and famine in the 1940s. Here, "*bushidō* baseball" became entangled with wartime Japanese national consciousness. However, this mentality and association did not survive in this form past 1945.

The day after the Japanese surrender in World War II, Japanese baseball players took whatever equipment they had and went out to play baseball, rebuild their community, and again transform society. The United States Occupation Forces, in an effort to quell militarism and promote democracy within Japan, dismantled Japan's existing physical education system and replaced it with a model styled upon American ethos and sporting culture. However, this effort suffered while facing the reality of shortages of material and space. The Japanese baseball community made gestures of adopting the American Occupation agenda and were rewarded with equipment and space. However, this reward came with the supposition that future generations of baseball fans in Japan would continue to espouse pro-American individualism and non-militarism, even as Japan re-armed to participate in the Cold War.

The United States continued to influence baseball culture in Japan and made overtures of controlling the Japanese professional leagues until the 1965 contract dispute over pitcher Murakami Masanori, which resulted in the cessation of formal relations between American and Japanese baseball until the mid-1990s. Now fully independent from American baseball, NPB demonstrated an interesting revival of nationalism under the discourse of *nihonjinron*, symbolized best by the non-Japanese baseball player, Oh Sadaharu. The cultural influence of non-Japanese players during the 1960s–1980s underscored the importance of post-colonial identities in shaping the discourses of Japanese uniqueness that flourished within nationalist discourse. However, this time of supposed baseball strength during the 1970s and 1980s was undermined by the failure of Japan to secure the hosting rights for the 1988 Summer Olympics to its former colony, South Korea. The poor performance of Japanese athletes at the 1988 Seoul Olympics, coupled with the massive salary increase seen in American professional baseball, caused Japanese baseball players to leave Japan for the United States in the mid-1990s. Although at first seen as a sign of weakness by the Japanese populace, in the early 2000s, Prime Minister Koizumi Junichirō spearheaded a re-invention of Japanese baseball players as diplomats and world-class businessmen. Instead of seeing the loss of Japanese baseball players to the United States as a weakness, Japanese baseball players in the United States became symbolic of Japanese global strength, a point that was underscored by Japan's victory in the inaugural World Baseball Classic under the moniker "Samurai Japan."

Bibliography

Books and Articles

Abe, Ikuo. "Muscular Christianity in Japan: The Growth of a Hybrid." *The International Journal of the History of Sport* 23, no. 5 (2006): 714–738.

Abe, Ikuo and J.A. Mangan. "The British Impact on Boys' Sports and Games and Japan: An Introductory Survey." *The International Journal of the History of Sport* 14, no. 2, (1997): 187–199.

Abe, Ikuo and J.A. Mangan. "'Sportsmanship'—English Inspiration and Japanese Response: F.W. Strange and Chiyosaburo Takeda." *The International Journal of the History of Sport* 19, no. 2-3 (2002): 99–128.

Abe, Ikuo, Yasuharu Kiyohara, and Ken Nakajima. "Sport and Physical Education under Fascistization in Japan." *InYo: The Journal of Alternative Perspectives on the Martial Arts and Sciences* 1 (2000): 1–18.

Abe, Isoo 安部磯雄 and Oshikawa, Shunrō 押川春朗. *Yakyū to gakusei* 野球と学生 [Baseball and Students]. Tokyo: Kobundō, 1911.

Ariyama, Teruo 有山輝雄. *Kōshien yakyū to Nihonjin: Media no tsukutta ibento* 甲子園野球と日本人:メディアのつくったイベント [Japanese People and Kōshien Baseball: A Media Created Event]. Tokyo: Yoshikawa Kobunkan, 1997.

Aydin, Cemil. *The Politics of Anti-Westernism in Asia: Visions of World Order in Pan-Islamic and Pan-Asian Thought*. New York: Columbia University Press, 2007.

Barshay, Andrew. *The Gods Left First: The Captivity and Repatriation of Japanese POWs in Northeast Asia, 1945-1956*. Berkeley, CA: University of California Press, 2013.

Balcomb, Theo. "Japanese Baseball Began on my Family's Farm in Maine." *National Public Radio: Parallels*. March 28, 2014. http://www.npr.org/sections/parallels/2014/03/28/291421915/japanese-baseball-began-on-my-familys-farm-in-maine.

Baseball Magazine Sha ベースボール・マガジン社. *Puro yakyū 70 nen shi* プロ野球70年史 [70 Year History of Professional Baseball]. Tokyo: Baseball Magazine Sha, 2004.

Befu, Harumi. *Hegemony of Homogeneity: An Anthropological Analysis of Nihonjinron*. Melbourne, Australia: Trans Pacific Press, 2001.

_____. "Internationalization of Japan and Nihon Bunkaron." In *The Challenge of Japan's Internationalization: Organization and Culture*, eds. Hiroshi Mannari and Harumi Befu. Hyogo, Japan: Kodansha International, 1983.

Benesch, Oleg. *Inventing the Way of the Samurai: Nationalism, Internationalism, and Bushidō in Modern Japan*. Oxford: Oxford University Press, 2014.

Bjarkman, Peter. *Baseball with a Latin Beat*. Jefferson, NC: McFarland and Co., 1994.

Bourdieu, Pierre. "Sport and Social Class." *Social Science Information* 17, no. 6 (1978): 819–840.

Burgess, Chris. "Maintaining Identities: Discourses of Homogeneity in a Rapidly Globalizing Japan." *Electronic Journal of Contemporary Japanese Studies* (May 2012): 1–17.

Carter, Thomas F. *The Quality of Homeruns: The Passion, Politics, and Language of Cuban Baseball*. Durham, NC: Duke University Press, 2008.

Carter, Thomas and John Sugden. "The USA and Sporting Diplomacy: Comparing and Contrasting the Cases of Table Tennis with China and Baseball with Cuba in the 1970s." *International Relations* 26, no. 1 (2011): 101–121.

Chūgaidō Publishers. *Oyatoi Gaikokujin Ichiran* 御雇外国人一覧 [Catalog of Oyatoi Foreigners]. Tokyo: Chūgaidō, 1872.

Claudy, Carl H. *The Battle of Base-Ball*. New York: The Century Co., 1912.

Craig, Albert. *Civilization and Enlightenment: The Early Thought of Fukuzawa Yukichi*. Cambridge, MA: Harvard University Press, 2009.

Cumings, Bruce. "The Origins and Development of the Northeast Asian Political Economy: Industrial Sectors, Product Cycles, and Political Consequences." *International Organization* 38, no. 1 (Winter 1984): 1–40.

Davis, Winston. "The Civil Theology of Inoue Testujirō." *Japanese Journal of Religious Studies* 3, no. 1 (March 1976): 5–40.

DeGroot, Gerard. *The Bomb: A Life*. Cambridge, MA: Harvard University Press, 2005.

Dower, John. *Embracing Defeat: Japan in the Wake of World War II*. New York: W.W. Norton and Company, 1999.

_____. "The San Francisco System: Past, Present, Future in U.S.-Japan-China Relations." *The Asia-Pacific Journal: Japan Focus* 12, 8, no. 2 (February 23, 2014). https://apjjf.org/2014/12/8/John-W.-Dower/4079/article.html.

_____. *War Without Mercy: Race and Power in the Pacific War*. New York: Pantheon Books, 1986.

Dreifort, John, ed. *Baseball History from Outside the Lines: A Reader*. Lincoln, NE: University of Nebraska Press, 2001.

Echevarría, Roberto González. *The Pride of Havana: A History of Cuban Baseball*. New York: Oxford University Press, 1999.

Elias, Norbert and Eric Dunning. *The Quest for Excitement: Sport and Leisure in the Civilizing Process*. Dublin: University of Dublin Press, 1986.

Elias, Robert. *The Empire Strikes Out: How Baseball Sold U.S. Foreign Policy and Promoted the American Way Abroad*. New York: The New Press, 2010.

Fitts, Robert K. "Babe Ruth and Eiji Sawamura," *Baseball Research Journal* 41, no. 2 (Spring 2012). http://sabr.org/research/babe-ruth-and-eiji-sawamura.

_____. *Banzai Babe Ruth: Baseball, Espionage, and Assassination during the 1934 Tour of Japan*. Lincoln, NE: University of Nebraska Press, 2012.

_____. *Remembering Japanese Baseball: An Oral History of the Game*. Carbondale, IL: Southern Illinois University Press, 2005.

Forsberg, Aaron. *America and the Japanese Miracle: The Cold War Context of Japan's Postwar Economic Revival, 1950–1960*. The University of North Carolina Press: Chapel Hill, 2000.

Fouse, David. "Japan's Dispatch of the Ground Self Defense Force to Iraq: Lessons Learned." *Asia-Pacific Center for Security Studies* (July 2007): 1–7.

French, Thomas. "Contested 'Rearmament:' The National Police Reserve and Japan's Cold War(s)." *Japanese Studies* 34, no. 1 (2014): 25–36.

Friedman, Sara. *Exceptional States: Chinese Immigrants and Taiwanese Sovereignty*. Oakland, CA: University of California Press, 2015.

Fujitani, Takashi. *Race for Empire: Koreans as Japanese and Japanese as Americans during World War II*. Berkeley, CA: University of California Press, 2011.

_____. *Splendid Monarchy: Power and Pageantry in Modern Japan*. Berkeley, CA: University of California Press, 1996.

Gainty, Denis. *Martial Arts and the Body Politic in Meiji Japan*. New York: Routledge, 2013.

Gallicchio, Marc. *The Cold War Begins in Asia: American East Asian Policy and the Fall of the Japanese Empire*. New York: Columbia University Press, 1988.

_____. *The Scramble for Asia: U.S. Military Power in the Aftermath of the Pacific War*. Lanham, Maryland: Rowman and Littlefield Publishers, 2008.

Gems, Gerald. "Anthropology Days, the Construction of Whiteness, and American Imperialism in the Philippines." In *The 1904 Anthropology Days and Olympic Games: Sport, Race, and American Imperialism*, edited by Susan Brownell. Lincoln, NE: University of Nebraska Press, 2008.

_____. *The Athletic Crusade: Sport and American Cultural Imperialism.* Lincoln, NE: University of Nebraska Press, 2006.

Gietschier, Steven P. "The Rules of Baseball." In *The Cambridge Companion to Baseball,* edited by Leonard Cassuto. Cambridge, UK: Cambridge University Press, 2011.

Gilman, Nils. *Mandarins of the Future: Modernization Theory in Cold War America.* Baltimore: The Johns Hopkins University Press, 2003.

Gluck, Carol. *Japan's Modern Myths: Ideology in the Late Meiji Period.* Princeton, NJ: Princeton University Press, 1985.

Gmelch, George, Ed. *Baseball without Borders.* Lincoln, NE: University of Nebraska Press, 2009.

Gordon, Andrew. *A Modern History of Japan: From Tokugawa Times to the Present.* Oxford University Press: New York, 2009.

_____. *Labor and Imperial Democracy in Prewar Japan.* Berkeley, CA: University of California Press, 1992.

Gotō, Takeo 後藤健生. *Kokuritsu Kyōgijyō no 100-nen: Meiji Jingū Gaien kara miru Nihon no kindai supōtsu* 国立競技場の100年:明治神宮外苑から見る日本の近代スポーツ [One Hundred Years of the National Athletic Stadium: Seeing Modern Japanese Sports from the Meiji Jingū Gardens]. Kyoto: Minerva Shobō, 2013.

Hamaguchi, Yoshinobu. "Innovation in Martial Arts." In *Japan, Sport, and Society: Tradition and Change in a Globalizing World,* eds. Joseph Maguire and Masayoshi Nakayama. New York: Routledge, 2006.

Harada, Cappy 原田キャッピ. *Taiheiyō no Kakehashi: Sengo Yakyū Fukkatsu no Rimenshi* 太平洋のかけはし：戦後・野球復活の裏面史 [Bridging the Pacific: The Secret History of Baseball Revival]. Tokyo, Baseball Magajin Sha, 1980.

Harimoto, Isao 張本勲. *Mō hitotsu no jinsei: Genbakusha toshite, Hito toshite*もう一つの人生：原爆者として、人として [Another Life: As an Atomic Bomb Survivor, As a Person]. Tokyo: Shin Nihon, 2010.

Harootunian, Harry. *Overcome by Modernity: History, Culture, and Community in Interwar Japan.* Princeton: Princeton University Press, 2000.

Harvey, Jean and Robert Sparks. "The Politics of the Body in the Context of Modernity." *Quest* 43, no. 2 (1991): 164–189.

Hata, Genji 秦源治. *Wagakuni yakyū wo rīdo shita: Dairen yakyū kai* わが国球界をリードした:大連野球界 [Our Country Was the Leader of Baseball: The Dalian Baseball World]. Kobe: Twentieth Century Dairen Conference, 2009.

Havens, Thomas R.H. *Fire Across the Sea: The Vietnam War and Japan, 1965–1975.* Princeton, NJ: Princeton University Press, 1987.

Hemmi, Masaaki 逸見勝亮. "Dai niji sekai taisengo no nihon ni okeru furōji・‐ Sensō koji no rekishi" 第二次世界大戦後の日本における浮浪児・戦争孤児の歴史 [Juvenile Vagrants and War Orphans after World War II in Japan]. *Nihon no kyōikushi gaku: Kyōikushi gakkai kiyō* [Japan Society for the Historical Studies of Education] 37 (1994): 99–115.

Hollerman, Leon. "International Economic Controls in Occupied Japan." *The Journal of Asian Studies* 38, no. 4 (August 1979): 707–719.

Howland, Douglas. "Samurai Status, Class, and Bureaucracy: A Historiographical Essay." *The Journal of Asian Studies* 60, no. 2 (May 2001): 353–380.

Huffman, James. *Modern Japan: A History in Documents*. New York: Oxford University Press, 2011.

Ichioka, Yuji. "The Meaning of Loyalty: The Case of Kazumaro Buddy Uno." *Amerasia Journal* 23, no. 3 (1997): 45–71.

Ienaga, Saburō. *The Pacific War*. New York: Random House, 1978.

Igarashi, Yoshikuni. *Bodies of Memory: Narratives of War in Postwar Japanese Culture, 1945–1970*. Princeton, NJ: Princeton University Press, 2000.

Ikegami, Eiko. *The Taming of the Samurai: Honorific Individualism and the Making of Modern Japan*. Cambridge, MA: Harvard University Press, 1995.

Inoue, Shun 井上俊. *Budō no Tanjyō* 武道の誕生 [The Birth of Budō]. Tokyo: Yoshikawa Kōbunkan, 2004.

Inoue, Tetsujirō 井上哲次郎. *Bushidō* 武士道 [The Way of the Samurai]. Tokyo: Heiji Zasshi Corporation, 1901.

Ishihara, Shintarō, *The Japan that Can Say NO,* translated by Frank Baldwin. New York: Simon and Schuster, 1991.

Irie, Katsumi 入江克己. *Shōwa supōtsu shi ron* 昭和スポーツ史論 [Discussions of Shōwa Sports History]. Tokyo: Fumidō Shuppan, 1991.

Itami, Yasuhiro 伊丹安広. *Yakyū no chichi: Abe Isoo Sensei* 野球の父: 安部磯雄先生 [The Father of Baseball: Teacher Abe Isoo]. Tokyo: Waseda Daigaku Shuppanbu, 1965.

Ivy, Marilyn. *Discourses of the Vanishing: Modernity, Phantasm, Japan*. Chicago: University of Chicago Press, 1995.

Iwabuchi, Koichi. "Complicit Exoticism: Japan and Its Other." *Continuum: The Australian Journal of Media and Culture* 8, no. 2 (1994): 49–82.

Izumino, Seiichi 五十公野清一. *Shōriki Matsutarō puro yakyū ikusei sanjyūnen* 正力松太郎プロ野球育成三十年 [Thirty Years of Shōriki Matsutarō's Professional Baseball]. Tokyo: Tsuru Shōbō, 1966.

Johnson, Chalmers. *MITI and the Japanese Miracle: The Growth of Industrial Policy, 1925–1975*. Stanford, CA: Stanford University Press, 1982.

Ka, Chih-Ming. *Japanese Colonialism in Taiwan: Land Tenure, Development, and Dependency, 1895–1945.* Taipei, Taiwan: SMC Publishing, Inc., 1995.

Kaga, Hideo 加賀秀雄. "Wagakuni ni okeru 1932 nen no gakusei yakyū no tōsei ni tsuite" わが国における1932年の学生野球の統制について [Regarding Our Country's 1932 Student Baseball Regulations]. *Hokkaidō Daigaku kyōiku gakubu kiyō* 51, no. 3 (1988): 1–16.

Katayama, Tetsu 片山哲. *Abe Isoo Den* 安部磯雄伝 [Biography of Abe Isoo]. Tokyo: Ōzorasha, 1991.

Kawai, Keiji and Brent McDonald. "Globalisation, Individualism and Scandal: New Directions in Japanese Baseball." *The International Journal of the History of Sport* 29, no. 17 (November 2012): 2450–2464.

Kawai, Keiji and Matt Nichol. "Labor in Nippon Professional Baseball and the Future of Player Transfers to Major League Baseball." *Marquette Sports Law Review* 25, no. 2 (2015): 491–529.

Kelly, William W. "Caught in the Spin Cycle: An Anthropological Observer at the Sites of Japanese Professional Baseball." In *Moving Targets: Ethnographies of Self and Community in Japan*, edited by Susan O. Long. Ithaca: Cornell University Press, East Asia Papers, 2000.

_____. "Learning to Swing: Oh Sadaharu and the Pedagogy and Practice of Japanese Baseball." In *Learning in Likely Places: Varieties of Apprenticeship in Japan*, edited by John Singleton. Cambridge, UK: Cambridge University Press, 1998.

_____. "Samurai Baseball: The Vicissitudes of a National Sporting Style." *International Journal of the History of Sport* 26, no. 3 (March 2009): 429–441.

Kikkawa, Takeo 橘川武郎 and Nara Takashi 奈良堂史. *Fan kara mita puro yakyū no rekishi* ファンから観たプロ野球の歴史 [History of Professional Baseball from a Fan's Point of View]. Tokyo: Nihon Keizai Hyōron Sha, 2009.

Kimball, Jeffrey P. "Richard M. Nixon and the Vietnam War: The Paradox of Disengagement with Escalation." In *The Columbia History of the Vietnam War*, edited by David L. Anderson. New York: Columbia University Press, 2011.

Klein, Alan. *Growing the Game: The Globalization of Major League Baseball.* New Haven, CT: Yale University Press, 2006.

_____. "Latinizing the 'National Pastime.'" In *America's Game: A Critical Anthropology of Sport*, edited by Benjamin Eastman, Michael Ralph, and Sean Brown. New York: Routledge, 2008.

_____. "Sport and Culture as Contested Terrain: Americanization in the Caribbean." *Sociology of Sport Journal* 8 (1991): 79–85.

Kobayashi, Ryūichi 小林竜一. "Dai Ichikō tōgakkō kōchō toshite no Nitobe Inazō" 第一高等学校校長としての新渡戸稲造 [Nitobe Inazō as Headmaster of Ichikō High School]. *Shigakken ronshū* (March 25, 2011): 70–85.

Kowner, Rotem. *The A to Z of the Russo-Japanese War*. Lanham, Maryland: Scarecrow Press, 2006.

Knopp, Japheth. "Negro League Baseball, Black Community, and the Socio-Economic Impact of Integration." *The Baseball Research Journal*. Phoenix, AZ: Society for American Baseball Research, 2016): 66–74.

Kuznick, Peter. "Japan's Nuclear History in Perspective: Eisenhower and Atoms for War and Peace." *Bulletin of Atomic Scientists*, 13 April 2011. http://thebulletin.org/japans-nuclear-history-perspective-eisenhower-and-atoms-war-and-peace-0.

Lee, Karam, Jung-Hee Ha, and Gwang Ok. "Extraterritorial Outlet of Korean Nationalism in the Far Eastern Championship Games, 1913–1934." *The International Journal of the History of Sport* 32, no. 3 (2015): 1–11.

Lie, John. *Multiethnic Japan*. Cambridge, MA: Harvard University Press, 2001.

Lin, Sheng-Lung 林勝龍. *Nihon tōchika Taiwan ni okeru bushidō yakyū no jyoyō to kaiten*日本統治下台湾における武士道野球の受容と展開 [The Infusion and Popularization of the Japanese Samurai Baseball Culture in Taiwan During the Period of Japan's Colonization], Dissertation, Waseda University, 2012.

Maguire, Joseph and Nakayama Masayoshi, eds. *Japan, Sport, and Society: Tradition and Change in a Globalizing World*. New York: Routledge, 2006.

Makito, Saya. *The Sino-Japanese War and the Birth of Japanese Nationalism*, translated by David Noble. Tokyo: International House of Japan, 2011.

Mangan, J.A. and Gwang Ok. "Seoul '88—Media, Politicians, Public: Confrontation, Cooperation and Democratic Consequences." *The International Journal of the History of Sport* 29, no. 16 (October 2012): 2276–2292.

Maruya, Takeshi 丸屋武士. *Kanō Jigorō to Abe Isoo: Kindai supōtsu to kyōiku no senkusha*嘉納治五郎と安部磯雄：近代スポーツと教育の先駆者 [Kanō Jigorō and Abe Isoo: Pioneers of Modern Sports and Education]. Tokyo: Akashi, 2014.

Maruyama, Masao. *Thought and Behavior in Modern Japanese Politics*. Oxford, UK: Oxford University Press, 1969.

Mawdsley, Evan. *World War II: A New History*. Cambridge, UK: Cambridge University Press, 2009.

McCormack, Gavan and Kim Dong-choon. "Grappling with Cold War History: Korea's Embattled Truth and Reconciliation Commission." *The Asia-Pacific Journal: Japan Focus* 7, 8, no. 6 (February 17, 2009). http://apjjf.org/-Gavan-McCormack/3056/article.html.

Medhurst, Martin. "Atoms for Peace and Nuclear Hegemony: The Rhetorical Structure of a Cold War Campaign." In *The Cold War: National Security Policy Planning from Truman to Reagan and from Stalin to Gorbachev*, Vol. 2, edited by Lori Lyn Bogle. New York: Routledge, 2001.

Miyatake, Kimio 宮武公夫. "*Jinruigaku to Orinpikku: Ainu to 1904 nen Sento Ruis Orinipikku Taikai*" 人類学とオリンピック：アイヌと１９０４年セントルイス・オリンピック大会 [Anthropology and the Olympics: The Ainu and the 1904 St. Louis Olympics]." *Hokkaido University Annual Report on Cultural Science* (2002): 1–22.

Morioka, Hiroshi 森岡浩. *Kōkō yakyū 100 nen shi* 高校野球100年史 [100 Year History of High School Baseball]. Tokyo: Tokyo Shuppudan, 2015.

Morris, Andrew D. *Colonial Project, National Game: A History of Baseball in Taiwan.* Berkeley, CA: University of California Press, 2011.

Murakami, Haruki. *Wind/Pinball: Two Novels.* New York: Alfred A. Knopf, 2015.

Murakami, Masanori 村上雅則. *Tatta hitori no dai-riga* たった一人の大リーガ [The Only Major Leaguer]. Tokyo: Kōbunsha, 1985.

Nagai, Yoshikazu. 永井良和. *Nankai Hawks ga atta koro: Yakyū fan to pa-rigu no bunkashi* 南海ホークスがあったころ：野球ファンとパ・リーグの文化史 [The Era of the Nankai Hawks: A Social History of Baseball Fans and the Pacific League]. Tokyo: Kawade Bunko, 2010.

Nagata, Yōichi 永田陽一. *Tokyo Giants Hokubei Tairiku enseiki* 東京ジャイアンツ北米大陸遠征記 [*Record of the Tokyo Giants North American Tour*]. Tokyo: Tohō Shuppan, 2007.

Nakamura, Takeshi 中村赳. *Oyatoi no gaikokujin no kenkyū* 御雇外国人の研究 [Research on the Oyatoi Foreigners]. *Journal of Hosei University Historical Society* (March 1964): 65–75.

Nakamura, Tetsuo中村哲夫 et al. "*Wagakuni sengo fukkōki niokeru supōtsu yōhin oroshi gyōkumiai no yakuwari to sono katsudō*" 我が国戦後復興期におけるスポーツ用品卸業組合の役割とその活動」 [The Roles and Activities of the National Association of Sporting-Goods Distributors in Postwar Japan], *Supōtsu sangyōgaku kenkyū* 18, no. 1 (2008): 1–15.

Nakazawa, Fujio 中澤不二雄. *Bokura no Yakyū* ぼくらの野球 [Our Baseball]. Tokyo: Yamanoki Publishing, 1948.

Nitobe, Inazō. *Bushido: The Soul of Japan*, 13th Edition. Tokyo: Teibi Publishing Company, 1908.

Noguchi, Hodaka 野口穂高. "1924 nen no daiichi zenkoku taiiku no de- no katsudō jōkyō ni kan suru—kōsatsu" 1924年の第一回全国体育デーの活動状況に関する一考察 [An Inquiry into the Conditions and Activities of the First All Japan Physical Education Day in 1924]. *Tamagawa Daigaku kyōiku gakubu* (2013): 47–79.

Ōbitsu, Takashi, 大櫃敬史. "Rīrando shohei ni kan suru keii: Amāsuto Daigaku shozō bunsho no bunseki wo chūshin toshite" リーランド招聘に関する経

緯：アマースト大学所蔵文書の分析を中心として [The Invitation of Dr. Leland: An Analysis of the Amherst Program]. *Daigaku kyōiku gakubu kiyō* 73 (1997): 1–34.

Oguma, Eiji. *A Genealogy of 'Japanese' Self-Images,* translated by David Askew. Melbourne, Australia: Trans Pacific Press, 2002.

Oguro, Richard S. *Senpai Gumi* [Our Teachers]. http://www.100thbattalion.org/wp-content/uploads/Senpai-Gumi.pdf.

Oh, Sadaharu 王貞治. *Yakyū ni tokimeite* 野球にときめいて [Prospering in Baseball]. Tokyo: Chūoronsha, 2011.

Ōjima, Katsutarō 大島勝太郎. *Chōsen yakyū shi* 朝鮮野球史 [Korean Baseball History]. Tokyo: Chōsen Publishing Co., 1932.

Ōkubo, Hideaki 大久保英明 and Yamagishi Kōji 山岸孝吏. "*Makkasa Gensui mai supōtsu kyōgikai no seiritsu to haishi*" マッカーサー元帥枚スポーツ競技会の成立と廃止 [The General MacArthur Cup Competitions: Regarding their Establishment and Dissolution]. Kanazawa: Kanazawa University Education Department Bulletin, 2004.

Ono, Yasuteru 小野安照. "Chōsen ni okeru yakyū juyō: Chōsen de 'bēsubōru' ha ikanishite 'yakyū' ni natta no ka" 朝鮮における野球の受容：朝鮮で「ベースボール」は如何にして「野球」になったのか [On the Reception of Baseball in Korea: How "Baseball" Became "Yakyū"]. In *Kanryū, Nichiryū: Higashi Ajia bunka kōryū no jidai* 韓流・日流:東アジア文化交流の時代 [Korean Flows, Japanese Flows: The Period of Exchange in East Asia], edited by Yamamoto Joho. Tokyo: Bensei Publishing Corporation, 2014.

————. *Shokuminchi Chōsen no Kōshien Taikai: Chōsen chikuyosen no setsuritsu to Chōsen no sanka wo megutte* 植民地朝鮮の甲子園大会：朝鮮地区予選の設立と朝鮮人の参加をめぐって [The Kōshien Tournament of Colonial Koreans: Concerning the Establishment of the Korean Qualifiers and Korean Participation at the Kōshien Tournament]. *Nijiseiki kenkyū* 二十世紀研究 [Twentieth Century Studies] 15 (December 2014): 43–67.

Pastreich, Emmanuel. "The Balancer: Rooh Moo-hyun's Vision of Korean Politics and the Future of Northeast Asia." *The Asia-Pacific Journal: Japan Focus* 3, no. 8 (August 3, 2005). http://apjjf.org/-Emanuel-Pastreich/2041/article.html.

Porteaux, Jonson N. "Reactive Nationalism and its Effect on South Korea's Public Policy and Foreign Affairs." *The Asia-Pacific Journal: Japan Focus* 14, 9, no. 5 (May 1, 2016). http://apjjf.org/2016/09/Porteux.html.

Port, Kenneth. *Transcending Law: The Unintended Life of Article 9 of the Japanese Constitution,* revised printing. Durham, NC: Carolina Academic Press, 2010.

Powers-Beck, Jeffrey. "'Chief': The American Indian Integration of Baseball, 1897–1945." *American Indian Quarterly* 25, no. 4 (Autumn 2001): 508–538.

Reaves, Joseph. *Taking in A Game: A History of Baseball in Asia*. Lincoln, NE: University of Nebraska Press, 2002.

Robinson, Greg. *A Tragedy of Democracy: Japanese Confinement in North America*. New York: Columbia University Press, 2009.

Roche, Maurice. *Mega-Events and Modernity: Olympics and Expos in the Growth of Global Culture*. London: Routledge, 2000.

Roden, Donald. "Baseball and the Quest for National Dignity in Meiji Japan." *The American Historical Review* 85, no. 3 (June 1980): 511–534.

Rostow, W.W. *The Stages of Economic Growth: A Non-Communist Manifesto*. Cambridge: Cambridge University Press, 1960.

Sayama, Kazuo 佐山和夫. *Nichibei rimenshi: Bishōjyo tōshū kara dai Bebu Rusu made* 日米野球裏面史：美少女投手から大ベーブルースまで [The Secret History of Japan-American Relationships: From Female Pitchers to Babe Ruth]. Tokyo: NHK Publishing, 2005.

Seaton, Philip A. *Japan's Contested War Memories: The 'Memory Rifts' in Historical Consciousness of World War II*. London: Routledge, 2007.

Selden, Mark. "A Forgotten Holocaust: US Bombing Strategy, the Destruction of Japanese Cities and the American Way of War from World War II to Iraq." *The Asia-Pacific Journal: Japan Focus*. http://www.japanfocus.org/-Mark-Selden/2414.

Sherif, Ann. *Japan's Cold War: Media, Literature, and the Law*. New York: Columbia University Press, 2009.

Shibusawa, Naoko. *America's Geisha Ally: Reimagining the Japanese Enemy*. Cambridge, MA: Harvard University Press, 2006.

Shinbō, Atsushi 新保淳. "Meijiki ni okeru 'taiiku' gainen no kenkyū: Ruiji gainen to no konran no genin ni tsuite" 明治期における「体育」概念の研究：類似概念との混乱の原因について [A Study on the Concept of "Physical Education" in the Meiji Era: On the Cause of Confusion with Similar Concepts]." *Shizuoka Daigaku kyōiku gakubu kenkyū hōkoku* 37 (1987): 19–27.

Sinclair, Robert. "Baseball's Rising Sun: American Interwar Baseball Diplomacy and Japan." *Canadian Journal of the History of Sport* 16, no. 2 (1985): 44–53.

Surdam, David. *The Postwar Yankees: Baseball's Golden Age Revisited*. Lincoln, NE: University of Nebraska Press, 2008.

Suzuki, Sōtarō 鈴木惣太郎. *Fumetsu no Daitōshu: Sawamura Eiji* 不滅の大投手：沢村栄治 [The Immortal Pitcher: Sawamura Eiji]. Tokyo: Kobunsha, 1975.

Suzuki, Yoshinori 鈴木良徳 and Kawamoto Nobumasa 川本信正. *Orinpikku shi* オリンピック史 [Olympic History]. Tokyo: Japan Publishing Association, 1952.

Takashima, Kō 高嶋航. *"Manchūkuo" no tanjyō to kyokutō supōtsu kai no saihen*「満州国」の誕生と極東スポーツ界の再編 [Reevaluating the Birth of Man-chūkuo and the Far East Sports World]. *Kyoto University Bulletin of Linguistic Research* 47 (2008): 131–181.

_____. *Teikoku Nihon to supōtsu* 帝国日本とスポーツ [Imperial Japan and Sports]. Tokyo: Hanawasho, 2012.

Takekawa, Shunichi. "Drawing a Line Between Peaceful and Military Uses of Nu-clear Power: The Japanese Press, 1945–1955." *The Asia-Pacific Journal: Japan Focus* 10, 37, no. 2 (September 9, 2012). http://apjjf.org/2012/10/37/Shuni-chi-TAKEKAWA/3823/article.html.

Takenaka, Akiko. "Mobilizing Death in Imperial Japan: War and the Origins of the Myth of Yasukuni." *The Asia-Pacific Journal: Japan Focus* 13, 38, no. 1 (September 21, 2015). http://apjjf.org/-Akiko-TAKENAKA/4377.

Tansman, Alan. *The Culture of Japanese Fascism*. Durham, NC: Duke University Press, 2009.

Thorn, John. "The Pittsfield 'Baseball' Bylaw of 1791: What It Means." *Our Game*, August 3, 2011. https://ourgame.mlblogs.com/the-pittsfield-baseball-bylaw-of-1791-what-it-means-940a3ccf08db#.uphpocsu3.

Tokyo Kaisei Gakkō 東京開成学校. *Tōkyō Kaisei gakkō ichiran* 東京開成学校一覧 [Summary of Tokyo Kaisei School]. Tokyo, 1875.

Tuman, John and Craig Emmert. "Explaining Japanese Foreign Direct Investment in Latin America, 1979–1992." *Social Science Quarterly* 80, no. 3 (September 1999): 539–555.

Tygiel, Jules. *Past Time: Baseball as History*. Oxford: Oxford University Press, 2000.

Villacorta, Wilfrido V. "Japan's Asian Identity: Concerns for ASEAN-Japan Rela-tions." *ASEAN Economic Bulletin* 11, no. 1 (July 1994): 79–92.

Whiting, Robert. *The Chrysanthemum and the Bat: Baseball Samurai Style*. New York: Dodd, Mead, and Company, 1977.

_____. *The Meaning of Ichiro: The New Wave from Japan and the Transforma-tion of Our National Pastime*. New York: Warner Books, 2004.

_____. *The Samurai Way of Baseball: The Impact of Ichiro and the New Wave from Japan*. New York: Warner Books, 2005.

_____. *You Gotta Have Wa*. New York: Vintage Books, 1989.

Wigen, Kären. *The Making of a Japanese Periphery, 1750–1920*. Berkeley, CA: Uni-versity of California Press, 1995.

Yamaguchi, Tomohisa 山口智久. *"Terebijyon jidai to supōtsu"* テレビジョン時代とスポーツ [The Television Era and Sports]. *Hitotsubashi University Depart-mental Report* (August 1994): 7–10.

Yamamura, Kozo, ed. *The Economic Emergence of Modern Japan*. Cambridge, UK: Cambridge University Press, 1997.

Yamamuro, Hiroyuki 山室寛之. *Puro yakyū fukkōshi* プロ野球復興史 [The History of the Revival of Professional Baseball]. Tokyo: Chūokōron Shinsha, 2012.

Yamamoto, Kōji 山本浩二. *Yakyū to Hiroshima* 野球と広島 [Baseball and Hiroshima]. Tokyo: Kadokawa, 2015.

Yoon, Young-Kwan. "The Political Economy of Transition: Japanese Foreign Direct Investments in the 1980s." *World Politics* 43, no. 1 (October 1990), 1–27.

Yōsensha 洋泉社. *Shōwa puro yakyū kyūjyō taizen* 昭和プロ野球「球場」大全 [Professional Baseball Stadiums of the Shōwa Era]. Tokyo: Yōsensha, 2014.

Yoshimi, Shunya. "'America' as Desire and Violence: Americanization in Postwar Japan and Asia During the Cold War," *Inter-Asia Cultural Studies* 4, no.3 (2003). 434–449.

Young, Louise. *Japan's Total Empire: Manchuria and the Culture of Wartime Imperialism*. Berkeley, CA: University of California Press, 1998.

Yu, Junwei. *Playing in Isolation: A History of Baseball in Taiwan*. Lincoln, NE: University of Nebraska Press, 2007.

National Diet Digital Materials

Asahi Shinbun Co., 朝日新聞社, *Undō nenkan: Taishō 8 nendo* 運動年鑑: 大正8年度 [Athletic Yearbook: Year Taishō 8]. http://dl.ndl.go.jp/info:ndljp/pid/955126.

Ishihara, Shintarō 石原慎太郎. *Nihon wo otoshireta jōhō kūkan no kai* 日本を陥れた情報空間の怪 [The Mystery of Japan Falling into the Information Gap]. *Bungei shūjun* 69, no. 2 (1991): 94–110.

Nihon Teikoku jinkō seitai tōkei 日本帝国人口静態統計 [Statistics of Imperial Japan Population]. http://dl.ndl.go.jp/info:ndljp/pid/805975.

Nihon Teikokuminseki kokōhyō 日本帝国民籍戸口表 [Report of Households in Imperial Japan], 1891. http://dl.ndl.go.jp/info:ndljp/pid/806017/29

Secretary of the Ministry of Education School Hygiene Section 文部大臣官學校衞生課, "*Taiiku de- jisshi gaikyō* 體育デー實施概況," [*Physical Education Day Implementation Guideline*], (1924). http://kindai.ndl.go.jp/info:ndljp/pid/939870

Olympic Reports and Pamphlets

Belgium Olympic Committee. *Olympic Games Antwerp 1920: Official Report*. Brussels: Belgium Olympic Committee, 1957.

Bergvall, Erik. *The Official Report of the Olympic Games of Stockholm 1912*. Stockholm: Wahlström and Widstrand, 1913.

Seoul Olympic Organizing Committee, *Official Report: Organization and Planning, Volume 1*. Seoul: Korea Textbook Co., Ltd, 1989.

Magazine and Newspaper Archives

Asahi Shinbun

Baseball Reference

Beijing Review

ESPN

The Japan Times

Kotaku

The Los Angeles Times

The New York Times

Nikkei Asian Review

Society for American Baseball Research

The Sporting News

Yakyūkai

Yomiuri Shinbun

Prange Collection Materials

Besuboru Magajin ("Baseball Magazine," Magazine, 1946–1952)

Gakusei Yakyū ("Student Baseball," Magazine, 1947)

Oru Besuboru ("All Baseball," Magazine, 1946–1949)

Shin Taiiku ("New Physical Education," 1946–1949)

Yakyūkai ("Baseball World," Magazine, 1946–1950)

Governmental Archives

National Archives and Records Administration
　　Record Group 331 (Materials from the Allied Occupation of Japan)
　　Record Group 263 (Files of the Central Intelligence Agency)

Supreme Court Cases

Flood v. Kuhn. 407 U.S. 258 (1972).

Websites, Blogs, Online Databases

Ballparks of Baseball. http://www.ballparksofbaseball.com.

Baseball Prospectus. http://www.baseballprospectus.com.

Baseball Reference. http://www.baseball-reference.com.

FanGraphs. http://www.fangraphs.com.

Hanshin Kōshien Stadium, "*Shisetsu gaiyou* 施設概要 [Facility Summary]". http://www.hanshin.co.jp/koshien/stadium_guide/seat.html.

The Imperial Household Agency. "Their Imperial Highness Prince and Princess Chichibu." http://www.kunaicho.go.jp/e-about/history/history12.html.

Japan Sports Association. http://www.japan-sports.or.jp.

The Japanese Baseball Hall of Fame and Museum. http://www.baseball-museum.or.jp.

"KANO 1931海の向こうの甲子園" [Kano's 1931 Overseas Trip to Kōshien]. http://kano1931.com/.

Pro Yakyu Now. http://www.japanesebaseball.com.

Society for American Baseball Research: BioProject. http:// http://sabr.org/bioproject.

Statistics Bureau of the Japanese Ministry of Internal Affairs and Communications. http://www.stat.go.jp/data/chouki/zuhyou/.

Thorn, John. *Our Game*. https://ourgame.mlblogs.com.

Vintage Ball. http://www.vintageball.com.

Waseda Baseball Team History. http://www.waseda.jp/9a-baseball-team/history.htm.

Index